THE SINGLE TAX MOVEMENT

IN THE

UNITED STATES

BY

ARTHUR NICHOLS YOUNG, Ph.D.

INSTRUCTOR IN ECONOMICS AND SOCIAL
INSTITUTIONS IN PRINCETON UNIVERSITY

PRINCETON UNIVERSITY PRESS
PRINCETON
LONDON: HUMPHREY MILFORD
OXFORD UNIVERSITY PRESS
1916

PREFACE

More than a generation has now elapsed since Henry
George published *Progress and Poverty,* but hardly any effort has been made to describe the single tax movement or
to appraise its significance. Substantially all of the literature devoted to the single tax question has been purely controversial. In the present volume the writer has undertaken
to give a complete historical account of the single tax movement in the United States, together with a discussion of the
tactics of the single taxers, their program, the present status
of the movement, and its influence upon economic thought
and upon fiscal and social reform.

A brief introductory survey of the chief anticipations of
Henry George's doctrines is presented in order to show the
place of the movement in the history of economic thought.
Then is traced the formulation of George's economic ideas
in the light of the economic environment amid which he
spent the formative years of his life, the California of the
two decades following the gold discovery of 1848. Next
follows a description of the reception of *Progress and
Poverty* in the eighties and of Henry George's activities in
the spreading of his gospel. Succeeding chapters describe
the development of the single tax movement through the
recent political campaigns undertaken with the aid of the
Joseph Fels endowment. Finally there is a consideration
of some general aspects of the movement, and an appraisal
of its significance.

Collection of the material upon which this study is based
has involved research in several parts of the country. The
writer spent several weeks in and around San Francisco

iii

securing data regarding the economic background of Henry George's life there, and had the opportunity of conferring with a number who had been intimately acquainted with him in the seventies. Important material was found in the Bancroft Library at the University of California and in the California State Library at Sacramento, particularly in the files of George's San Francisco *Evening Post* (1871-75) and contemporary newspapers. The writer also in the years 1913-15 has personally visited several of the localities where the single tax movement has been most prominent, including Portland, Ore., Seattle and Everett, Wash., Chicago, Ill., Cincinnati, Ohio, and New York City; also in Canada, Victoria and Vancouver, B. C., and Edmonton, Alberta. Information regarding the movement in places not visited has been secured mainly through conferences and correspondence with single taxers and others, from the propaganda literature used, and from periodicals. Searches for material relating to the single tax movement have been carried on in the following university libraries: California, Leland Stanford, Jr., Minnesota, Wisconsin, Chicago, Columbia, and Princeton; in the public libraries of San Francisco, Los Angeles, Minneapolis, Chicago, and New York; and in the John Crerar Library of Chicago and the Library of Congress, Washington, D. C. The writer has worked through the files of the chief single tax periodicals: *The Standard, Justice, The National Single Taxer, The Single Tax Review,* and *The Public.* He has had the opportunity of discussing various aspects of the movement and its program with a considerable number of those most active in the movement today.

For aid the writer is under obligation to many. Where possible, acknowledgment has been given in the footnotes. Special acknowledgment, however, is due to the following single taxers: Mr. Joseph Dana Miller, editor of the *Single*

Tax Review, Mr. C. B. Fillebrown of Boston, Mr. Daniel Kiefer, chairman of the Joseph Fels Fund Commission, Mr. Louis F. Post of Washington, D. C., Mr. Harold Sudell of Philadelphia, Mr. John Z. White of Chicago, Mr. O. T. Erickson of Seattle, and Mr. C. E. Todd and Mr. F. W. Lynch of San Francisco; also to Mr. Benjamin C. Marsh of New York City, secretary of the Society to Lower Rents and Reduce Taxes on Homes. The writer also is under obligation to Mrs. Richmond Plant of Los Angeles for the gift of material collected by the late Richmond Plant; to Mr. H. I. Priestley, Assistant Curator of the Academy of Pacific Coast History, Berkeley; and to Professor C. C. Plehn of the University of California.

For valued criticism the writer is grateful to his colleagues, Professors F. A. Fetter, E. W. Kemmerer, and W. M. Adriance, to Mr. W. W. Cumberland, and to Professor R. G. Cleland of Occidental College, Los Angeles. Professor Fetter has painstakingly read the entire manuscript, and the writer is especially grateful for the opportunity of discussing with him most of the points considered. Finally, the writer is indebted to his wife for invaluable aid rendered in many ways.

ARTHUR NICHOLS YOUNG.

Princeton
New Jersey
April, 1916

CONTENTS

CHAPTER I
ANTICIPATIONS OF HENRY GEORGE'S IDEAS
Introduction

Few movements of any sort bear such a striking relation to the life and work of a single individual as the single tax movement bears to the life and work of Henry George. Scarcely anything in the history of social reform movements is more remarkable than the spectacle of this unknown California printer setting foot in New York City in 1880, poor in pocket, equipped solely with a book and the consciousness of a message, to become the founder of a new world-wide crusade against world-old evils. Like the founder of a new religion, Henry George believed that he had been called to be a prophet to his age. The task to which he set himself was to be the bearer of an economic revelation, to point the way to social salvation, to show the "great primary wrong" which causes a shadow to accompany our advancing civilization. He sent forth his gospel with unwavering faith that his message would find friends who would take "the cross of a new crusade". That faith has been realized and to-day thousands of his disciples in all parts of the world are devoted to his memory and turn for the final solution of economic problems to *Progress and Poverty*.

In order to reach a clearer understanding of the place which Henry George's single tax doctrines occupy in the history of economic thought, we shall consider in the present chapter the extent to which they were anticipated. A discussion of the anticipations, however, must be confined within limits. An attempt to consider the numerous manifestations of the idea to which land reformers of all times have appealed—that all men have a "God-given" or "natural" or "equal" right to the earth—would take us too far afield. Hardly any agrarian movement fails to exhibit some manifestation of this idea, which dates back at least to the time when the author of Ecclesiastes wrote that "the profit of the earth is for all". We must confine ourselves to considering (1) some of the more specific anticipations of George's characteristic doctrines, and (2) the relations between these doctrines and the doctrines of the leading economists, from the Physiocrats to Cairnes.[1] We shall then examine the question of George's originality, his knowledge of and dependence upon former writers while formulating the ideas which, first presented in 1871 in *Our Land and Land Policy*, were worked out more fully eight years later in *Progress and Poverty*. In the second chapter we shall consider the influence which the environmental conditions of early California exerted upon Henry George.

[1] A detailed consideration of these points would take us too far afield. The precursors here discussed are representative; the list is by no means exhaustive.

For further discussion of precursors of Henry George see: Dollfus, Über die Idee der einzigen Steuer, Basel, 1897; Gide and Rist, Histoire des Doctrines Économiques, Paris, 1913, pp. 654-76; Escarra, Nationalisation du sol et Socialisme, Paris, 1904; Henry George, Political Economy, New York, 1898, bk. 2, ch. 7; E. H. Crosby, The Earth-for-All Calendar, in the National Single Taxer, New York, each month of 1900 (a list of quotations from many anticipators of George); and J. M. Davidson, Concerning Four Precursors of Henry George and the Single Tax, London, 1899.

The first two accounts mentioned are the most valuable. Davidson's partisanship for the single tax has led him at times to strain a point in discovering similarities between George's doctrines and those of Spence, Ogilvie, Paine, and Dove, the precursors whom he discusses.

Anticipations by isolated writers, non-economists

Spinoza, the Dutch philosopher (1632-1677), in his *Tractatus Politicus* proposed that the rents of the soil, supplemented perhaps by the rents of houses, should defray the expenditures of the state.

"The fields, and the whole soil, and, if it can be managed, the houses should be public property, that is, the property of him who holds the right of the commonwealth: and let him let them at a yearly rent to the citizens, whether townsmen or countrymen, and with this exception let them all be free, or exempt from every kind of tax in time of peace. And of this rent a part is to be applied to the defences of the state, a part to the king's private use."[2]

Marshall Vauban published in 1707 his *Projet d'une Dixme Royale*. His travels through France had given him an opportunity to see the poverty of the peasants, which he believed was due largely to heavy and unequal taxation.[3] He proposed a reform of France's tax system which some have regarded as entitling him to rank as "a pioneer of the single tax".[4]

The title of Vauban's book, however, is misleading as regards his reform project. The *dixme royale,* or royal tithe, was not, as its name might indicate, a single income tax. It was a comprehensive proposal for simplifying the existing tax system, but yet far from a single tax proposal. It called for proportional taxes on the produce of land and on the revenue of wealth in general, but definitely proposed to continue (not without improvements in method, however) the raising of revenue from salt duties, and to retain certain other imposts.[5]

It is better, therefore, to regard Vauban as a reformer

[2] Spinoza, Tractatus Politicus, ch. 6, sec. 12.
[3] Vauban, Projet d'une Dixme Royale, 1708 ed., p. 3.
[4] E. g. Haney, History of Economic Thought, New York, 1911, p. 135.
[5] Vauban, op. cit., premiere partie.

who made an earnest and worthy plea for greater simplicity, justice, and uprightness in taxation, rather than as
a pioneer advocate of the single tax.[6]

Thomas Spence, of Newcastle-on-Tyne, advocated ideas
strikingly like those of Henry George in a lecture before
the Philosophical Society of Newcastle on the 8th of November, 1775, for the printing of which, wrote Spence,
"the Society did the Author the honour to expel him".[7]

Spence believed in the natural right of all men to land,
and his views on the effects of its private appropriation are
suggestive of *Progress and Poverty.*

"For as all the rivers run into the sea, and yet the sea is
not full, so let there be ever so many sources of wealth, let
trade, foreign and domestic, open all their sluices, yet will no
other but the landed interest be ultimately the better."[8]

Spence's remedy was "to administer the landed estate of
the nation as a joint-stock property, in parochial partner-
ships, by dividing the rent."

"There are no tolls or taxes of any kind paid among them,
by native or foreigner, but the aforesaid rent.   The government, poor, roads, &c. &c. . . . are all maintained by the
parishes with the rent: on which account all wares, manufactures, allowable trade, employments, or actions, are entirely
duty-free."[9]

---

[6] For a thorough discussion of this point see Dollfus, Über die Idee
der einzigen Steuer, Basel, 1897, pp. 15-25.

[7] Spence's two chief pamphlets are, The Meridian Sun of Liberty,
or, the Whole Rights of Man Displayed and most Accurately Defined,
a twelve page pamphlet which, Spence stated (1796 ed., p. 4), he had
been "publishing in various editions for more than twenty years";
and The Rights of Infants, or the Imprescriptable Right of Mothers
to such a Share of the Elements as is sufficient to enable them to
suckle and bring up their Young.   The latter, which was written in
1796, has been reprinted in the Single Tax Rev., Oct. 15, 1907, pp. 11-16.
Copies of these pamphlets are in the New York City Public Library.

[8] Spence, The Rights of Infants, p. 3.

[9] Spence, The Whole Rights of Man, p. 11.

When all necessary expenditures of government have been met comes "the most pleasant part of the business to everyone", the equal division of the surplus.

A contest between the Corporation of Newcastle and the freemen of the borough probably suggested to Spence his proposal. The Corporation had enclosed and leased a part of the common land, but were defeated in the law courts and obliged to allow the rent to the freemen as dividends.[10]

The result of Spence's advocacy of this proposal was that he was forced to remove to London. There he continued his propaganda and at one time gained a considerable following. But the government laid a heavy hand upon his agitation and the societies of his followers were suppressed.[11]

William Ogilvie, Professor of Humanities in King's College, Aberdeen, was another eighteenth century thinker who anticipated certain of Henry George's ideas. In 1782 he published anonomously *An Essay on the Right of Property in Land with respect to its Foundation in the Law of Nature.*[12] He believed that the equal right of all men to the earth was "a birthright which every citizen still retains",[13] and as a means for securing that right he proposed a "progressive agrarian law", under which men were to be permitted to claim their birthright share from unoccupied lands, and those holding more than this share were grad-

[10] Foxwell, Introduction to Menger, The Right to the Whole Produce of Labour, London, 1899, p. xcv.
[11] See Menger, op. cit., p. 147 et seq. It is of interest to note that Spence's pamphlet came to New York in 1829 and that some of his ideas were incorporated in the platform of the first workingmen's political party. See Commons, Documentary History of American Industrial Society, vol. 7, p. 30.
[12] Ogilvie's book was reprinted by W. Dugdale, London, 1838, with a notice that "the book attracted considerable attention" at the time of publication, but was suppressed. It also has been reprinted by D. C. MacDonald under the title, Birthright in Land, London, 1891.
[13] Ibid. (MacDonald reprint), p. 9.

ually to be deprived of their surplus of land, retaining, however, the title to any improvements which they might have made.[14]

Ogilvie's ideas on taxation were somewhat vague, but he wrote in a footnote that he believed a land tax to be the most equitable form of tax.[15] The landowner, he believed, enjoyed a revenue without performing a corresponding social service.[16] He suggested a tax on barren lands to force the owner either to cultivate or dispose of them.[17] Ogilvie was probably the first to suggest definitely a tax on the increment of land values. He wrote:

"A tax on all augmentation of rents, even to the extent of one half the increase, would be at once the most equitable, the most productive, the most easily collected, and the least liable to evasion of all possible taxes, and might with inconceivable advantage disencumber a great nation from all those injudicious imposts by which its commercial exchanges are retarded and restrained, and its domestic manufactures embarrassed."[18]

Thomas Paine's pamphlet, *Agrarian Justice opposed to Agrarian Law, and to Agrarian Monopoly,* appeared in 1797.[19] Paine distinguished, as did Henry George, between natural property and artificial property.

"There are two kinds of property. Firstly, natural property, or that which comes to us from the Creator of the universe,—such as the earth, air, water. Secondly, artificial or acquired property,—the invention of men."[20]

"Equality of natural property", wrote Paine, "is the sub-

[14] Ibid., p. 93 et seq.
[15] "If the original value of the soil be the joint property of the commonwealth, no scheme of taxation can be so equitable as a land tax." Ibid., p. 16, note. See also p. 95, note.
[16] "It [the rent of land] increases also without any effort of his, and in proportion to the industry of those who cultivate the soil." Ibid., p. 35.
[17] Ibid., p. 58.
[18] Ibid., pp. 58-59.
[19] Thomas Paine's Works, New York, 1895, vol. 3.
[20] Ibid., p. 324.

ject of this little essay."[21]   Since the private appropriation
of land "has dispossessed more than half the inhabitants of
every nation of their natural inheritance," justice demands
an indemnification.[22]   This was best to be managed, Paine
believed, by a tithe upon all inheritances to create a "National Fund", which should give to each the sum of fifteen
pounds sterling at the age of twenty-one and an annuity
of ten pounds at the age of fifty.[23]

Patrick Edward Dove, a Scotchman, was the most remarkable anticipator of Henry George.   In 1850 he published anonomously *The Theory of Human Progression,
and Natural Probability of a Reign of Justice*.[24]   This is
a diffuse work largely taken up with philosophical and
theological speculation; economic problems hardly seem to
be the main issue.   However, Dove referred to the land
question as "the main question of England's welfare."[25]

Dove stated the problem with all the vigorous fervor of
Progress and Poverty.

"How comes it that, notwithstanding man's vast achievements, his wonderful efforts of mechanical ingenuity, and the
amazing productions of his skill, . . . a large portion of the
population is reduced to *pauperism?* . . . To charge the poverty of man on God, is to blaspheme the Creator.   . . . *He*

[21] Idem.

[22] Ibid., p. 331.

[23] Idem.   Paine's plan was criticized by Spence in his Rights of Infants (p. 3) as being "an execrable fabric of compromissory expediency, as if in good earnest intended for a Swinish Multitude".

[24] The original of Dove's work is rare.   There is a copy in the Library of Princeton University.   It has been reprinted, edited and
abridged by Julia A. Kellogg, New York, 1910.   The essence of Dove's
argument in his Theory of Human Progression is in the third section
of ch. 3, On the Theory of Man's Practical Progression.   Dove also
wrote The Elements of Political Science, Edinburgh, 1854, in which
he made known his authorship of the earlier work.

George was later charged with plagiarizing from Dove.   See infra,
p. 24.

[25] The Theory of Human Progression, p. 322.

has given enough, abundance, more than sufficient; and if man has not enough, we must look to the mode in which God's gifts have been distributed."[26]

Dove diagnosed the cause of poverty as the denial of the natural right of all to the land of their birth, "the alienation of the soil from the state, and the consequent taxation of the industry of the country."[27]

Dove believed that the actual division of the land, even if possible, would be futile as a remedy. The solution was to be found in *"the division of its annual value or rent,"* which could best be done "by taking the whole of the taxes out of the rents of the soil, and thereby abolishing all other kinds of taxation whatever."[28] If this were done "all *industry* would be absolutely emancipated from every burden, and every man would reap such natural reward as his skill, industry, or enterprise rendered legitimately his, according to the natural law of free competition."[29]

Herbert Spencer, in his *Social Statics,* published in 1850, the same year as Dove's work, gave the fullest exposition of the natural rights theory applied to land prior to Henry George's writings.   In chapter IX, The Right to the Use of the Earth, he declared that "equity . . . does not permit property in land".[30]

"The right of each man to the use of the earth, limited only by the like rights of his fellow-men, is immediately deducible from the law of equal freedom.   We see that the maintenance of this right necessarily forbids private property in land.   On examination, all existing titles to such property turn out to be invalid."[31]

Spencer believed that equal apportionment of the earth among its inhabitants and common property in land would

[26] Ibid., p. 311 et seq.
[27] Ibid., p. 320.
[28] Ibid., p. 387.
[29] Idem.
[30] Spencer, Social Statics, New York, 1865, p. 132.
[31] Ibid., p. 143.

be alike unfeasible. But the change could be effected with
no serious disturbance of the existing order.

"The change required would be simply a change of landlords. Separate ownerships would merge into the joint-stock
ownership of the public. Instead of being in the possession
of individuals, the country would be held by the great corporate body—Society. Instead of leasing his acres from an
isolated proprietor, the farmer would lease them from the
nation. Instead of paying his rent to the agent of Sir John
or his Grace, he would pay it to an agent or deputy-agent of
the community. Stewards would be public officials instead of
private ones; and tenancy the only land tenure."[32]

Spencer admitted that the question of compensation to
present proprietors of land was complicated and difficult.[33]
But he declared that "the theory of the co-heirship of all
men to the soil is consistent with the highest civilization,
and . . . however difficult it may be to embody that theory
in fact, Equity sternly commands it to be done."[34]

In the eighties, when discussion of *Progress and Poverty*
was at its height, Spencer's name was frequently coupled
with George's as an advocate of land nationalization. But
Spencer had modified the views set forth in 1850 in *Social
Statics,* and in 1892 he withdrew the original volume,
issuing in its place *Social Statics, abridged and revised,*
a book from which his radical utterances on the land question were omitted.[35] For his retraction he was sharply
criticized by George in *A Perplexed Philosopher,* published
in 1892.

Anticipations by the socialists

Socialist writers before the time of Henry George had
regarded private property in land, together with private
property in other forms of wealth, as exploitative. Some

[32] Ibid., p. 141.
[33] Ibid., pp. 142-43.
[34] Ibid., pp. 143-44.
[35] See George, A Perplexed Philosopher, New York, 1892, pp. 132-35.

had held that land ownership was peculiarly exploitative, because it infringed the natural right of all men to the earth, the heritage of the race. Proudhon gave forcible expression to this thought in his *Qu'est-ce la Propriété?* published in 1840, when he wrote: "Qui a fait la terre? Dieu. En ce cas, propriétaire, retire-toi!"[36]

Likewise the socialists, desiring collective ownership of most forms of wealth, had regarded collective ownership of land as a fundamental plank in their program. The famous *Communist Manifesto* of 1848, written by Karl Marx and Frederick Engels, has the following as first in the list of measures "pretty generally applicable" in "the most advanced countries":

"Abolition of property in land and application of all rents of land to public purposes."[37]

Some socialist writers had placed particular emphasis upon the abolition of private ownership of land. Among these were the Belgian socialist, Baron de Colins, a voluminous writer of the middle of the nineteenth century,[38] and François Huet, a Christian socialist.[39]

Anticipations by the German "Bodenreformers"

The first of the German Bodenreformers was Hermann Heinrich Gossen.[40] In 1854 he proposed that the state should purchase all land and lease it to the highest bidders.[41]

[36] Proudhon, Qu'est-ce la Propriété? p. 74.

[37] Marx and Engels, Manifesto of the Communist Party, Chicago, n.d., p. 45.

[38] See Laveleye, Socialism of Today, pp. 245-53.

[39] Ibid., pp. 253-56, also Laveleye, Primitive Property, pp. 333-36.

[40] Regarding Gossen see Jevons, Preface to the 2d (1879) and subsequent editions of The Theory of Political Economy; Walras, Un économiste inconnu, Jour. des Économistes, 1885; Handwörterbuch der Staatswissenschaften, article on Gossen; Dollfus, Über die Idee der einzigen Steuer, p. 103, note; and Gide and Rist, Histoire des Doctrines Économiques, Paris, 1913, pp. 669-71.

[41] Gossen, Entwicklung der Gesetze der menschlichen Verkehrs und

The state could acquire land advantageously, he believed, because it would be able to borrow the purchase money at low rates of interest. If collective ownership of land were introduced, society instead of private individuals would get the advantage of any future increase in land values.[42]

In 1871 August Theodor Stamm, in his *Die Erlösung der darbenden Menschheit,* presented views similar to those of Henry George.[43] Stamm believed that private property in land was the cause of nearly all human ills. In its abolition was to be found the complete solution of the social problem. Collective ownership might be effected in several ways, but the best means, Stamm believed, was gradually to absorb the rent of land by increasing the land tax. Stamm differed from George, however, in holding that, since the original wrong of private appropriation of land was not that of the present but of previous generations, the rights of present owners should receive some consideration.[44]

In 1879 Adolph Samter, in his *Das Eigentum in seiner socialen Bedeutung,* advocated land nationalization.[45]

When, in 1879, *Progress and Poverty* was published, it was early translated into German and attracted considerable attention in Germany.[46] The result of the discussion it aroused was the development of a group of Bodenreformers, who have worked assiduously for proposals similar to George's. The leaders among the Bodenreformers have

der darausfliessenden Regeln für menschliches Handeln, Brunswick, 1854.

[42] Dollfus, op. cit., p. 103, note.

[43] For an account of Stamm's views see Dollfus, op. cit., p. 101 et seq.

[44] Dollfus, op. cit., p. 102.

[45] See Menger, The Right to the Whole Produce of Labour, London, 1899, p. 151, note.

[46] See Henry George, Jr., The Life of Henry George, pp. 330, 343 (referred to hereafter as The Life of Henry George), and Dollfus, op. cit., p. 101.

been Michael Flürscheim, Theodor Hertzka, and Adolph Damaschke.[47]

Proposals similar to George's single tax have not found much favor in Germany. But the Germans have taken the lead in taxing the "unearned increment" of land values.[48]

Anticipations in movements for special taxation of land

Movements for special taxation of land together with exemption of improvements from taxation are met independently in several newly settled countries. It is not strange that settlers who improve their farms should resent the fact that the result of their labor is to add to the value of land held by non-improving or absentee speculators.

In Iowa in the thirties and forties there was a considerable movement for the exemption of improvements from taxation.[49] The actual settlers felt that non-resident speculators and big land-holders were bearing too little of the burdens of taxation. The outcome of the agitation against "land monopoly" was the passage of the act of January 14th, 1840, which made it the duty of the county assessor to assess real estate at "the actual value which such real estate would bear without the improvements thereupon."[50]

---

[47] For accounts of the German Bodenreform movement, see Dollfus, op. cit., pp. 101-08; Gutzeit, Die Bodenreform, Leipzig, 1907; articles in the special German number of the Single Tax Rev. (New York), Mar.-Apr., 1912, especially an article by W. Schrameier, Land Reform in Germany, Single Tax Rev., May-June and Jul.-Aug., 1912; and the files of Bodenreform, the organ of the Bodenreformers, published at Berlin.

See also Flürscheim, Auf friedlichem Wege, 1884; Hertzka, Freiland, ein soziales Zukunftsbild, Leipzig, 1890; and Damaschke, Die Bodenreform, Berlin, 1902.

[48] For an account of the German land increment taxes see Seligman, Essays in Taxation, New York, 1913, pp. 505-15.

[49] See Brindley, History of Taxation in Iowa, vol. I, pp. 8, 24-29, and 370-73 for an account of this movement.

[50] See Brindley, op. cit., pp. 8 and 361, note 16.

This law, however, was soon repealed as a majority of the legislature held it to be contrary to the Organic Law of the Territory.[51]

But the repeal did not put a stop to the agitation. It continued after Iowa had been admitted to the Union in 1846. The advocates of exempting improvements urged that the existing system encouraged "land monopoly" and speculation, and discouraged improvements.

"These lands of the capitalists [held for speculation] are now being more valuable by the labor of the settler, whose improvements are increasing the same, and the fruits of whose industry under the present law, are taxed to support that very government, which protects these lands, and without which they would be measurably valueless. . . .

"Assessments on land for taxes should be levied and graduated according to the relative value and quality of the same, whether selected in the country or towns, and . . . the value of improvements on such lands or town lots should not be included in the assessments unless it should be for corporation purposes in towns."[52]

The agitation, however, did not result in further legislation.

Similar ideas were advocated by a Wisconsin tailor, Edwin Burgess, of Racine.[53] In 1848 he wrote a letter from Racine which appeared in "Excursion No. 45, Clearance No. 3, of the Portland [Maine] Pleasure boat, J. Hacker, Owner, Master, and Crew,"[54] in which he said:

"I want now to say a few words on the best means of raising revenue or taxes so as to prevent land monopoly. I know not what are your views on the subject, but should like to have you inquire *whether raising all the taxes off the land*

[51] Ibid., pp. 24-25.
[52] Ibid., pp. 372, 373.
[53] See The Edwin Burgess Letters on Taxation, first published in the Racine (Wis.) Advocate, 1859-60, reprinted by W. S. Buffham, Racine, Wis., n.d. The introductory note gives a brief account of the life of Burgess.
[54] This letter was quoted in The Standard, Aug. 5, 1891, pp. 6-7.

*in proportion to its market value would not produce the great-
est good to mankind with the least evil,* of any means of raising revenue.   Taxing personal property has a tendency to limit
its use by increasing its price, and the consequent difficulty of
obtaining it."

In 1859-60 Burgess gave a more extensive presentation
of these ideas in a series of eleven letters to the Racine
Advocate, in which he urged that land should be taxed and
improvements exempted.[55]   These letters aroused considerable discussion and some opposition.   Burgess believed that
his policy would force idle land into use, would encourage
the production of wealth and increase opportunities for employment, and would do away with the evasion and fraud
which accompany other taxes.

"Were all the taxes on the land, and the people's land free,
then the hitherto landless could soon build their own homes on
their own land, and raise all they needed to consume or exchange, and no longer need the land, house, or capital of
others; then rent, interest, and even usury would cease for
want of poverty to sustain them, for the curse, land monopoly,
being removed, the effect would cease with the cause.   Thus
would the happiness of mankind be immeasurably increased,
and misery be proportionately diminished; then would earth
be redeemed from the giant sin of land robbery, and the
Paradise of the present or future be far above that of the
past."[56]

In the seventies similar ideas were expressed in Australia.
When Henry George was editing the San Francisco *Post,*
a copy of a tract written by Robert Savage, of the "Land
Tenure Reform League of Victoria," came to his attention.
He published an extract from it in an editorial in the *Post,*
April 16th, 1874.   The author of the tract declared that
"the allocation of the rents of the soil to the nation is the
only possible means by which a just distribution of the
created wealth can be effected."

[55] Cf. note 53, supra.   The arguments of "S.S." against Burgess's
proposal are included in the reprint.
[56] The Edwin Burgess Letters on Taxation, p. 14.

The movement for the exemption of improvements in western Canada dates from 1874, in which year the town of Nanaimo, on Vancouver Island, British Columbia, received a special charter permitting the total exemption of improvements from taxation.[57] Nanaimo has never taxed improvements.

Anticipations in the writings of the leading economists from the Physiocrats to Cairnes

Thus far we have considered anticipations of Henry George's ideas apart from the theories of the economists. But since it was from the doctrines of the classical economists, particularly from their theory of rent, that George drew many of the materials to frame his theory of distribution, it will be worth our while to examine briefly their ideas of the social significance of the rent of land, its taxation, and private property in land. We shall consider first the French Physiocrats, who formed the first real "school" of economists.

A cardinal doctrine of the Physiocrats[58] was that of the

[57] Haig, The exemption of improvements from taxation in Canada and the United States, a report prepared for the Committee on Taxation of the City of New York, New York, 1915, pp. 170-71. This report gives a full account of Canada's experiments in special taxation of land. For accounts of Australasian experience with land taxes see the British Blue Book of 1909, Taxation of Land, etc. Papers bearing on land taxes and on income taxes, etc., in certain foreign countries, and on the working of taxation of site values in certain cities of the United States and in British colonies, together with extracts relative to land taxation and land valuation from reports of Royal Commissions and Parliamentary Committees. Cd. 4750. See also an account by Knibbs in The Financial Yearbook of the Commonwealth of Australia, 1901-10, Melbourne, 1911; and Seligman, Essays in Taxation, New York, 1913, pp. 516-31.

[58] For accounts of the Physiocrats and their doctrines see Gide and Rist, Histoire des Doctrines Économiques, Paris, 1913, bk. 1, ch. 1, and Higgs, The Physiocrats, London, 1897. Regarding the relations between George's ideas and those of the Physiocrats see Rivaud, Henry George et la physiocratie, Paris, 1907.

impôt unique, a single tax upon land, which was proposed to supplant the complex and burdensome taxes of the *ancien régime.* The *impôt unique* occupies a much more prominent place in the history of economic thought than do other anticipations of George's doctrine. The term "single tax", the commonly used designation of George's doctrine, is a literal translation of *impôt unique.* So striking are the resemblances between these two single tax proposals that in 1886 Henry George, believing the Physiocrats to be his precursors, dedicated his *Protection or Free Trade* "to the memory of those illustrious Frenchmen of a century ago, Quesnay, Turgot, Mirabeau, Condorcet, DuPont and their fellows, who in the night of despotism foresaw the glories of the coming day", and in *Progress and Poverty* (1879) he wrote: "Without knowing anything of Quesnay or his doctrines, I have reached the same practical conclusion."[59] But he candidly stated that, since he was only acquainted with the works of the Physiocrats at second hand, he was unable to say how far their peculiar doctrines resembled his.

Some of his followers and critics, however, have been less cautious, and, misled by a superficial similarity, have assumed an unwarranted degree of correspondence between the two doctrines. It is true that the concrete proposals were the same—to do away with all taxes except upon land. But even here there was an important difference. George proposed that the state should absorb by taxation the entire rental value of land, while the Physiocrats believed that the *impôt unique* should not take more than a third of the *produit net* of agriculture.[60]

[59] Progress and Poverty, bk. 8, ch. 4, p. 422. Page references to Progress and Poverty refer to the 25th anniversary edition, New York, 1905.
[60] "La loi de la justice et celle de la sagesse se réunissent donc pour attribuer au moins les deux grand tiers du produit net, on revenu

This quantitative difference, however, was not the main one, for the Physiocratic conception of the significance of the *impôt unique* was fundamentally different from George's conception of his single tax. The Physiocrats urged their tax proposal, not because they saw a wrong in the private appropriation of the income from land, but because they believed that the *produit net* of agriculture was the sole source of increase in national wealth, the source from which all taxes, no matter how levied, must in the last analysis be paid.[61] The Physiocrats, it is true, regarded all taxes excepting upon land as indirect, as do the single taxers. But from widely different reasons. The Physiocrats regarded other taxes as indirect because they believed that they were ultimately shifted to the *produit net* of agriculture, regardless of the manner in which they may have been levied. The single taxers, on the other hand, believe that all taxes other than those upon land are indirect because they are shifted so as to become burdens on industry, taxes on labor, and a hindrance to the production of wealth; taxes upon land, they believe, are not shifted, and do not restrict the production of wealth.[62]

Furthermore the Physiocratic conception of the social effects of private property in land was directly opposite to that of present day single taxers. Far from seeing in this

---

clair et liquide, à chaque propriétaire foncier." Baudeau, Introduction a la Philosophie Économique, p. 760. Baudeau suggests a rate of six twentieths, i.e., thirty per cent (p. 760).

[61] "Ainsi, de quelque façon qu'on s'arrange, la classe productive, les propriétaires des terres, et l'impôt même, comme premiers distribuuers des dépenses, payent inévitablement la totalité de l'imposition indirecte." Quesnay, Second Probléme Économique (Daire's ed.), p. 135.

"Tous les impôts, sous quelque forme qu'ils soient perçus, retombent nécessairement à la charge des propriétaires des biens fonds, et sont toujours en dernière analyse payés par eux seuls, ou directement, ou indirectement." Turgot, Ouvres (Daire's ed.), vol. i, p. 416.

[62] Cf. Shearman, Natural Taxation, New York, 1895.

institution the fundamental cause of social injustice, the
Physiocrats believed in it thoroughly.   DuPont went so
far as to say: "La proportion de l'impôt avec le produit
net doit être telle que le sort du propriétaire foncier soit le
meilleur possible et que leur état soit préférable à tout autre
dans la société."[63]

One of the points of closest resemblance between George's
beliefs and those of these eighteenth century thinkers—a
point which has often escaped attention—is to be found in
the fact that each plan was proposed as the plan to usher
in the "natural order".

In Adam Smith's *Wealth of Nations* we find the germs
of the idea that land rent is peculiarly an unearned and
exploitative income.

"As soon as land becomes private property, the landlord
demands a share of almost all the produce which the labourer
can either raise, or collect from it.   His rent makes the first
deduction from the produce of the labour which is employed
upon the land."[64]

The idea of land rent as an income which, altogether
apart from any special activity of the land owner, tends to
increase spontaneously with the progress of society, yielding to its recipients a relatively increasing share in the
distribution of wealth, is also found in the *Wealth of Nations*.   We read there:

"Every improvement in the circumstances of the society
tends either directly or indirectly to raise the real rent of land,
to increase the real wealth of the landlord, his power of purchasing the labour, or the produce of the labour of other
people.

[63] Dupont, Physiocratie ou Constitution essentielle du gouvernement
le plus avantageous au genre humain (Daire's ed.), p. 356.
[64] Adam Smith, Wealth of Nations (McCulloch ed., 1850), bk. 1,
ch. 8, p. 29.   Smith goes on to say, however, that a second deduction
from the produce of labor is the profits of stock, which the master
receives from the laborer in return for advancing his maintenance or
supplying him with tools, etc.

" . . . The real value of the landlord's share, his real command of the labour of other people, not only rises with the real value of the produce, but the proportion of his share to the whole produce rises with it."[65]

Adam Smith referred to the propriety of taxing the rent of land in a peculiar way.

"Both ground-rents and the ordinary rent of land are a species of revenue which the owner, in many cases, enjoys without any care or attention of his own. Though a part of this revenue should be taken from him in order to defray the expenses of the state, no discouragement will thereby be given to any sort of industry. . . . Ground-rents, and the ordinary rent of land, are therefore, perhaps, the species of revenue which can best bear to have a peculiar tax imposed upon them. "Ground-rents seem in this respect a more proper subject of peculiar taxation than even the ordinary rent of land. . . . Ground-rents, so far as they exceed the ordinary rent of land, are altogether owing to the good government of the sovereign. . . . Nothing can be more reasonable than that a fund which owes its existence to the good government of the state should be taxed peculiarly, or should contribute something more than the greater part of other funds towards the support of that government."[66]

David Ricardo, whose theories of value and wages furnished the economic groundwork for Lasalle and Karl Marx, developed also the doctrine of rent which became the cardinal principle in the system of Henry George. It is one of the ironies of history that the theories of Ricardo, who was such a staunch exponent of the interests of the moneyed classes, should have been employed to justify radical attacks upon the economic interests of these classes. Professor H. S. Foxwell has well said that, whatever qualifications Ricardo may have made in his own mind upon his use of the term "labour", "ninety-nine readers out of a hundred took him literally, and the main impression left by his book was that while wealth was almost exclusively due

[65] Adam Smith, op. cit., bk. 1, ch. 11, p. 115.
[66] Ibid., bk. 5, ch. 2, pp. 380-81.

to labour, it was mainly absorbed by rent and other pay-
ments to the unproductive classes."[67]

"In a progressive country", argued Ricardo, . . . "the
landlord not only obtains a greater produce, but a larger
share." Hence, "the interest of the landlord is always opposed to the interest of every other class in the community.
His situation is never so prosperous as when food is scarce
and dear."[68] The difficulty of providing food for a growing population and the extension of the margin of cultivation to poorer lands assures to the landlord an indefinitely
increasing income. His gains are anti-social, secured at
the expense of the rest of the community.

Ricardo's followers have persistently held up the rent
of land as an anomalous income, an economic phenomenon
of an exceptional and somewhat mysterious nature. They
have represented it as an income pre-eminently not earned,
a charge whose payment is in no way essential to continued
production.[69] Since the step is so short from this idea to
the proposition that land rent should be intercepted from
land owners for the benefit of the rest of society, who do
contribute to production, the Ricardian economists must
shoulder a considerable part of the responsibility for the
single tax arguments. Cannan in his *Theories of Production and Distribution* wrote:

"The movement for 'nationalizing' land without compensation to present owners, on which Mr. Henry George and others
have wasted immense energy, would probably never have
been heard of, if the Ricardian economists had not represented

[67] Foxwell, Introduction to Menger, The Right to the Full Produce
of Labour, London, 1899, p. xlii.
[68] Ricardo, On the Influence of a Low Price of Corn on the Profits
of Stock, Works (McCulloch ed., 1871), pp. 375, 378.
[69] E. g. Carver writes in his Distribution of Wealth: "It is not
necessary that anyone should receive rent in order that there may
be land, and rent is not therefore necessary in order that there may
be production" (p. 208).

rent as a sort of vampire which continually engrosses a larger and larger share of the produce, and if they had not failed to classify rent and interest together as two species of one genus."[70]

George's doctrine that "rent or land value does not arise from the productiveness or utility of land," that "it in no wise represents any help or advantage given to production, but simply the power of securing a part of the results of production,"[71] looks remarkably like a corollary of the ordinary statements of the famous "law of rent".

James Mill discussed land taxation much more fully than did Adam Smith or Ricardo. In his *Political Economy,* 1821, he suggested that in a new country the rent of land would be a source peculiarly adapted to defray the expenditures of the state without burdening anyone.[72]   But in old countries

"where land has . . . been converted into private property, without making rent in a peculiar manner answerable for the public expenses; where it has been bought and sold upon such terms, and the expectations of individuals have been adjusted to that order of things, rent of land could not be taken to supply exclusively the wants of the government without injustice."[73]

James Mill's *Political Economy* is noteworthy in that it contains the earliest thorough consideration of the merits of a tax upon the "unearned increment" of land values. Much of the credit for the idea of taxing the increment of land values should be given to James Mill rather than, as is usual, to his more distinguished son.   James Mill wrote in his *Political Economy:*

"This continual increase, arising from the circumstances of the community, and from nothing in which the land-holders

[70] Cannan, Theories of Production and Distribution, London, 1903, p. 393.
[71] George, Progress and Poverty, bk. 3, ch. 2, p. 166.
[72] James Mill, Political Economy, p. 243.
[73] Ibid., p. 244.

themselves have any peculiar share, does seem a fund no less peculiarly fitted for appropriation to the purposes of the state, than the whole of the rent in a country where land had never been appropriated."[74]

John Stuart Mill, in his *Political Economy,* 1848, definitely proposed a tax on the future increment of land values. He urged that "the future increment of rent should be liable to special taxation; in doing which all injustice to the landlords would be obviated, if the present market price of their land were secured to them; since that includes the present value of all future expectations."[75]   Mill was largely instrumental in founding the "Land Tenure Reform Association", which, in 1870, commenced a definite program of propaganda for "the interception by taxation of the future unearned increase of the rent of land."[76]

Mill, in his *Political Economy,* definitely took the position that land ownership is less justifiable than the ownership of other wealth. "Landed property", he said, "is felt, even by those most tenacious of its rights, to be a different thing from other property."[77]

"When the 'sacredness of property' is talked of, it should always be remembered, that any such sacredness does not belong in the same degree to landed property. No man made the land. It is the original inheritance of the whole species. Its appropriation is wholly a question of general expediency. When private property in land is not expedient, it is unjust. It is no hardship to anyone to be excluded from what others

---

[74] Ibid., p. 247.

[75] John Stuart Mill, Political Economy, bk. 5, ch. 2, sec. 5.

[76] Mill, Dissertations and Discussions, vol. 5, p. 225, et seq.   The Programme of the Association is on pp. 225-26.

[77] Mill, Political Economy, bk. 2, ch. 2, sec. 6. It has been the theory of English law that land is not property in the same sense as is other wealth. Sir Frederick Pollock wrote that land does not belong to its owner "in the same sense as money or a watch"; that the law does not recognize its absolute private ownership, but regards it as "held, immediately or mediately, of the Crown". (The Land Laws, London, 1883, p. 12.)

ANTICIPATIONS 23

have produced: they were not bound to produce it for his use, and he loses nothing by not sharing in what otherwise would not have existed at all. But it is some hardship to be born into the world and to find all nature's gifts previously engrossed, and no place left for the new-comer."[78]

J. E. Cairnes followed Mill in his views, taking the position that property in land was fundamentally different from other forms of property, since "no man made the land". In his essay, *Political Economy and Land,* published in 1870 with reference to the Irish land question, he wrote:

"Sustained by some of the greatest names—I will say by every name of the first rank in Political Economy, from Turgot and Adam Smith to Mill—I hold that the land of a country presents conditions which separate it economically from the great mass of the other objects of wealth,—conditions which, if they do not absolutely and under all circumstances impose upon the State the obligation of controlling private enterprise in dealing with land, at least explain why this control is in certain stages of social progress indispensable."[79]

Conclusion

Summing up the results of our survey, we see that Henry George was anticipated in all the essential ideas of his economic and political philosophy: that the land, to which all men have equal natural rights, should not be engrossed by the few; that private property in land is peculiarly exploitative, and that private receipt of its income is a chief cause of poverty and misery; that, with the progress of society, this income tends to become larger both absolutely and relatively; and that land incomes should be liable to special treatment in taxation, even to being made the sole source of government support. Even in the relating of

[78] Mill, op. cit., bk. 2, ch. 2, sec. 6.
[79] Cairnes, Essays in Political Economy, Theoretical and Applied, London, 1873, p. 189. The essay here quoted was first published in 1870, in the Edinburgh Rev.

these ideas in a comprehensive system, Spence, Burgess, and, more completely, Dove anticipated him.

But to say that Henry George was anticipated on these points is far from saying that he was not original in his statements of them. Fortunately, we have his own full testimony regarding the extent of his indebtedness to others for the ideas which he first expressed in 1871 in his little book, *Our Land and Land Policy, National and State.* In 1874, while editing the San Francisco *Post,* he wrote editorially:

"So far as we know, we were the first upon the American continent or anywhere else, to enunciate the principle which will some day be an accepted axiom, that land is the only thing which should be taxed for purposes of revenue. And when we did, it was some time before we could find anyone else who thought the same way."[80]

The references to Malthus, Ricardo, and Mill in *Our Land and Land Policy* show that at this time George had some knowledge of their writings.[81] But, according to Henry George, Jr., he undertook no very thorough study of the economists until engaged in writing *Progress and Poverty.*[82]

Fifteen years later, when *Progress and Poverty* had become famous, Henry George was accused of having plagiarized from Patrick Edward Dove, and the charge was given some currency.[83] In replying, George wrote:

"I had worked out the whole thing for myself without conscious aid that I can remember unless it might have been for the light I got from Bisset's 'Strength of Nations' as to the economic character of the feudal system. When I published

[80] San Francisco Post, April 16, 1874.
[81] George, Our Land and Land Policy, pp. 82, 110.
[82] See Henry George, Jr.'s comment in a footnote in Henry George's Our Land and Land Policy, p. 82.
[83] J. W. Sullivan made this charge in a magazine called The Twentieth Century. See the Life of Henry George, p. 520.

'Our Land and Land Policy', I had not even heard of the
Physiocrats and the impôt unique."[84]

And in his *Political Economy,* published posthumously,
he stated that Herbert Spencer's *Social Statics* was the
only work of the kind that had come to his notice before
the writing of *Progress and Poverty.*[85]

Henry George unquestionably is to be ranked as one of
the boldest and freshest thinkers on economic problems.
He worked out a compact and unified theory of the distribution of wealth, making it his own by right of synthesis
and emphasis. The fact that the skeleton of ideas contained in *Progress and Poverty* is to be discovered in
Spence's pamphlets and Dove's wordy system has little
more than historical significance. Dr. E. R. Taylor, Henry
George's friend, writing in the *Single Tax Review,* point-
edly compared the precursors of Henry George to those
Norse wanderers whose ships touched the American shores
in the centuries before Columbus.[86]

Henry George's own words, written in reply to the
charge of plagiarism, may be final in this connection:

"It is not necessary for me to defend 'Progress and Poverty'
from a charge of plagiarism. What that book has done is a
sufficient answer.
"If it had been such a book as those it has rescued from
forgetfulness, it would have shared their fate."[87]

It was not *Progress and Poverty* alone, however, but
Progress and Poverty coupled with the energy and personality of its author, that gave rise to the single tax movement. No book sent forth unaided could have motivated
such an intense movement for social reform. From the

[84] The Standard, New York, Oct. 19, 1889.
[85] George, Political Economy, p. 189. In the seventh chapter of bk. 2
George discusses anticipations of his ideas and disclaims knowledge of
them.
[86] Single Tax Rev., July-Aug., 1912, p. 8.
[87] The Standard, Oct. 19, 1889.

publication of *Progress and Poverty* in 1879 until the very hour of his death Henry George gave himself unsparingly to the spreading of the faith. Speaking and writing, he carried his message from one end of the United States to the other and even around the world.[88]

[88] For a full discussion of Henry George's. personal activities in founding and spreading the single tax movement, see Henry George, Jr., The Life of Henry George, New York, 1900.

CHAPTER II

THE ECONOMIC BACKGROUND OF HENRY GEORGE'S DOCTRINE

On the 27th of May, 1858, Henry George first set foot in San Francisco after a stormy voyage of one hundred and fifty-five days around the Horn. A lad of eighteen, he had left his Philadelphia home to come to the Pacific Coast in search of his fortune. But California with all its famed wealth offered no easy road to success, and through years of poverty and hard knocks Henry George was compelled to struggle for a livelihood.[1]

It was during the years 1858 to 1870 that he formulated his views upon economic and social questions. Possessed though he undoubtedly was of remarkable originality as an economic thinker, it can not be questioned that California's peculiar economic conditions exercised a profound influence upon the course of his thought. Judge James G. Maguire, George's friend before *Progress and Poverty* was written and later prominent in the single tax movement, has said that George "could not have discovered the great truths of political economy but for the social and industrial phenomena which transpired within his experience", and that had it not been for "the marvelously rapid evolution manifested in California, in which was shown every stage of land monopolization that was developed in Europe and

[1] See The Life of Henry George, by Henry George, Jr. Referred to hereafter as The Life of Henry George.

27

America in many centuries, we would now have no single-tax agitation."[2]

Regarding the formulation of his economic philosophy Henry George himself wrote in 1880:

"I certainly neither picked it up second-hand nor got it by inspiration.[3] I came to it by a long, laborious, and most conscientious investigation. I came to it by the very same road over which I have essayed in this book [Progress and Poverty] to lead my readers.

". . . If I have been enabled to emancipate myself from ideas which have fettered far abler men, it is, doubtless, due to the fact that my study of social problems was in a country like this [California], where they have been presented with peculiar directness, and perhaps also to the fact that I was led to think a good deal before I had a chance to do much reading."[4]

A consideration of some of these social problems which presented themselves with such "peculiar directness" in the California of the quarter century following the gold discoveries serves to shed considerable light upon the conception and development of Henry George's ideas.

Spanish and Mexican land grants

The land question, always at the fore in new communities, was peculiarly prominent in California for forty years after the American occupation. This prominence resulted in large part from two causes. The first was the liberal land grant policy of Spain and (after 1822) of Mexico. The second was the policy—or perhaps lack of policy—in regard to the settlement of claims to these grants which the United States adopted after the acquisition of California in 1848.

---

[2] See Justice, a Philadelphia (and Wilmington, Del.) single tax weekly, Jan. 5, 1895, p. 3.

[3] But see infra, p. 45.

[4] In the Sacramento Record-Union, Mar. 27, 1880, replying to a review of Progress and Poverty.

The original Spanish settlement of California in 1769 was a scheme of colonization. The Franciscan missions, extending from San Diego to the Golden Gate, were "stepping-stones, over which to pass to the true civilization of the new land".[5] Likewise the *pueblos* and *presidios* had their part in the plan of settlement. During the period from 1769 to 1846 the problem had been to get the country peopled, and accordingly the authorities usually stood ready to grant unoccupied lands to any native or naturalized citizen who might apply and meet simple requirements.[6] Under the Spanish régime the number of grants was probably not more than thirty. But the Mexican authorities were more liberal, particularly after 1833, and when the United States took possession of California in 1846 more than eight million acres of the choicest lands of the state were in the hands of some eight hundred Mexican grantees.[7]

During the interregnum American military officials promised the preservation of existing property rights.[8] The treaty of Guadaloupe Hidalgo reaffirmed this guarantee. But what these rights actually amounted to in the case of the land grants was almost past finding out. Grants had been made loosely and in general terms—often for a given number of leagues at a place indicated by name only. Titles, descriptions, and boundaries adequate for the Mexican régime could hardly meet the standards of American law.

[5] Royce, California, p. 22.

[6] See pages 2 to 5 of the Report on the subject of land titles in California, by William Carey Jones, in the Senate Documents, 31st Congress, 2nd session, vol. 3, no. 18. The limit of area which might be granted to a single individual was eleven square leagues, the square league being 4,428.4 acres. Ibid., p. 3.

[7] Bancroft, History of California, vol. 6, pp. 529-30. Donaldson states in The Public Domain (p. 381) that the area of these grants confirmed to 1880 was more than eight million acres.

[8] Bancroft, op. cit., p. 533.

When California "broke out" in 1848, the situation became far more acute. From every quarter of the earth came thousands of eager immigrants, drawn to the magic land by the rumors of its golden treasure. California, in the active imaginations of the gold seekers and of the bulk of the American populace as well, existed as a land where, interspersed with valuable farming lands, fabulous gold deposits abounded.[9] Such an earthly paradise should not be allowed to remain unchallenged in the hands of a few hundred despised Mexican grantees.

The years following 1848 were years of bitter conflict—on the one side the land-grant holders with their vague and extensive claims, and on the other the newcomers, eager to locate on desirable land. The impatience of these would-be settlers is well set forth in the following letter of L. W. Hastings to the California *Star,* March 13, 1847:

"[Let the settlers] apply wherever they may, and to whomsoever they may, and the result is invariably the same: they are repulsed with an indignant 'This is all mine'. This all-embracing occupant, after the very expressive and exclusive declamation here alluded to, goes on to describe his unbounded premises. 'That mountain', says he, 'on the east is the southeast corner of my farm, and that timbered country which you see in the distance is my northwest corner; the other corners of my farm are rather indefinitely marked at present, but I shall endeavor to have the *rope* applied to them also, as soon as the *alcalde* is at leisure.' "[10]

[9] "It was not of 500 or 1,000 rancheros, living on stock farms owned by themselves and their fathers, and of little value by American standards, that the Senate was thinking, but of a marvelous land of gold-mines, great towns, and limitless prospects; not of a quiet pastoral people, but of a horde of speculators, hungry for gold and power and land; not so much of the valid claims as of the fraudulent ones; of the unknown more than the known." Bancroft, op. cit., pp. 539-540,

[10] Cited in Royce, California, p. 209. We should perhaps discount Hasting's opinion. He was active in anti-Mexican propaganda before the American occupation, and naturally hostile to all things Mexican, including the grants.

The American policy regarding the land grants

The matter of quieting California land titles came up in Congress in 1848 and again in 1849, but nothing was done. At length, the discussion of the session of 1850-51 resulted in the Land Act of March 3, 1851.[11] This act provided that the grantees should appear before a board of commissioners with their titles, claims, and witnesses. But the decision of this board was not final, since either party might take appeal to the district court, and to the United States Supreme Court.

International obligation and common sense alike should have shown that the plain duty of Congress was to devise a means for the prompt settlement of titles in the interests of the orderly progress and development of California's resources. But, after delaying action from 1848 to 1851, Congress passed an act as a contemporary Californian characterized it, "nominally to 'settle' private land claims in California, but really to unsettle them and the whole country, and keep them unsettled."[12]

It is not worth while to review at length the dreary history of the prolonged litigation which resulted from this

[11] Preparatory to the execution of the guarantee of titles promised by the treaty with Mexico, two investigations were made. Capt. H. W. Halleck submitted a report March 1, 1849, detailing the laws and regulations under which the Spanish and Mexican governments had granted lands. (31st Cong., 1st sess., H. Ex. Doc. no. 17) On April 10th, 1850, Wm. Carey Jones submitted to the Secretary of the Interior an able report on the subject of land titles in California. (31st Cong. 2nd sess., Sen. Doc. no. 18) The burden of his report was that "the grants in California . . . are mostly perfect titles"; that although some are not technically perfect, they "have the same equity as those which are perfect, and were and would have been equally respected under the government which has passed away." (p. 34) Jones recommended an authoritative survey of the grants, the United States reserving the right to proceed against those which seemed questionable.

[12] Hittell, The Resources of California, San Francisco, 1863, pp. 455-56.

act.[13] Suffice it to say that the real working-out of the law
was that, instead of the United States complying with its
treaty obligation to confirm equitable titles, the grantees
were compelled to defend their claims against a stubborn
opposition by the legal agents of the United States.[14] The
reason for this was that the "squatter" interests, which desired to oust the grantees, were "masquerading in the name
of the United States" and brought about numerous appeals
even where the titles were the clearest.[15] These interests,
says Bancroft, "in a majority of cases continued the contest when all proper motives had ceased to exist."[16] The
plan of settlement needs no further condemnation than the
fact that the litigation dragged along for more than thirty
years.

Meanwhile, the effects of unsettled land titles and un-
marked boundaries appeared—doubt, fraud, bloodshed, and
general insecurity. As Bancroft has well said: "In a
sense there was no government land to be purchased; every
occupant felt that his possession was threatened by squatters on the one hand, or by grant owners on the other;
neither squatters nor grant owners could sell, or dared to

[13] An excellent contemporary account is that of Hittell, op. cit., pp.
453-61, also the same writer's History of California, vol. 2, bk. 7,
ch. 10; see too, Bancroft, History of California, vol. 6, ch. Mexican
Land Grants, and Royce, California, ch. 6.

[14] Hittell says sarcastically (op. cit., p. 457): "All the law agents
were competent men, and no one can justly complain that the interests of the United States were neglected by any one of them."

[15] Bancroft, op. cit., p. 571.

[16] Ibid., p. 577. The following figures tell the story: 813 claims
were presented, 591 of which were confirmed, 203 rejected, and 19
dropped. 264 were finally settled by the board, 450 by the district
court, and 99 by the U. S. Supreme Court. (Ibid., p. 542.)
Patents were issued as follows:

1856 to 1860— 96	1871 to 1875—135
1861 to 1865— 91	1876 to 1880— 64
1866 to 1870—141	(Ibid., p. 571, note)

invest in extensive improvements."[17]   Such conditions
drove away, or prevented from coming, the best class of
farmers, thereby greatly retarding the development of agriculture, which, rather than mining, was bound to be the
permanent main industry of the state.

Under conditions such as these began California's "land
monopoly". The Californians were unable to retain their
huge estates. They were persecuted and plundered by
squatters, who seized on part of their lands and resisted
expulsion, refusing to leave except for blackmail.[18] Forced
to pay in land the costs of the seemingly endless litigation,
the owners handed over large tracts to their lawyers. A
contemporary considered that in this manner the original
owners lost at least two-fifths of their holdings.[19]

The concentration of land ownership in California is not
chargeable directly to the fact that in 1846 a few hundred
unambitious native Californians held several million acres
of the best lands of the state. Had their titles been
promptly confirmed, they would likely have sold much of
this to settlers at less than government prices.[20] It was due
rather to the land policy of the United States, which, far

[17] Ibid., p. 577.

[18] "The squatters took the land, occupied it, drove away the owner's
cattle, cut down his trees, fenced in his springs, paid him no rent, paid
no taxes, by their influence forced him to pay the taxes on the land
they were occupying, and assessed the taxes at most exorbitant rates.
This system was not rare, but frequent—it was practised on not one,
but a hundred ranches. And then, with the money derived from the
land thus obtained, they paid lawyers to appear in the name of the
United States, contest the owner's title, and delay a decision; and,
after decision, to get up a contest about the survey and delay a settlement of the boundaries." Hittell, Resources of California, 1863, p. 459.
See too Royce, California, p. 488, et seq.

[19] Hittell, op. cit., p. 460. See also Bancroft, op. cit., p. 571.

[20] Bancroft tells of men who would have willingly sold land for
25 or 50 cents per acre (op. cit., p. 635). The best recorded price of
land to 1846 was $1,000 per league (op. cit., p. 533, note).

from executing the sacred promises of the treaty, really, as
Bancroft has said, resulted in "confiscation, and that not in
the real interests of the United States, or of American settlers, but of speculating land sharpers".[21]

The public land policy of the United States

At the same time the federal public land policy tended
to encourage "land monopoly". The Act of March 3, 1853,
admitted California lands to preëmption, with all of its
opportunities for fraud and land-grabbing, from which
California suffered along with the other parts of the
West.[22]   Other lands were located with the Agricultural
College scrip of eastern states and with "Half Breed
scrip" (issued to Indians in lieu of their lands), located
by speculators as "attorneys" for the Indians.[23]

A further factor in the situation was the granting of
large tracts within the borders of California to railways.
The total area of these grants is estimated by Donaldson
at 16,387,000 acres, or more than sixteen per cent of the
entire area of the state.[24]   The chief railways favored were
the Western Pacific, Central Pacific, Southern Pacific, Atlantic and Pacific, Texas and Pacific, and California and
Oregon.   These grants included some of the richest lands
of the state.

The public land policy of California

The policy of the state of California in the disposal of
its lands was no better than the policy of the United States.

[21] Op cit., p. 577. See too Royce, California, p. 491.
[22] See Hill, The Public Domain and Democracy, Columbia Univ.
Studies, 1910, p. 46.
[23] Henry George describes this in Our Land and Land Policy, 18/1
(1900 reprint, pp. 51-52).
[24] The Public Domain, p. 287. "The above estimate is for the quantity of land which will be given by the United States to the various
roads *if they are constructed.*" Italics the present writer's.

Acquiring a rich endowment of land under the several Land Acts, California squandered it through the extravagance of the legislatures of the first twenty years.[25]   The Act of September 28, 1850, gave to each state the swamp and overflowed lands within its bounds.[26]   The Legislature of 1854 promptly provided for their sale at the uniform price of one dollar per acre.[27]   Under the Act of March 3, 1853, California received the 16th and 36th sections for school purposes, a grant under which, 6,719,324 acres had been patented to June 30, 1880.[28]   The same act granted two townships for a state university.

The following is Bancroft's account of California's use of these grants:

"In relation to these several grants of land, in 1869 . . . all of the seventy-two sections . . . had been sold.   Very little swamp land remained, and only the least desirable of the surveyed common-school lands. . . .   By an act of the legislature of 1868, . . . provision was made for the sale of all **the lands** of every kind owned by the state, or in which she had any interest, the maximum price being fixed at $1.25 an acre.

"Thus in eighteen years the state had disposed of her vast landed possessions, making no attempt to increase their value by improvements, nor leaving any to rise in value along with the development of the country about them.   The money realized was . . . dissipated by the extravagance of the early legislatures, or fraudulently disposed of by political tricksters in collusion with dishonest officials."[29]

---

[25] See Bancroft, op. cit., vol. 6, ch. 22, Finances.

[26] See Donaldson, op. cit., p. 219 et seq.   He says (p. 220): "The swamp land acts have been the subject of much complaint of fraud, actual fraud, and deceit."

Henry George charges in Our Land and Land Policy (p. 60), that half of the land sold as swamp is good dry land.   "Lands thousands of feet above the level of the sea have been purchased as swamp; lands over which a heavily loaded wagon can be driven in the month of May; and even lands which cannot be cultivated without irrigation."

[27] Bancroft, op. cit., p. 615.

[28] Donaldson, op. cit., p. 228.

[29] Bancroft, op. cit., pp. 640-41.

The concentration of land ownership

Testimony abounds as to the effect of the above-mentioned factors in bringing about in California during the first fifteen years of statehood an unusual concentration of land ownership in the hands of a comparatively few holders. But concrete statistics as to the process of development of these conditions are almost entirely wanting. The United States Census reports of 1860 and 1870 are incomplete and manifestly unreliable as regards the listing and classification of California farms.[30] The most adequate statistics are those compiled in 1872 by the first California State Board of Equalization. The figures are compiled from the Assessors' reports of 1872 "for the purpose of showing the number of farms in the state containing 100 acres and upwards." This report, says the Board, "exhibits the size and locality of the farms with sufficient certainty to enable a correct idea to be formed respecting the extent of the alleged evils of land monopoly in this state."[31]

Classification of holdings of farms.[32]

Class	Size (acres)			No. of farms
1	100	to	500	23,315
2	500	to	1,000	2,383
3	1,000	to	2,000	1,126
4	2,000	to	3,000	363
5	3,000	to	4,000	189
6	4,000	to	5,000	104
7	5,000	to	10,000	236
8	10,000	to	20,000	158
9	over	20,000		122

[30] The California State Board of Equalization wrote of the census figures: "They do not come near representing all the farms either in the aggregate or in the classes in which they are subdivided" (1872-73 Report, p. 24).

Compare the figures cited in the 1870 Census volume Industry and Wealth, pp. 340-41, with those here cited from the Report of the California State Board of Equalization.

[31] Report of the State Board of Equalization, 1872-73, in Appendix to the Journals of Senate and Assembly, 20th session, vol. II, p. 22.

[32] Ibid., pp. 22-23.

The total acreage of the farms in each class is not given. But if we take the average size of the farms in each class to be one third of the way between the maximum and minimum (e.g. in class four, 2333 acres, etc.), with the average in class nine as 30,000 acres,[33] we should obtain an approximate estimate. This method, applied to the farms classed as larger than 5,000 acres, would give the total area of such holdings as 7,340,000 acres. Applied to holdings larger than 2,000 acres, their total area would appear as 9,267,000 acres. The total area assessed is stated as 20,029,890 acres.[34] According to the above estimate, the 516 holdings larger than 5,000 acres would form 36.6 per cent of the total, while the 1,172 holdings larger than 2,000 acres would form 46.3 per cent of it.

The census of 1870 gave California's population as 560,000. If the above rough estimate is correct, and one five-hundredth of the population held nearly one half of the available agricultural land, there was surely a real basis for the popular charge of "land monopoly".

Land speculation

As regards the speculative withholding of land from the market a singular stupidity was often shown. The charge made by Henry George in 1873 that the large landowners of the state were "dogs in the manger, who will not use the land themselves or let anybody else use it", was more than mere rhetoric.[35] The desire to wait for the unearned increment led to the withholding of so much land from the market that the development of California was held back.

[33] In Our Land and Land Policy, 1871, (1900 reprint, pp. 71-72), Henry George mentions a dozen holdings of from 100,000 to 450,000 acres. An average of 30,000 does not appear excessively high.
[34] Report of the California State Board of Equalization, 1872-73, p. 27.
[35] San Francisco Post, Apr. 7, 1873.

J. M. Days, in a speech delivered in the Legislature in 1875,
charged that immense tracts were held by those who would
neither sell nor pay taxes: "It is the land monopolist who
gathers toll everywhere and puts a blight on everything.
He holds millions of acres of uncultivated land, refusing to
sell except at an enormous price. He pays comparatively
no taxes, shifting the burden on industry. He drives the
poor into cities to compete with one another for bread."[36]
The railroads too, it appears, for a time failed to see the
great possibilities of building up traffic by disposing of their
lands at liberal prices.[37]   So it was difficult in many sections for California's growing population to purchase land
at prices which they regarded as reasonable.

It is evident that the holding of large tracts of unused
land would be difficult were these holdings assessed at the
same value as that at which they were held for sale, and
likewise difficult were they assessed at a value approaching
that of improved land of similar character and situation.
But the difference in appearance between unimproved land
and land on which a man has done a year or so of work was
greater than the difference in value, and assessors were
more likely to consider the difference in appearance, assessing the unimproved holding at a merely nominal sum, and
making the assessment of the improved farm inordinately
high.   It was a system whose workings offered a "premium
for monopolization" of land, and which seemed to penalize
the maker of improvements.[38]   It was the belief of the 1872
State Board of Equalization that the most marked inequality in assessment was "in the failure, in many counties, to
assess lands at their full value, and in assessing large tracts
at a much less rate per acre than small ones, and also in

[36] See California Speeches, vol. 5, in State Library, Sacramento.
[37] Statement of Mr. J. A. Filcher, Sept. 1913.
[38] See the San Diego Union, quoted in the San Francisco Post, Dec.
16, 1871.

permitting considerable amounts of land to escape assessment altogether."[39]

Growth of population and land values

Another distinctive feature of the early years of California was the unusual rapidity of the growth of population. Lured by the golden treasure, thousands found their way around the Horn, across the Isthmus, or over the prairies, mountains, and deserts to the land of promise, peopling it as rapidly as any portion of the United States has been peopled. The following figures tell the story:

	Population of California	Population of San Francisco
1848	20,500[40]	800[41]
1850	112,097[40]	16,500[40]
1860	379,994	56,802
1870	560,247	149,473
1880	864,694	233,959

With the coming of these immigrants real estate values mounted by leaps and bounds. The San Francisco *Directory* for 1852 (p. 9) describes in a striking manner the arrival of the brig *Belfast* from New York, laden with a valuable cargo of goods. "She hauled up to the Broadway wharf, the only wharf accessible to such a vessel, and there discharged. No sooner was she known to be landing her cargo than goods of all kinds fell twenty-five per cent, and real estate rose fifty per cent. A vacant lot on the corner of Washington and Montgomery streets at that time bordering on the water, which had been offered for $5,000 and refused, sold readily the very next day for $10,000."

This period exhibited increases in the value of land which were beyond all precedent.[42] With the discovery of

[39] Report, p. 7.
[40] Bancroft's estimate, History of California, vol. 6, pp. 158-59.
[41] Royce, California, p. 220.
[42] However, increase in the value of California land was by no means

gold, the time when the highest recorded price of land was
$1,000 per league passed forever.[43]   The authors of the
Annals of San Francisco, after recounting the big gains
which men got in gold-mining, merchandising, and loaning
capital at thirty or sixty per cent, say:

"But chiefly it was the holders of real estate that made the
greatest fortunes. The possession of a small piece of building
ground in or about the centre of business was a fortune in
itself. Those lucky people who held lots from the times before
the discovery of gold, or who shortly afterwards managed to
secure them, were suddenly enriched, beyond their first most
sanguine hopes. The enormous rents paid for the use of
ground and temporary buildings in 1849 made all men covetous
of real estate. . . .
"The temptation to perpetrate any trick, crime, or violence,
to acquire real estate, seemed to be irresistible, when the great
returns drawn from it were considered. . . . The rents of the
larger hotels, of the restaurants, coffee saloons, gambling and
billiard rooms, and of the finer stores and warehouses, would
appear almost incredible to the distant reader. Ordinary
stores, offices, and dwelling-houses were rented at equally extravagant sums. . . . In a couple of years, the building speculator in real estate had all his outlay (which, since labor and
materials were so very high, was exceedingly great) returned
to him in the shape of rents. Henceforward his property was
a very mine of wealth. As rents rose, so did the prices of such
property. The richest men in San Francisco have made the
best portion of their wealth by the possession of real estate."[44]

Henry George and these conditions

Such was the background of Henry George's experience,
such were the peculiar economic circumstances amid which
from early manhood he struggled for livelihood for a score
of years.   He witnessed intimately perhaps the most dis-

steady, there being many and rapid fluctuations in population and
prosperity. See Bancroft, History of California, vol. 6, pp. 781-82,
and Royce, California, p. 422 et seq.
[43] Bancroft, op. cit., p. 533, note.
[44] Soule, Gihon, and Nisbet, The Annals of San Francisco, 1855.
The citations here are from pages 498 to 500.

creditable episodes in all our checquered public land history:
the seizure by greedy land grabbers of half of California's
choicest lands; the speculative withholding of much of this
land from the market. Uncertain land titles and conflict-
ing claims conspired with these conditions to make it hard
for the average man to get a foothold upon the land, and
thereby held back the material progress of the state.

George's theory of progress becomes better understood
in the light of these peculiar California conditions. In the
first years after the gold discovery deserted ships rotted in
San Francisco Bay, and city artisans commanded fabu-
lously high wages. But as the exceptional opportunities
for stumbling upon fortunes or for taking up rich lands
were seized by those first on the ground, as multitudes of
men came in, eager to compete for what they regarded as
the opportunities of a century, the inevitable leveling down
process commenced and rates of wages began slowly to re-
cede toward the levels obtaining elsewhere.[45] Prevented
from taking up land in the rural districts by California's
extreme "land monopoly" and by the instability of land
titles, men drifted to the cities as the chance of an individual's "washing out" big gains became rarer, and as hy-
draulic and quartz mining gradually took the place of
simpler and cruder methods. During the decade, 1860 to
1870, more than half of the increase of California's population was in San Francisco. In 1860, fifteen per cent of
the population of the state was in its largest city; in 1870,
twenty-seven per cent. The evils of poverty and vice, always most conspicuous in cities, manifested themselves in
San Francisco.

Henry George was more than a mere observer of these

[45] Hittell states that the wages of carpenters fell from sixteen dollars per day in 1849 to five dollars in 1856, and to four dollars in
1862. Resources of California, p. 305.

conditions. He was himself a working-man, who had thought the thoughts of wage workers and looked upon life from their point of view. He had worked before the mast and at the printer's bench. In California he had lived the life of a poor man and had walked the streets of San Francisco in search of employment. He had himself grappled with untoward conditions and had been distressed by the problem he attempted to solve. The opposite of the closet philosopher, he got his ideas from immediate experience and observation.

CHAPTER III

THE FORMULATION OF GEORGE'S ECONOMIC IDEAS

In a pamphlet published in San Francisco in 1871 with the title *Our Land and Land Policy, National and State,* Henry George first presented his idea that "the pursuance of a wrong policy in regard to land"[1] is the fundamental cause of poverty and social injustice. But it is evident that from boyhood he had been thinking on economic problems. In a speech of February 4, 1890, in San Francisco, he recalled two interesting incidents which reveal the trend of his early thoughts.[2] The first was of a conversation, when he was a boy of nineteen, with a group of miners on a schooner bound for the Frazer gold fields. He had asked what harm the much-maligned Chinese were doing in the mines if they were only working the cheap diggings.

"And one old miner turned to me, and he said [sic], 'no harm now; but it will not be always that wages are as high as they are today in California. As the country grows, as people come in, wages will go down and some day or other white men will be glad to get these diggings that the Chinamen are now working.' And I well remember how it impressed me, the idea that as the country grew in all that we are hoping that it may grow, the condition of those who had to work for their living must grow, not better, but worse."

[1] George, Our Land and Land Policy, National and State, p. 121. The original edition of this is very rare. The citations here are from Henry George, Jr.'s reprint of 1900.

[2] This address is printed in J. H. Barry's single tax weekly, the San Francisco Star, Feb. 8, 1890. See also The Life of Henry George, pp. 80, 100.

The other incident was his seeing, a year or so later, on a new theatre drop curtain "what was then a dream of the far future—the overland train coming into San Francisco." "After we had shouted ourselves hoarse", he said "I began to think what good is it going to be to men like me—to those who have nothing but their labor?"

Henry George's first formal writing on an economic subject was an article *What the Railroad Will Bring Us,* in the *Overland Monthly,* October, 1868. Although "single tax" ideas are not evident, we find several passages which foreshadow ideas later set forth in *Progress and Poverty.* After observing that the high rates of wages and interest then prevailing in California were "indications that the natural wealth of the country was not yet monopolized",[3] he forecasted that the tendency of the approaching era of denser population and development would be toward a lowering of the rates of interest, and especially of wages, and to increasing economic inequality.

"As a general rule . . . those who have, it will make wealthier; for those who *have not,* it will make it more difficult to get. Those who have lands, mines, established businesses, special abilities of certain kinds, will become richer for it and find increased opportunities; those who have only their own labor will become poorer, and find it harder to get ahead."[4]

Henry George's trip to New York in 1868-69 was a most significant event in the formulation of his economic ideas. Fresh from the new West, this thoughtful young man of thirty was shocked by the sight of old-world poverty in the very shadow of the homes of wealth. "The contrast of luxury and want that I saw in New York appalled me", he wrote nearly thirty years later, "and I left for the West feeling that there must be a cause for this, and that if possible I would find out what it was".[5]

[3] Overland Monthly, Oct. 1868, p. 302.
[4] Idem.
[5] George, The Science of Political Economy, p. 201. See too The Life of Henry George, p. 191, et seq.

The answer was not long in appearing. The latter part of 1869 saw George once more in California, and engaged in editing the Oakland *Transcript*.[6] On the tenth of May of that year, the driving of the golden spike had marked the completion of the Pacific railway, and California was filled with high hopes. Sacramento was then the California terminus of the Central Pacific, but the prospect of extending the line to Oakland had led to a great speculation in lands. Fancy prices were set on land from the eastern shore of San Francisco Bay for miles back among the Oakland hills. It was under such conditions that Henry George rode out on horseback on a memorable afternoon to pass through what he later described as "one of those experiences that make those who have had them feel thereafter that they can vaguely appreciate what mystics and poets have called the 'ecstatic vision' ".[7] Regarding this experience, he said in after years:

"Absorbed in my own thoughts, I had driven the horse into the hills until he panted. Stopping for breath, I asked a passing teamster, for want of something better to say, what land was worth there. He pointed to some cows grazing off so far that they looked like mice and said: 'I don't know exactly, but there is a man over there who will sell some land for a thousand dollars an acre'. Like a flash it came upon me that there was the reason of advancing poverty with advancing wealth. With the growth of population, land grows in value, and the men who work it must pay more for the privilege. I turned back, amidst quiet thought, to the perception that then came to me and has been with me ever since."[8]

Henry George's opportunity to develop and present his ideas did not at once occur. In February, 1870, shortly after his "vision", he accepted the editorship of the Sacramento *Reporter*,[9] and commenced an aggressive opposition

[6] The Life of Henry George, p. 197.
[7] George, The Science of Political Economy, p. 163.
[8] See The Life of Henry George, p. 210.
[9] Ibid., p. 211.

to the Central Pacific Railway's campaign for state and
county subsidies, to be secured by means of "taxation for
railroad companies".[10]   The editorial columns of the *Reporter,* primarily engaged in attacks on the railway power,
took up the question of railway land grants, opposing land
subsidies, both national and state, and pointing out the
abuses to which they gave rise.

So vigorous was George's fight that within a few months
the railway interests bought control of the paper, forcing
his retirement.   But his retirement did not mean his silence.
A pamphlet soon appeared from his pen, *The Subsidy Question and the Democratic Party,* an able and effective arraignment of the policy and principle of subsidization.[11]
Land grants squandered "the public domain, the patrimony
of the people, the birthright of millions yet to come".   Hot-
house methods of railway extension would, it is true, create
an increase in the value of land, but this "can only in small
degree be considered any actual increase in wealth".[12]   And
George did not lose the opportunity during this fight to
say a word against "individual monopolization of public
lands".   "It is cheap land that has given us our rapid
growth, that has made us an intelligent, active, free, independent people. . . . When the day comes that land in
the United States is monopolized . . . as in England or
Ireland . . . we may bid good-bye to those traits of character and those institutions which have been our peculiar
glory."[13]

[10] This is the title of an editorial in the Reporter, May 7, 1870.
[11] There is a copy of this pamphlet in the Library of the University
of California.
[12] George, The Subsidy Question and the Democratic Party, pp. 13, 6.
[13] Editorial, "The public lands", Sacramento Reporter, May 4, 1870.

"Our Land and Land Policy"

It was in the latter part of 1871 that *Our Land and Land Policy, National and State* appeared in San Francisco. In this booklet of forty-eight closely typed pages, Henry George for the first time gave to the world his solution for the problem he had set himself to solve. His attitude as a reformer is well set forth in the following quotation from this little book:

"There is a problem which must present itself to every mind which dwells upon the industrial history of the present century; a problem into which all our great social, industrial, and even political questions run—which already perplexes us in the United States; which presses with still greater force in the older countries of Europe; which, in fact, menaces the whole civilized world, and seems like a very riddle of the Sphinx, which fate demands of modern civilization, and which not to answer is to be destroyed—the problem of the proper distribution of wealth."[14]

This little book comprised five parts: I The Lands of the United States, II The Lands of California, III Land and Labour, IV The Tendency of Our Present Land Policy, V What our Land Policy Should Be. Parts I, II and IV call attention to the reckless prodigality of the land policy of nation and state, and its tendency to concentrate ownership in the hands of the few. Parts III and V contain the argument later developed and clarified in *Progress and Poverty*, that land-owners receive the lion's share of the benefits of economic advance, and that the placing of the chief weight of taxation upon land would solve most of our social problems.[15]

We need not review this familiar argument, but some differences between Henry George's ideas as here set forth and as eight years later embodied in his more famous work

[14] Our Land and Land Policy, p. 118.
[15] See especially pp. 117-24.

deserve attention. Although Henry George considered
property in land to be different from property in other
wealth, he stated here that "the recognition of private
ownership in land is necessary to its proper use—is, in fact,
a condition of civilization."[16] He would only have his reform assure that "there should be no monopolisation—no
standing between the man who is willing to work and the
field which nature offers for his labour."[17] He also proposed that unoccupied lands should be given to actual settlers in lots of forty or perhaps eighty acres, thereby insuring
regular and normal settlement.[18]

It is of interest, too, to note that the land tax as here
proposed was not to absorb all the rent of land;[19] it was
only to supplant most of the existing taxes. Nor was the
land tax to be a uniform, proportional tax—the sole fiscal
dependence of the state. Each land-holder was to enjoy a
limited exemption "for the purpose of still further counter-
acting the tendency to the concentration of wealth, and for
the purpose of securing as far as possible to every citizen
an interest in the soil."[20] Furthermore, two additional
sorts of taxation were suggested, namely, an inheritance
tax, which "should be a very heavy duty, amounting to a
considerable part of the whole [estate]", and license taxes
for purposes of restriction.[21] It is plain to see that in 1871

[16] Ibid., p. 88. It is difficult to reconcile this passage with others
here on property in land, e.g. this on p. 121: "The ownership of the
land gives the power of taking all that labour upon it will produce,
except enough to keep the labourer in condition to work."
[17] Ibid., pp. 87-88.
[18] Ibid., pp. 98-101.
[19] "The same amount of rent will be paid, but a portion of it will
now go to the State instead of to the landlord" (p. 105). "Were our
whole revenue raised by a direct land tax." (p. 115). "The proposition
to put the bulk of taxation on land exclusively." (p. 131).
[20] Ibid., p. 111.
[21] Ibid., pp. 111-12.

Henry George was less radical than when writing *Progress and Poverty.*

"I sold of this book probably a thousand copies at a good price", Henry George said later, "but feeling that I should go to greater length and more thoroughly into the question, I refrained from sending it east."[22] It was hardly heard of outside of San Francisco, and even there it made little impression. "It was generally approved by those interested in land reform", Hon. James G. Maguire has said.[23] But the California of the seventies was not the place where new theories of distribution were most likely to receive a critical hearing. Land speculation, railway speculation, and gambling in mining stocks were all-pervasive. Men were kept poor or driven mad by the hope of being one among ten thousand. At the first stroke of the clock at twelve and five, men would rush to investigate the bulletins of mining stocks. In their feverish desire to "get rich quick", they were simply not interested in questions of fundamental social philosophy. What Josiah Royce has characterized as "a general sense of social irresponsibility" was the spirit of the times.

The beginnings of the single tax movement date from the publication of this unpretentious little book by this then obscure California printer. From that time to the last day of his life, Henry George devoted himself to forwarding his economic gospel through the medium of his editorial columns, his books, and his speeches.

The California land agitation

California had had a land agitation from the days when the squatters, fresh from their trip around the Horn or across the plains and Rockies, rioted in their protest against

---

[22] Statement to Arthur McEwen, in San Francisco Examiner, Oct. 30, 1897.

[23] In conversation with the writer, August, 1913.

the immense Mexican grants. Although the bitter strife over uncertain titles had in the main relaxed by 1870, there had developed a widespread dissatisfaction over the peculiarly aggravated land situation which was the result of the unfortunate land policy of nation and state—the passing of a large share of the fairest lands of the state into the hands of a few individuals and corporations.[24] For years there had been an agitation against "land monopoly", James McClatchy of the Sacramento *Bee* being perhaps the most conspicuous worker for land reform.[25] It has been through newspaper agitation, said the *Bee,* that there "has arisen and been carried into popularity that great question relative to the taxation and the holding of lands, now [1873] so prominent in California."[26] Land reform was in the air, and many had become interested in breaking up the big ranches and the railroad holdings.[27]

To this end divers proposals were made. Since the underassessment of big tracts was all too common, many urged as a sufficient remedy the taxing of land at its "true value". The San Diego *Union* states that forty "ranchos", comprising 600,000 acres in San Diego County, are taxed on "$450,000, or seventy-five cents per acre, and the total tax upon it, at the present rate amounts to $12,892.25, of which about one half only has been paid."[28] Some urged that assessors should not be allowed to value land at less. than the Government's price, $1.25 or $1.50 per acre.[29]

[24] Supra, ch. 2.

[25] "It was James McClatchy who instilled into George those ideas antagonistic to land monopoly, which were afterwards so brilliantly woven in Progress and Poverty. In fact, George insisted that James McClatchy should be the man to write that work." J. H. Barry in the San Francisco Star, Nov. 6, 1897.

[26] Sacramento Bee, Nov. 18, 1873.

[27] Statements of Judge James G. Maguire, J. A. Filcher, Joseph Leggett, and P. J. Healy, August, 1913.

[28] Quoted in the San Francisco Post, Dec. 16, 1871.

[29] Ibid., Feb. 24, 1874.

Others suggested that a sure way to break up the ranchos
was to have a law which would provide for self assessment
and allow a man to buy what land he desired by paying ten
per cent more than its assessed valuation.[30]   A proposal
frequently heard was the enactment of an absolute limit to
the amount of land which any individual might hold.   "Has
any man a natural right to more than 1,000 acres of land?"
inquired the Sacramento *Union*.[31]

But most prominent of all suggested remedies was the
special treatment of land in the matter of taxation.[32]   Governor Newton Booth, in his inaugural in December, 1871,
urged a special land tax, "so adjusted as to discourage the
holding of land in large bodies for purposes of speculation."[33]   "The only remedy we can suggest," said the San
Francisco *Chronicle,* "is to tax these lands for the full
value of what they would be worth in the possession of
farmers. . . . The Board of Supervisors and the local
Assessor should run roads, build stone culverts and bridges,
erect school-houses and tax—tax heavily; tax to their full
value.   If one man or a half dozen men are ambitious to
own a county let them pay for it."[34]   Said the Sacramento
Union:

"If 600 men out of 600,000 own half the land in this State,
refusing to partition it out and sell it at reasonable rates, and
conspiring from year to year to prevent its being taxed so as
to yield its share of the burdens of government, nothing is
clearer to our minds than that the 599,400 of landless citizens

[30] Statement of Mr. J. A. Filcher, Sept., 1913.
[31] Sacramento Union, Nov. 4, 1873. See also Sacramento Bee, Nov.
4 and 10, 1873; Sacramento Union, Nov. 1, 1873; San Francisco Post,
March 6, 1874.
[32] Under the title of "Stupid instructors" an editorial in the conservative San Francisco Call (Nov. 12, 1873) said that "the most
absurd propositions ever put forth in relation to taxation, perhaps,
have appeared from time to time in several California journals."
[33] Quoted in the San Francisco Post, Dec. 8, 1871.
[34] San Francisco Chronicle, May 5, 1873.

and small and overtaxed farmers have the right to lay such taxes upon the estates of the land monopolists as will compel them either to support the government or to divide up and sell their vast estates."

The *Union* urged a progressive land tax, under which fifty per cent should be added to the ordinary tax for ranches of from 1,000 to 2,000 acres; seventy-five per cent, from 2,000 to 3,000; one hundred per cent, from 3,000 to 5,000; one hundred fifty per cent, from 5,000 to 8,000; and two hundred per cent, above 8,000.[35]

A number of land reform bills, more or less radical, were introduced into the legislature from time to time, but they failed of passage. In December, 1873, the Assembly appointed a committee of five "to take into consideration the subject of land monopoly, and to offer some remedy therefor." But their report was of no consequence.[36]

Complaint against the relatively light taxation of the land speculator as compared with the heavier burden of the man who improved his land was naturally heard. It is a general phenomenon that settlers in new countries who improve their farms should look with jealous eyes upon non-improving, absentee speculators, who reap unearned increment as an indirect result of the labor of the actual settlers. These do not overlook the plain fact that when one man improves his farm, the value of neighboring lands is enhanced. California was not the first place where such considerations had led to agitation for the exemption of improvements and the taxation of land alone. There was a considerable agitation for this in Iowa in the forties.[37] In 1859-60 it was proposed by Edwin Burgess in Wisconsin along almost the same lines as by Henry George in Cali-

---

[35] Sacramento Union, Nov. 4, 1873.

[36] This report is in the Appendix to the Journals of the Senate and Assembly, 21st session, 1876, vol. 4.

[37] Supra, ch. 1, pp. 12-13.

fornia in 1871.[38]   Later there have been manifestations of
the same idea in Australasia and western Canada.[39]

There were peculiar conditions in the California of this
period which made the taxation of improvements appear excessive relative to the taxation of lands.   Because of the
uncertain nature of the land titles[40] much land escaped taxation, and, besides, there were many "possessory claims"
to national or state land for which no patent had issued.[41]
The taxing of these claims, while speculative holdings were
generally underassessed, easily suggested the thought that
men were penalized for their improvements.   Said Assemblyman J. M. Days, in 1872: "In California nothing but industry is taxed, the large land-owner paying a mere nominal
sum. . . . If an individual was to buy one hundred acres,
and build a house and barn and fence upon it, . . . he would
be taxed on an amount of three or four thousand dollars.
Now, what is taxed? Any person with common sense can
see that nothing but the labor expended upon the place is
taxed."[42]

[38] Edwin Burgess, Letters on Taxation, reprinted by W. S. Buffham,
Racine, Wis.   These letters first appeared in the Racine Advocate,
1859-60. Burgess first made his proposal as early as 1848. See ch. 1,
pp. 13-14.

[39] In the Post of Apr. 16, 1874, George quoted the platform of the
"Land Tenure Reform League of Victoria", as set forth in a tract by
Robert Savage.   The seventh plank said: "The allocation of the
rents of the soil to the nation is the only possible means by which a
just distribution of the created wealth can be effected."
In commenting on this, George claimed originality for his own
idea. Supra, ch. 1.
For references to works describing the experience of Australasia
and Canada with special taxation of land cf. ch. 1, supra, note 57.

[40] Supra, ch. 2.

[41] For the bearing of the assessment of these "possessory claims" on
the origin of the practice of separately assessing land and improvements, see infra, p. 63.

[42] Speech on his bill for a graduated land tax, quoted in the San
Francisco Post, Mar. 18, 1872.

The San Francisco "Evening Post", 1871-75

In December, 1871, Henry George and two of his friends started the San Francisco *Evening Post*. The editorship of this small daily gave George an organ for propaganda, and for four years he participated vigorously in the discussion of the land question. The *Post* favored the strict enforcement of the assessment laws and was sympathetic toward the backers of schemes for the graduated taxation of large estates. It opposed the limitation of holdings; practically, on the ground that a limit could be easily evaded, and in principle on the ground that no just arbitrary limit could be set. The *Post* preferred its own remedy: "Put all taxation on land values, and this curse would melt away like snow before a July sun."[43]

No opportunity to urge the policy of putting heavier taxes upon land[44] escaped Henry George. Sometimes editorials about it appeared several days in succession, and rarely did a week pass without some reference to the subject. From every conceivable side the *Post* attacked the existing system. It declared that assessments were necessarily faulty; that the taxation of personal property was morally and practicably indefensible; that the poll tax was illogical; that tariff taxes were oppressive to the poor and wrong in principle; that the main burden of taxation lay upon the shoulders of those least able to bear it. "If one

[43] San Francisco Post, Apr. 7, 1873. See too Nov. 3, 1873, and Mar. 6, 1874.

[44] Strictly speaking, George's proposal at this time was not for a *single* tax. "We would tax but three things", he said, "the value of land (exclusive of improvements), above a certain small amount exempt to each individual; the estates of deceased persons, passing by succession or will; and such businesses as it is deemed good policy to restrain and regulate, such as liquor saloons, gaming houses, etc." The Post, Jan. 2, 1873. See too Mar. 6, 1873, and supra, ch. 3. The name "single tax" was not in general use as applied to George's proposal until after 1887. Infra, ch. 6.

would see where taxation is really felt, he must go to the people whom the tax-gatherer never visits; . . . where in heathen ignorance, little children are toiling out their lives amid the clatter of wheels and looms; to the slums and tenement rows, where the man from the new West cannot go without a sinking and sickening of the heart."[45]   The most common type of editorial in the *Post* was one mainly taken up with direct, able, and cutting criticism of specific evils in the existing tax system, or with a fling at the land abuses, and whose conclusion tersely pointed to the advantages which Henry George believed would result from his land-value tax.

The propaganda which accompanied George's striking criticism of evils and abuses was equally forceful.   From many sides he defended his idea that "the income from the land should support the Government, and not go to the enriching of one small class of the population."[46]   In fact, it was in the editorial columns of the *Post,* during these four years, that Henry George developed and elaborated his arguments from the form in which they appeared in *Our Land and Land Policy* to the form which they took in *Progress and Poverty.*   We find here worked out George's theory of the "natural" right of men to land, and his labor theory of property; his attack upon the current doctrines of wages and population; his doctrine that land rent was a social product, whose private appropriation, coupled with the taxation of the products of labor, was the basal economic wrong; in short, his whole theory of progress under systems of private property in land.   Here also were elaborated his ideas as to the beneficent, remedial effects of his land-value tax.[47]

[45] Editorial, "Where taxation falls", Sacramento Reporter, May 12, 1870.

[46] San Francisco Post, Apr. 16, 1874.

[47] See, especially, the following editorials in the Post: Feb. 8, June 28, 1872; Mar. 17, Apr. 28, 1873; Feb. 25, Apr. 7 and 21, July 14, 1874.

An editorial entitled "A Problem for Workingmen" contains in a nutshell the argument of *Progress and Poverty,* and is worthy of being quoted at length.

"Is it not universally true that as population grows and wealth increases the condition of the laboring classes becomes worse, and that the amount and depth of real poverty increases? . . . The explanation that as population increases there is a greater strain on natural resources, and that labor in the aggregate becomes less productive, does not suffice, for the economies of production and exchange . . . more than compensate for any greater strain on natural resources. . . . Why is it, then, . . . as population increases, and wealth increases, that the largest class of the community not only do not get any of the benefit, but become actually poorer?

" . . . As population increases, land, and hardly anything else but land, becomes valuable. . . . Land ownership levies its tax upon all the productive classes.

"What is the remedy?

"To make land-owners bear the common burdens—tax land and exempt everything else."[48]

The adversaries of the "Evening Post"

Needless to say, this radical land reform agitation did not go unchallenged. In January, 1872, appeared *Green's Land Paper,* a monthly sheet, edited, the *Post* remarks, by the author of the land law "which still disgraces our statute books". The *Land Paper* intimated its intention of going after certain "communistic notions" such as those tincturing the *Post* and stated its platform as follows: "We hold that a man has a right to buy and hold, as long as he sees proper, just as much land as he sees proper, just as much land as he has the ability to control, and any talk about discriminating laws about him is the sheerest nonsense—the most disgusting demagoguery."[49]

[48] Ibid. Apr. 21, 1874.
[49] It is to be regretted that Green's Land Paper and some other contemporary publications which would prove of great interest are not to be found today. The San Francisco fire of 1906 destroyed the city

So conspicuous was the *Post's* advocacy of George's plan that it made it a target for criticism by contemporary dailies. The plan was, of course, labelled with those most serviceable adjectives "agrarian" and "communistic", and was denounced as "revolutionary and destructive"—a project which, if carried out, "would lead only to ruin".[50] But, along with mere denunciation, the most important of the arguments since urged against George's theory were here adduced in the course of this first period of discussion.

From the time of the earliest mention of the use of a special land tax as a means of land reform, the argument that such a tax would be a confiscation of property was insistently urged.[51] Men urged, too, that it would not be fair to saddle the expenses of government upon a single class, the land-owners, while others, who owned other wealth and were well able to pay, went free. "This is to us a new kink in political economy", said the San Francisco *Chronicle* in commenting upon the *Post's* proposal.[52]

"Let us see how this will work. All the railroads would be simply taxed for the narrow strip over which they have the right of way! All their iron, rolling stock, . . . and valuable franchises are personal property, and must not be taxed! The palatial residences of Messrs. —— [etc.] . . . and the hundreds of other wealthy ones, with their furniture, decorations, works of art, their fast horses, and splendid carriages, not to be taxed! The rich merchant with his millions of personal

libraries, with their invaluable collections of newspapers and other historical data. The above citations from Green's Land Paper are taken from the Post of Jan. 2, 1872. In certain other cases hereafter it has been found necessary to quote the Post's citation of its contemporaries for the same reason—the originals are incomplete or missing altogether.

[50] See the San Francisco Examiner, Nov. 15, 1875; the Post, June 26, 1874; the San Jose Argus, quoted in the Post, April 6, 1874; the Colusa Sun, quoted in the Post, May 1, 1874.

[51] Statements of Mr. Joseph Leggett and Mr. P. J. Healy, August, 1913.

[52] San Francisco Chronicle, Feb. 16, 1873.

property, his goods in bonded warehouse, his ships at sea, are not to be taxed! . . . The whole burden of our state and general government, of our city and municipal expenditure, is to devolve upon the owners of land and lots."

Some believed that George's plan would check investment in land, causing it to become "a drug on the market". To this the *Post* replied that to increase the taxes on land would in no way prejudice its functioning as an instrument of production, as would be the effect of tax increases upon other wealth. "Would we have any the less land?"[53] In reply to the charge of the San Jose *Argus* that the price of land would be injuriously affected and the number of land-holders lessened, Henry George admitted that his scheme would make land "less desirable to hold", but claimed that it would be "therefore much easier to get", saying, "Will not a larger number of the people be enabled to become land-holders?"[54]

The most frequent argument brought against the land tax proposal was that it would be hard on the farmer, whose wealth consists chiefly of land, and on the owner of a small city home. "What an idea it is", exclaimed the San Francisco *Call,* "that the farmer, who is already too heavily taxed, is to be rid of his burdens only by having lands pay all of his tax!"[55] The San Francisco *Examiner* remarked that the prevalent ideas upon the subject were that the adoption of George's proposal "would enhance the cost of agricultural productions, put our farmers at a disadvantage, and cause a greater pro rata taxation of the owners of small city homesteads than at present."[56]

The *Post* replied to this objection with the usual single tax rebuttal that land speculators and the owners of valu-

---

[53] San Francisco Monitor, quoted in the Post, Feb. 26, 1873.
[54] The Post, April 6, 1874.
[55] Quoted by the Post, Apr. 17, 1874.
[56] Ibid., Mar. 28, 1873.

able sites in cities would pay relatively more, while the farmer, whose wealth consisted, not merely of his land, but of "his house and barn, his fences and tools, his stock and growing crops, his own labor, and that of his family", would pay relatively less.[57]

The place of peculiar significance given to land in Henry George's theory of the distribution of wealth elicited attention in the course of these early discussions. We find the San Francisco *Examiner* challenging the attempt to distinguish between natural and artificial wealth, and urging that economically land and other wealth were not different in kind. Taking up George's labor theory of property in goods other than land, the writer argued that in the case of all property alike man has historically appropriated natural wealth. "The truth is, in both cases, the man has, by his labor, brought a natural product into a condition where it will serve his wants."[58]

The *Examiner* also questioned the *Post's* doctrine that land values alone increase with progress. "Population increases the value of land, as said by the *Post,* but that is no reason why it should be exclusively taxed. Rents, manufactures, and the productiveness of money employed in every branch of business, are enhanced from the same cause."[59] To this the *Post* replied: "We should like the *Examiner* to tell us what other thing than land increases in value with the increase of population, except where its increased value is caused by or is swallowed up by the increased value of land. Interest . . . does not increase with the increase of population; labor, other things being equal, would certainly not be higher if this city had a population of 500,000, instead of 188,000."[60] And as to the source of

[57] San Francisco Post, Apr. 6, 1874.
[58] San Francisco Examiner, Nov. 15, 1875.
[59] Ibid., quoted by San Francisco Post, Mar. 31, 1873.
[60] San Francisco Post, Mar. 31, 1873.

great fortunes, the *Post* stated its belief that "the ownership of land makes ten, yes, twenty millionaires, where
labor, personal talents, invention, manufacturing or trade
makes one."[61]

Ephemeral nature of the land agitation

The agitation of the land question to which Henry
George was contributing his part was, as has been pointed
out, the outgrowth of the peculiar land situation existing
in California in the period following the gold discovery.
Its immediate aim was little more than the breaking up of
the immense holdings of land. In so far as Henry George's
purpose was the attacking of this extreme concentration of
land ownership, many were with him.[62] But his purpose
was more than this. "The reasons for taxing land, and exempting improvements and personal property", he said, "do
not arise from any peculiarity in the present distribution
of land in California, and they are not temporary, but
permanent."[63]

In the seventies there were relatively few who were willing to follow Henry George for the single land tax which
he urged. In April, 1873, he wrote in the *Post* that "there
is only one paper that we know of—the Sacramento *Bee*—
which has adopted our view."[64] However, he was hopeful,
writing in April, 1874, that his doctrine was "rapidly making converts", and prophesying that it would some day be
"an accepted axiom".[65] But there is no reason to think
that the propaganda gained a very extensive acceptance for

[61] Ibid., Apr. 13, 1874.
[62] Statements of Joseph Leggett, P. J. Healy, and Judge J. G.
Maguire.
[63] San Francisco Post, Mar. 24, 1873.
[64] San Francisco Post, April 17, 1873. See editorial in the Bee, Oct.
29, 1873, also supra, ch. 3.
[65] San Francisco Post, Apr. 16, 1874.

George's ideas, or that his particular agitation was ever near to issuing in a political movement.

In 1890 a California newspaper man remarked to Henry George: "California hasn't taken to your gospel with enthusiasm."[66] He replied that there were two reasons for that: "One is that real estate has been a very active commodity among you. You have been in the boom stage and multitudes have been endeavoring to find profit in the exchange of land. The other reason is that California is out on the world's edge. . . . The struggle for existence is not yet so fierce here as elsewhere and the pressure of poverty not so painful."

After four years of active and able work as editor, Henry George was obliged to give up the *Post* as the result of a difference with Senator John P. Jones, who had become financially interested in the paper.[67] Governor Irwin appointed George State Inspector of Gas Meters in January, 1876, a position which he held for four years and which gave him leisure to think and to write *Progress and Poverty*.[68] Deprived, by the loss of the *Post*, of his means of propaganda, he took a considerable interest in politics during this period. In the Hayes-Tilden campaign of 1876 he became prominent as a Democrat orator, and incidentally acquired valuable training in public speaking.[69]

When, in 1878, it was decided to revise the state constitution, he become a Democratic candidate for the convention. Since one of the important causes of the revision was the prevailing dissatisfaction with the existing tax laws, Henry George was eager for the opportunity of contending for his views on tax reform. But, with the defeat of the Democrats, his chance was lost.[70]

[66] San Francisco Examiner, Feb. 4, 1890.
[67] The Life of Henry George, p. 247.
[68] Ibid., pp. 262, 326.
[69] Ibid., p. 266 et seq.
[70] Ibid., p. 298 et seq.

Land and taxation clauses in the California constitution of 1879

The California constitution of 1879 exhibits results of thirty years of land agitation in several of its clauses.[71] Article XVII, Section 2, reads like a plank from a political platform:

"The holding of large tracts of land, uncultivated and unimproved, by individuals or corporations, is against the public interest, and should be discouraged by all means not inconsistent with the rights of private property."

A member of the convention has told the writer that when the Convention voted on this, it was "passed with a laugh, for political ends."[72] The third section of this same article declared that state lands "shall be granted only to actual settlers, and in quantities not exceeding three hundred twenty acres." This was a case of locking the stable door when the horse was stolen. Article XIII, Section 3, was designed to secure better assessment of large tracts by providing for their assessment "by sections or fractions of sections".

The second Section of this last mentioned Article provided for separately assessing land and improvements on land, and for assessing at the same value "cultivated and uncultivated land, of the same quality, and similarly situated". Since this is similar to propositions since urged by single taxers as an entering wedge for their measures, some have supposed that George and his followers were responsible for it.

The evidence, however, is to the contrary. The Cali-

---

[71] The Debates of the Convention show that much attention was given to the land question. More than twenty proposals for more or less radical land reforms were brought in, and memorials on the subject of land monopoly appear in the records. See, e.g., p. 602.

[72] J. A. Filcher, Sept., 1913.

fornia Political Code of 1872 had already required the separate assessment of land and improvements.[73] As early as 1852, six years before Henry George came to California, the makers of the first assessment of Los Angeles County had stated separately the value of land *sin mejoras* and the value *de las mejoras,*[74] and the San Francisco assessment figures for 1853-54 made the same distinction.[75] The origin of the practice of separately assessing land and improvements is not clear, but it may be found, as Professor Plehn has suggested to the writer, in the necessity of taxing improvements made on "possessory claims" to United States or to state land, for which no patent had issued, and in the taxation of mines, many of which were on land for which no patent had been acquired. Three members of the convention which framed the constitution have stated that George's ideas were not mentioned on the floor of the convention.[76] Examination of the *Debates* bears out this statement. It is also a pertinent fact that Henry George was opposed to the adoption of the constitution, believing that it "would strengthen the land and railroad monopolies and that it had many other serious faults".[77]

The *Debates* show that the inclusion of this provision for separate assessment of land and improvements occasioned little discussion. Its inclusion appears to have been taken for granted by the Convention, as it was only placing in the organic law a requirement already imposed by the Po-

[73] Political Code of California, 1872, pt. 3, title 9, ch. 3, sec. 3650.
[74] See the assessment rolls in the County Hall of Records, Los Angeles.
[75] Bancroft (History of California, vol. 6, p. 775) cites the assessed valuation of San Francisco property in the fifties. The distinction between the total values of land and of improvements appears for the first time in the figures for 1853-54.
[76] Messrs. J. A. Filcher, Justice Schomp, and Thomas McConnell. Statements to the writer, Sept., Oct., and Nov., 1913.
[77] See The Life of Henry George, pp. 316-17.

litical Code. But the clause which provided for assessing
at the same value cultivated and uncultivated lands, of like
quality and similarly located, elicited a great deal of discussion.[78] The aim of this provision was evidently to place
an increased weight of taxation upon the man who did not
improve his land. The official copy of the completed constitution, issued by the Convention with an explanatory
supplement addressed "To the people of the State of California", said that "the effect of this provision will be that
extensive landed proprietors, unless they choose to pay the
increased tax, will have to cultivate their lands or dispose
of them to someone who will".[79]

These constitutional provisions, then, were the result of
the above-discussed feeling of the homesteaders and others
against the land speculators and the holders of big ranches.
They were not embodied in the constitution as the result of
Henry George's land agitation alone, but were the outgrowth of a generation of land agitation, of which his agitation was but a single phase. No direct results from
George's propaganda appeared either in political action or
in legislation at that time in California, except in so far as
his propaganda was merged with the general agrarian
movement.

"The Land Reform League of California", 1878

Early in 1878 the first society to further Henry George's
views was organized by a number of his San Francisco
friends.[80] It bore the title "The Land Reform League of

[78] In reality the separate assessment clause was but a corollary of
this provision. Investigation of the Debates and the statements of
Messrs. Filcher, Schomp and McConnell make it clear that in the
minds of the framers of the constitution the term "improvements"
referred primarily to agricultural improvements, and not to buildings
upon city lots.
[79] Constitution of the State of California, adopted in Convention at
Sacramento, "printed by order of the Constitutional Convention", p. 46.
[80] See the Life of Henry George, p. 293 et seq.

California". Joseph Leggett became the first president. Mr. Leggett has said that the society had twenty or twenty-five adherents, with perhaps ten active members.[81] The society held weekly meetings. It was under the auspices of this organization that Henry George delivered his first formal propaganda lecture, in the Metropolitan Temple of San Francisco, March 26, 1878. His subject was: "Why work is scarce, wages low, and labour restless." Although the audience was not large, the lecture was well received.[82]

In September, 1877, Henry George began the writing of *Progress and Poverty*.[83] For a year and a half he was occupied with the writing of this remarkable book, which was completed about the middle of March, 1879. Its reception we shall consider in the next chapter.

[81] Statement to the writer, Aug., 1913.
[82] Idem. See also The Life of Henry George, p. 294 et seq.
[83] Ibid., p. 289.

CHAPTER IV

THE RECEPTION OF PROGRESS AND POVERTY

Henry George described *Progress and Poverty* in its sub-title as "an Inquiry into the Cause of Industrial Depressions and of Increase of Want with Increase of Wealth". In 1880 the times were propitious for such an inquiry. An era of apparently great general prosperity had been rudely disturbed by the crash of 1873, whose sequel was a period of prolonged depression—"hard times". Falling prices brought uneasiness and tended toward the stagnation of enterprise. Labor outbreaks in 1877 directed attention to unconsidered problems of the new industrialism. The material progress growing out of industrial advances and the rapid exploitation of new resources had indeed brought wealth and prosperity to many. But great individual riches only set forth in higher relief the contrast between wealth and want; the new-built cities each contained its slum; "old world poverty" was manifesting its unwelcome presence in free America. With such conditions, a fearless and attractively presented re-examination of the fundamentals of economic life, challenging accepted ideas, was sure to gain a hearing, while a militant optimism such as that of Henry George could not fail to find disciples.

Progress and Poverty like many other now famous books had difficulty in finding a publisher. George's manuscript, completed in March, 1879, was rejected by the eastern publishers to whom he submitted it. They laughed at the idea of there being a sale for a work on political economy

66

which had been written in San Francisco. "I could get no one to print the work", he wrote in his *Political Economy,* "except my old partner in San Francisco, William M. Hinton, who had gone into the printing business, and who had sufficient faith in me to make the plates."[1] On the 17th of May, George set the first sticks of type himself, and in the fall of 1879 *Progress and Poverty* appeared in San Francisco as an author's edition of five hundred copies.

The reception of "Progress and Poverty" in California

Opinion of the reviewers in contemporary California newspapers was divided as to the future of *Progress and Poverty.* One sort of opinion was that represented by the *Alta California,* that the book would be "dropped out of view in a short time as a blunder of a mind more active than wise".[2] The contrary view was that Henry George had written "a very remarkable book", which was "destined to have a very great success". "We recognize in it one of those invaluable attempts to throw more light upon the scheme of civilization, which are always so prolific of intellectual progress. . . . It is from friction that fire springs, and it is from the sharpest and most sweeping challenges of received hypotheses that the greatest enlightenment is to be expected."[3] The reviewer for the San Francisco *Chronicle* believed that "notwithstanding the comparative obscurity of this writer as compared with Ricardo, Adam Smith, Mill, Spencer and others on the same subject, his volume will attract much attention among advanced minds".[4] Commendation of George's brilliant style and of his book's "sincere sympathy with humanity, its

[1] George, Political Economy, p. 203. See also The Life of Henry George, p. 315 et seq.
[2] San Francisco Alta California, Jan. 26, 1880.
[3] Sacramento Record-Union, Feb. 21, 1880.
[4] San Francisco Chronicle, Feb. 1, 1880.

tenderness, its passionate desire for better things" is general in these reviews.[5]

One of the earliest magazine reviews was that in the *Californian* of February, 1880, from the pen of Dr. E. R. Taylor, Henry George's close friend. While the reviewer did not undertake a criticism of the basal ideas of the book, his views as to its future are deserving of mention. "Here, if we mistake not, is one of those original works which open fresh discussions and draw new lines. . . . Whether the theories which it lays down are right or wrong, they cannot be treated with contempt. Political Economists cannot ignore a book which, even if it be erroneous, presents error in such a form that it is likely to become a new gospel in every radical club, and to find apostles in every knot of dissatisfied workingmen."[6]

In California, however, the book made but little impression beyond the group of Henry George's friends. In 1880 he was a man of no particular distinction in San Francisco. James H. Barry, now editor of the San Francisco *Star,* who set type on *Progress and Poverty,* has said that most of the printers thought it "a damned piece of audacity that Harry George should write a book at all".[7] While enjoying some reputation as a facile writer, he had as a journalist only the standing of the insurgent, radical editor of a paper which had had a hard struggle to exist. "What business has an inspector of gas meters to write a book?" was the view of some. His fellow-members of the Bohemian Club pooh-poohed the book, claiming that the scheme was not new, having been tried in India, Japan, and elsewhere. "Few

[5] Sacramento Record-Union, Feb. 21, 1880.
[6] The San Francisco Alta California, Jan. 26, 1880, finds fault with this review for "elaborate praise of minor merits, and silence about fundamental errors." The citation here is from The Californian, Feb. 1880, p. 183.
[7] Statement to the writer, August, 1913.

thought that it would make anything of a stir in the world",
said Judge James G. Maguire.[8] It was the same old story
—"Can any good thing come out of Nazareth?" Even
when the book was beginning to gain recognition in the
East it made but little impression in George's home city.
One of his friends, P. J. Healy, who kept a book store in
San Francisco and was the chief distributor for *Progress
and Poverty,* has said that he sent for two hundred copies,
but that more of these were given away than were sold
during the first two years after publication.[9] California
later learned to be proud of Henry George when he had
become a celebrity; but even then he was given recognition
not because California had examined him and found him
worthy of distinction, but because he had made a stir in
the outside world.[10]

Henry George comes to New York

The receipts from the sale of the author's edition of
Progress and Poverty proved nearly sufficient to pay for
the plates.[11] With this initial expense met, Henry George
undertook to secure a publisher who would print the book
from these plates. He sent unbound copies of the author's
edition to various publishers and at length Appleton & Co.
agreed to issue the book. In the latter part of 1879 the
plates were forwarded to New York.[12]

In August, 1880, Henry George left San Francisco for
New York to commence the wide spreading of his economic
gospel, a work which was to engage him without ceasing
until the very hour of his death. His faith never wavered

[8] Idem.
[9] Idem.
[10] The data for this paragraph were given to the writer by Messrs.
J. H. Barry, P. J. Healy, J. G. Maguire, Joseph Leggett, and E. R.
Taylor of San Francisco.
[11] George, Political Economy, p. 203.
[12] Idem.

as to the greatness of his mission and the efficacy of his remedy for regenerating society. Never for a moment did he doubt that to him destiny had granted the discovery of a wonderful truth, which was forever to free the lives of men from the dread of wretched poverty. "With want destroyed; with greed changed to noble passions; with the fraternity that is born of equality taking the place of the jealousy and fear that now array men against one another; with mental power loosed by conditions that give to the humblest comfort and leisure; and who shall measure the heights to which our civilization may soar? Words fail the thought! It is the Golden Age of which poets have sung and high-raised seers have told in metaphor!"[13] Such were his hopes and his ideals.

He himself believed firmly from the first that *Progress and Poverty* would gain recognition as a book of the greatest importance. In September, 1879, he wrote to his father: "It will not be recognized at first—maybe not for some time—but it will ultimately be considered a great book, will be published in both hemispheres, and be translated into different languages." To his friend John Swinton he wrote: "It is the most important contribution to the science of political economy yet made". And to John Russell Young: "But whether it is at first applauded or denounced makes little difference, provided it is treated with attention. The book, fairly started, will go. This is not merely my judgment; it is my experience. I have put out enough copies to thoroughly test it, and I am more than satisfied of that."[14]

At the time of Henry George's arrival in New York in

[13] Progress and Poverty, bk. 10, ch. 5, p. 549. References to Progress and Poverty are to the Twenty-fifth anniversary edition, Doubleday, Page & Co., 1905.
[14] These citations are from The Life of Henry George, pp. 321, 322, 332.

August, 1880, *Progress and Poverty* was slowly beginning to gain recognition. About the first of April, 1880, three months after publication, Appleton & Co. had suggested the issuing of a cheaper paper-cover edition.[15] January 4, 1881, George wrote:

"When I came East I found that it had hardly got started here. And during the campaign [Garfield-Hancock] and until the last two weeks in December it went very slow. But then a movement began, and on the last day of the year every copy of the previous editions and every copy of the 1,000 of the cheap edition were gone, and orders and inquiries came piling in from every quarter. Appleton & Co. begin to realize for the first time that I have been telling them the truth, and that they have got hold of a book capable of an enormous sale. . .

"Comparatively speaking, the success of the book is already tremendous—for, so far as I can learn, no book on political economy has ever yet been published in the United States (or to my astonishment, I learn in England either) that has sold 1,000 copies in the first year (unless forced into the schools), and in fact the entire sales of most of them are to be counted in hundreds, not thousands."[16]

And January 21, 1881, he wrote:

"The book is a success. The sale seems now to have commenced in good earnest, and orders are coming from all parts of the country—in ones, two and tens and twenties."[17]

The first reviews in the East

Examination of the comments of contemporary reviewers sheds further light on the reception of *Progress and Poverty*. While some of these reviewers of 1880 discussed the book in a prosaic, perfunctory way, with little criticism,[18] the most of them recognized that here was a book out of the ordinary.[19] The writer of a leading article on

[15] Ibid., p. 333.
[16] Ibid., pp. 342-43.
[17] Ibid., p. 343.
[18] E.g. the New York Independent, Jan. 29, 1880, p. 12.
[19] See the collection of press notices printed with the fifth (1882) edition of Progress and Poverty, and with a number of later editions.

"Progress and Poverty" in the *Popular Science Monthly* of April, 1880, characterized the book as "a remarkable answer" to the problem of poverty, and "one of the most important contributions yet made to economic literature".[20]

The concensus of views was that here was "a book destined to create a great deal of discussion",[21] that it was "not a work to be brushed aside with lofty indifference or cool disdain",[22] and that it would "neither be ignored, nor sneered down, nor laughed down."[23] M. W. Hazeltine wrote in the New York *Sun's* review, March 14, 1880: "However rudely this resolute investigator may disturb and irritate the partisans of current theories, and however sharp and vehement the opposition he may kindle, they cannot afford to neglect his plea or ignore his argument. . . . His conclusions, however strange and revolutionary they may seem in their bearing upon society, will not be rejected by sober and impartial men without mature deliberation."

Those first disposed to smile at the idea that any book worth while on political economy should emanate from the western frontier were in turn surprised that a California economist should write such a book as *Progress and Poverty*. Said the reviewer in the New York *Times:* "From the El Dorado of modern times, from a new country . . . which is described to us by its people in the most extravagant language as regards its natural resources, climate, productions, etc., there comes now a book on the alleged connection between progress and poverty, wealth and want."[24] To this writer it seemed a "paradox" that the

[20] Pages 722, 737.
[21] Boston Transcript, cited, see note 19, supra.
[22] New York Sun, Mar. 14, 1880.
[23] New York Evening Mail, cited, see note 19, supra.
[24] New York Times, June 6, 1880.

evils of old communities should present themselves in such a land of limitless promise.

Recognition of the power and appeal of Henry George's literary style was general. Here was a book hard to lay down when once begun, a book which treated social questions in a vital and interesting manner, which attracted by its earnestness and sympathy. Here too was a book with an appeal to men whom the dryness or technical character of so many works on economic questions would repel. The very title, "Progress and Poverty", was a big asset.

If praise of its style was general, so was recognition of the urgency of the issues discussed. As one reviewer put it, "Why poverty persists is the fundamental social question of our time".[25]

Securing attention

Meanwhile, Henry George was becoming well-known through the magazines. In March, 1880, he contributed to the *Popular Science Monthly* an article on "The study of political economy" which he had presented in the form of a lecture at the University of California in 1877.[26] This same magazine reviewed *Progress and Poverty* at length in the March and April numbers. The *Nation* had a notice from the pen of Horace White which appeared in two parts, July 22 and August 12, 1880. The December *Atlantic* had two articles discussing the book, written by W. B. Weeden and Willard Brown. In June, 1881, Henry George contributed "The taxation of land values", an able summary of his views, to *Appleton's,* and in July he wrote for the *North American Review* an article on "Common sense in taxation".

That *Progress and Poverty* was already attracting a

[25] Popular Science Monthly, Apr. 1880, p. 722.
[26] See The Life of Henry George, p. 274 et seq.

good deal of attention appears from the incidental comments of newspapers and magazines, beginning in the latter
part of 1880. In January, 1881, the New York *Sun* refers
to Henry George as "the author of 'Progress and Poverty',
an economic work now attracting the attention of thinking
men on both sides of the Atlantic".[27] The *Popular Science
Monthly*, commenting upon the appearance of a seventy-
five cent edition, said in February, 1881 : "We are happy
to note . . . that it has proved a very considerable success.
Four editions have been called for in this country; the Germans are printing a translation in parts; it is discussed in
French and Italian periodicals; and an English edition is in
preparation. The work is everywhere looked upon as an
important contribution to Political Economy, and as an
eloquent and vigorous discussion of imminent social problems. It is a wholesome sign of the growing liberality of
the times that a work should be so cordially received and
highly appreciated, while at the same time there is general
and decisive dissent from its main conclusions."[28]

This same comment averred that, though *Progress and
Poverty* was "read and enjoyed for its humane spirit and
the novelty and independence of its views", Henry George
did not make converts who endorsed his essential doctrines.
Of this charge, Henry George said in a letter of January
23, 1881 :[29] "I find them [converts] in all directions.
Every day I get letters." One of these enthusiastic converts, in what was perhaps the first of a long line of single
tax letter discussions which have been contributed gratis to
the (more or less) open columns of newspapers, wrote to
the New York *Sun,* January 7, 1881 : "I do not believe the

[27] New York Sun, Jan. 6, 1881.
[28] Popular Science Monthly, Feb., 1881, p. 565.
[29] The Life of Henry George, p. 344.

arguments in 'Progress and Poverty' have been answered, or ever can be answered".[30]

Increasing reputation

The land question was especially prominent about 1880 because of the Irish land troubles, then at their height. Not slow to take advantage of this fact, Henry George published about the first of March, 1881, *The Irish Land Question, What It Involves and How Alone It can be Settled*.[31] The purpose of this little book was "to show the importance and true character of the land question everywhere, and especially in the United States".[32] Its central thought is shown by the striking question posed by the author in the opening chapter: "What would the Irish tenants gain, if, tomorrow, Ireland were made a State in the American Union and American law substituted for English law?"[33]

The reviews and comments on *The Irish Land Question* in the spring of 1881 show that Henry George had already won distinction as a writer and that *Progress and Poverty* had gained a wide hearing for his views. The New York *Sun* remarked that George's doctrines had "attracted a great deal of attention not only in this country but in Europe", and said that *The Irish Land Question* was "distinguished by the substantial and literary merits which have gained for the author a high and wide reputation".[34] The New York *Times* referred to *Progress and Poverty* as "a masterly book on the reasons for the spread of pauperism in the modern social fabric", and said that "the honors that 'Progress and Poverty' obtained here and abroad cannot

[30] For this discussion of Jan., 1881, see the New York Sun, Jan. 7, 17, 21, 22, 27, 29.
[31] This book was later issued with the title, The Land Question.
[32] Preface to edition of 1884.
[33] The Irish Land Question, p. 8.
[34] New York Sun, Mar. 27, 1881.

fail to be reinforced by this treatise, for it speaks to all
Europe, as well as to Great Britain and Ireland".[35]   In
April, 1881, *The Critic,* reviewing the two books, spoke of
Progress and Poverty as George's "deeply interesting, his
exceedingly able and glowing book", which was "now in its
fourth American edition with translations into German and
French, and encomiums from the most thoughtful journals
of England, France, Germany, and the United States".[36]
Popular Science in May, 1881, referred to George's "now
well-known work";[37] *Appleton's* said in the same month
that it "has recently attracted considerable attention among
economists and all persons interested in questions of social
science".[38]   Of the probable reception of *The Irish Land
Question,* the reviewer in the New York *Herald*[39] inferred
from the success of *Progress and Poverty* that "Mr. Henry
George . . . has something to say which many will hasten
to read, and multitudes will presently discuss".

In the summer of 1881, Henry George made a visit to
California.   On the 11th of August he lectured for the second time in Metropolitan Temple, San Francisco.   At his
lecture three years before he had spoken to a "beggarly
array of empty benches", but on this occasion he was
greeted by a crowded house.[40]   The *Alta California,* which
a year and a half before had prophesied that his book would
be "dropped out of view in a short time as a blunder of a
mind more active than wise",[41] referred to him now as the
"author of 'Progress and Poverty', a book that has made
him a great name as a political economist".[42]

[35] New York Times, Mar. 23, 1881.
[36] The Critic, vol. 1, p. 90 (1881).
[37] Popular Science, May, 1881, p. 119.
[38] Appleton's, May, 1881, p. 472.
[39] New York Herald, Mar. 21, 1881.
[40] The Life of Henry George, p. 352.
[41] Supra, p. 67.
[42] San Francisco Alta California, July 21, 1881, p. 2.

George's first visit to Great Britain

In the fall of 1881, Henry George sailed for the British
Isles as special correspondent for the New York *Irish
World*.[43] Radical ideas regarding land tenure were in the
air. Not merely a reduction of rents or "fixity of tenure at
fair rents" was being demanded. Many were urging the
abolition of the existing landlord class.[44] *Progress and
Poverty* was even more opportune in Great Britain than in
the United States. The land question was the question of
the hour, and Henry George was eager to make propaganda
for his own proposed solution as well as to study Irish
conditions.

Progress and Poverty had met with a reception in England similar to that in the United States. Introduced there
in the latter part of 1880, it had rapidly attracted attention.[45] George wrote to Francis G. Shaw in February,
1882: "Paul, of Kegan Paul, Trench & Co., says it is the
most astonishing success he *ever* knew. When they first
got it out no one would touch it. They laughed at the idea
of selling an American book on political economy. It was
a long while before they got rid of twenty copies. Then, as
he says, purely on its own strength, the book to their astonishment began to make its way. Their first edition was
out early in December (1881). They have got another;
that is going faster and they anticipate a big sale."[46] Early
in 1882, six-penny and three-penny editions of the two
books were printed and widely circulated.[47] Such was the
impression made by George's writings and addresses during
this and subsequent visits to England that in 1897 J. A.

[43] The Life of Henry George, p. 354.
[44] San Francisco Bulletin, Sept. 29, 1879, p. 4.
[45] See The Life of Henry George, pp. 341, 343.
[46] Ibid., p. 390.
[47] Ibid., pp. 390, 391.

Hobson characterized him as having had "a more directly powerful formative and educative influence over English radicalism of the last fifteen years than any other man."[48]

It is certain that George's tremendous influence in Great Britain, his reaching all classes of men there, and the vigorous discussion which he aroused,[49] reacted upon the public mind of America. When, in August, 1882, he and a friend were arrested in Ireland as "suspicious strangers," it was featured in the headlines of American papers and furnished a touch of the spectacular which advertised him further.[50] An amusing testimony to this fact is a statement in a notice of *Progress and Poverty* in the New York *Tribune* of February 2, 1883, to the effect that "the work is chiefly interesting as an Irishman's attempt to apply the abstract principles of political economy to the land question".

Passages of Francis A. Walker's *Land and Its Rent,* written in 1883 as a reply to *Progress and Poverty,*[51] indicate clearly the effect which the success of George's book in England was having in furthering the extension of his ideas at home.

"Unfortunately there is too much evidence of a profound popular effect produced by this work upon the public mind of Great Britain, and, though *more tardily,* upon the public mind of the United States.[52]

"The work was, in fact, published in 1879; but though it had a ready sale and attracted not a little attention, and even elicited some heedless commendation by reason of the eloquence and picturesqueness of its style, it created its first sen-

[48] J. A. Hobson, The Influence of Henry George in England, Fortnightly Review, vol. 68, p. 844 (1897).

[49] See the Quarterly Review, Jan. 1883. Alfred Russel Wallace believed that by July, 1883, nearly 100,000 copies of Progress and Poverty had circulated. McMillan's Magazine, vol. 48, p. 361 (1883).

[50] See The Life of Henry George, p. 392, et seq., also the New York Times, Aug. 10, 11, and 12, 1882.

[51] See infra, pp. 83-84. The citations here are from pages 7 to 9.

[52] The italics are the present writer's.

sation when reprinted abroad. In Great Britain the success of
this book has been truly remarkable. . . .

"Such a reception could hardly be accorded an American
book abroad, without awakening new interest and stimulating
a wider demand at home."

"The distinguished author of 'Progress and Poverty' "

In October, 1882, Henry George returned to America
after a year's absence. On his arrival at New York he
received a truly remarkable welcome. Newspapers referred
to him as "the author of *Progress and Poverty*";[53] as
"the writer on political economy, whose 'Progress and Poverty' created such a stir";[54] as "Henry George, the distinguished author of 'Progress and Poverty' ".[55] On the
20th of October, the Central Labor Union welcomed him
at Cooper Institute with a most enthusiastic demonstration.
Banners on the walls bore such legends as "Land, the Common Property of the People", and Edward King, of the
Type Founders Union, welcomed him as the man who "had
converted Political Economy from a dismal science into a
science radiant with hope".[56] In his speech, George said:
"I am convinced that the greatest struggle of the century
has already begun. The flame has been lit, the fire is
burning on, and in a few months there will be a great
movement all over the civilized world. Everywhere there
is distress and disquiet."[57]

A reception of a different sort but not less remarkable
was the banquet given in George's honor the following evening at Delmonico's: a gathering which the New York
Times characterized as "a distinguished assemblage".[58]

[53] New York Sun, Oct. 21, 1882.
[54] New York Herald, Oct. 16, 1882.
[55] Ibid., Oct. 21 and 22, 1882.
[56] Ibid., Oct. 21, 1882.
[57] New York Tribune, Oct. 21, 1882.
[58] New York Times, Oct. 22, 1882.

Hon. Algernon S. Sullivan, the toastmaster, in introducing
Henry George said that the banquet was remarkable in that
for the first time in New York representative men gathered
to do honor "to one whose sole claim to recognition was
that he was a philosopher and an author".[59]

"In the ante-room was an elegantly engrossed and framed
address to Mr. George, in which were particularly recognized
his personal work, his sympathy with mankind, his intellectual
vigor and his literary attainments. It was explicitly stated that
not all of the signers of the address were sympathizers with
Mr. George's views upon the nationalization of land; it was
simply a testimonial of esteem and not a complete indorsement
of the theories which Mr. George espoused, but they honored
the brilliancy of his performances and the value of his intellectual services as a philosopher and philanthropist."[60]

Henry Ward Beecher in his address said that he came from
a desire "to join in a token of respect to one of that class
of men who contribute some service to the commonwealth
besides material wealth".[61]

Henry George was in a fair way to become the literary
lion of the hour. To quote an incident narrated in *Frank
Leslie's Illustrated Newspaper,* March 3, 1883: "Only a
few nights ago in the parlors of a wealthy but thoughtful
New York citizen, on Gramercy Park, Mr. George was
listened to for hours by an audience of fashionable ladies
and gentlemen in full dress, and several wealthy men arose
at the close of his address and announced their concurrence
in his views! Nothing more strange and anomalous has
recently taken place in our society. When millionaires become agrarians, the fact is not to be ignored."[62] The writer
foresaw, however, that the author of *Progress and Poverty*
might not be thus lionized if conditions should arise in
which his theories became an issue.

[59] Idem.
[60] New York Herald, Oct. 22, 1882.
[61] New York Times, Oct. 22, 1882.
[62] Frank Leslie's Illustrated Newspaper, Mar. 3, 1883, p. 18.

In February, 1883, Henry George gave *Progress and Poverty* to John W. Lovell & Co. for a twenty cent, paper-covered, edition.[63]   The New York *Times,* January 28, 1883, in announcing this, referred to it as "a still cheaper popular edition of a book which has made and justly made its mark in the United States, in Germany, in France, and in Great Britain". The first edition numbered fifteen thousand copies and was exhausted in less than a week.[64]   In April, 1883, George wrote: "The 20-cent edition of 'Progress and Poverty' got out in February and is working powerfully. We are gaining rapidly in every direction. It will not be long now before the movement will show in politics."[65]   George's desire to make converts and organize them is seen from the statement in the front of this cheap edition which gives his address and says that he will "be glad to hear from those who share the views expressed in this book, and who desire to advance them".

At about this time also, the first distinctive organization outside of California[66] to further George's ideas was formed in New York, the "Free Soil Society", Mr. Louis F. Post being the president.[67]   Mr. Post has said of this society that although it was "national in its scheme, it never advanced much beyond the 'paper' stage".[68]

[63] See The Life of Henry George, p. 404.

[64] This is the statement of Tit-Bits, which was published by Lovell. The clipping from which it is taken is found in the clipping files of the New York World. It is undated, but evidently belongs in 1883 or 1884.

[65] The Life of Henry George, p. 406.

[66] See supra, ch. 3.

[67] The Life of Henry George, p. 406, et seq.

[68] Post, Origin and History of the Single Tax Movement, in The Public, Nov. 26, 1904.

Professor Sumner's criticism

It was hardly to be expected that a radical book creating such a stir should long escape attack from the side of economic orthodoxy, when George had emphatically disputed some of its doctrines and taught that others of them led logically to ideas from the enunciation of which its exponents had unknowingly or willfully shrunk. Professor W. G. Sumner led the attack of the schoolmen with a scathing and somewhat arrogant review of George's book in *Scribner's Monthly,* June, 1881.[69]

"It has been declared several times, in regard to Mr. George's 'Progress and Poverty', and by various reviewers, that its appearance marks an epoch or constitutes an event. We are cordially of the same opinion, although for a somewhat different reason. Nothing could more distinctly mark the absence of any true body of criticism in social science and political economy than the respectful consideration which has been given to this book. It now appears in paper covers in a popular edition, and is going on its way to propagate still more social folly and prejudice where there is already so much that common sense scarcely has a chance."

Professor Sumner regretted that sociology was "yet the free arena for all the people with hobbies, crude notions, world philosophies, and schemes", and declared that George had not fitted himself for his task "by any *correct* study of sociology".[70] He lamented the fact that "as respectful attention is given to a book like this as to the most careful work of a highly trained and scientific observer". To him "the unkindest cut of all was that Professor Cliffe Leslie should take notice of this book as a special and representative product of American Political Economy". His conclusion is that the refutation of the misunderstandings and misrepresentations of *Progress and Poverty* would require the writing of "a correct treatise on sociology from

[69] Scribner's Monthly, June, 1881, pp. 312-13.
[70] Italics the present writer's.

the first principles up to some of the most refined applications", and that the proposition in George's latest book
"is not a contribution to the solution of the Irish question;
it is only a gauge of the philosopher who made it."

Also in the *Princeton Review* of November, 1881, Professor Sumner in a weighty article entitled "Sociology"
condemns those "sentimentalists" who preach "notions of
rights and equality, of the dignity, wisdom, and power of
the proletariat, which have filled the minds of ignorant men
with impossible dreams."[71]   At the time at which this
article appeared, *Progress and Poverty* had just been made
available for further stirring up the "proletariat" with "notions of rights and equality" by being republished serially
in *Truth,* a one cent workingman's daily of New York
which had a circulation of from 75,000 to 100,000.[72]

Walker's "Land and Its Rent"

By the middle of 1883, six months after Henry George's
return from his English campaign, his theories were not
merely widely discussed, they were producing an unprecedented sensation.   In May, 1883, General Francis A.
Walker delivered a series of lectures at Harvard University, chiefly by way of replying to George.   These lectures, published under the title *Land and Its Rent,* were the
first substantial criticism which *Progress and Poverty* had
received from the economists.   The spirit of Walker's criticism was as unfortunate as that of Sumner's review.[73]   The
following citations from *Land and Its Rent* show plainly
the amount of influence Henry George was exerting.

"Altogether unexpectedly, and, so far as one can see, without any cause existing in the economic relations of society, the

[71] Princeton Review, Nov. 1881, p. 321.
[72] See The Life of Henry George, p. 355.   This republication of
Progress and Poverty was commenced Oct. 9, 1881.   Louis F. Post
was at that time editor of Truth.
[73] Supra, pp. 82-83.

questions of the rightfulness and the expediency of private property in land, and of the influence of rent upon the distribution of wealth, have been precipitated upon us. . . . In the United States, where practically the question of the private ownership of the soil has not heretofore even been raised, we find popular attention bestowed in a remarkable degree upon a book, now perhaps in its hundredth edition, . . . whose practical proposals embrace the virtual abolition of private property in land through the confiscation of rents by the State—the author of this work appearing as a welcome contributor to influential journals and reviews, and receiving the greeting of crowded assemblies as the apostle of great sociological and economical reforms.

"It will be said: 'The publication of such a work is certainly a curious phenomenon of the times, and a very disagreeable phenomenon; but surely the work itself cannot call for any serious consideration. . . . Surely, society must long since have passed the point where it was necessary to discuss propositions like these, or to refute a writer who gives such ample warning of the dangerous nature of his doctrines.'

"But I think we cannot deal quite in this spirit with Mr. Henry George's 'Progress and Poverty'. As the London Quarterly Review remarks: 'False theories . . . claim our attention . . . in proportion to the extent to which action is likely to be influenced by them; and since action in modern politics so largely depends on the people, the wildest errors are grave, if they are only sufficiently popular'. . . .Unfortunately there is too much evidence of a profound popular effect produced by this work upon the public mind.

. . . "It is said that 'Progress and Poverty' has reached an enormous circulation. The author has certainly come to be one of the lions of the hour. There is no reason to suppose that his doctrines have yet deeply infected the public mind of this country; yet the ingenuity and eloquence of this writer must produce no inconsiderable effect upon any reader, however intelligent, and however fortified by economic study."[74]

George's "Social Problems"

In the spring of 1883 *Frank Leslie's Illustrated Newspaper* engaged Henry George to write for it a series of thirteen weekly articles under the caption "Problems of the

[74] Walker, Land and Its Rent, pp. 5, 6, 7, 9.

Time", a series of articles expanded and published in book form a few months later under the title *Social Problems*. The first of these articles appeared in the issue of April 14, 1883, the magazine stating on the same page that it was in no way to be understood as approving "the views which may be from time to time expressed" in articles on political and economic questions.

But notwithstanding this initial declaration, as the articles began to appear it would seem that some sort of pressure was brought to bear on the management, possibly by advertisers or other patrons whose sentiments the doctrines set forth in the articles may have stirred up. At any rate, the management deemed it incumbent upon them to supply an antidote to Henry George in the form of editorial criticisms of his views. These attempted refutations were pitifully weak, at times amusing in their gross misrepresentations of George's positions, or harsh in their denunciation.[75] For example, an editorial of July 28th tilts furiously against George's supposed doctrine of the "equal division of land", finding it impracticable on the grounds that "land of itself has no equality of value", and that an increase of population would mix things. Henry George, says the writer, "prefers the squalor of nomadic solitude to the larger movements of civilization". The conclusion of the whole matter as expressed in the editorial of August 25th was to the effect that the serial they were engaged in publishing was "a sham and a fraud on the simplicity of people who, like himself, have not a competent faculty of thinking." Such refutation must manifestly have helped to make converts for Henry George, were it taken to be indicative of the strength of the position of his opponents.

---

[75] The chief of these editorials are in the following numbers: May 26, June 2, 16, July 14, 28, Aug. 25, 1883.

From philosopher to propagandist

As Henry George and his theories came more and more into prominence through discussion the comments became distinctly more critical. It is very apparent that discussion was beginning to take on a different character. Rather than "Henry George, the distinguished author of 'Progress and Poverty' " it was "Henry George, the social agitator."[76] This change appears in the reviews of *Social Problems* as compared with the earlier reviews of *Progress and Poverty*,[77] as well as in the tone of other comments or references to Henry George and to his doctrines.[78] This changed attitude was due in part to the fact that the tone of *Social Problems* was not quite the same as that of the earlier book, that, as Arthur T. Hadley said, it had "less restraint, less attempt at sustained argument, more rhetoric, more fervent appeals to feeling and action";[79] in part it was due to the realization that Henry George was more than a mere literary lion, that he was a propagandist who made his proposal not as an abstract, purposeless scheme, but as a measure for the securing of which he would leave no stone unturned.

Often the comments were denunciatory or abusive, inveighing against George's theory as "immoral", as proposing "revolution based on robbery", and branding George himself as a dangerous, socialistic-minded citizen. Some of

[76] New York Herald, Apr. 29, 1884.

[77] Mr. Horace White, reviewing Social Problems for the Nation, said that it was " 'Progress and Poverty' over again, with less argument and more passion, less political economy and more tirade and bombast," vol. 38, p. 238 (1884). See too A. T. Hadley's review in the New York Independent, May 1, 1884, p. 11, and the review in the New York Tribune, Feb. 18, 1884.

[78] For newspaper comments see the New York Tribune editorials, Aug. 26, 1883, Jan. 15, Apr. 23, 1884; the New York Times, Feb. 4, Aug. 4, 1884.

[79] Reviewing Social Problems in the New York Independent, May 1, 1884, p. 11.

these attacks took the form of ridicule, such as the following editorial in the New York *Times,* February 25th, 1885,
on "The nationalization of trousers".

"The great project of the nationalization of trousers, so ably
urged by the eminent reformer, Mr. Jacob Isaacs, cannot be
lightly dismissed. . . . It is Mr. Isaac's opinion that trousers
are the source of all wealth. This is demonstrated in three
ways: (1) No man can gain employment in civilized countries
unless he wears trousers, and (2) no man can, in the changing
conditions of the climate of countries inhabited by civilized
races, work without trousers, and at the same time preserve
his health. Hence, while wealth is the result of labor, it is
also the result of trousers. Again, (3) wealth, or money,
which is its representative and concrete expression, is universally carried in the trousers pocket."

However, George's ideas were being seriously and respectfully considered by multitudes. The circulation of his
writings, powerfully aided by his speeches, had gained a
wide hearing for his ideas. These formed the subject for
numerous newspaper editorials and magazine articles.
Books of refutation were beginning to appear. Henry
George was making converts and, according to one of his
critics, he had "arrayed on his side not a few of our ablest
literary men, magazine writers, Presidents and Professors
in colleges and universities, statesmen and jurists of recognized ability and integrity, together with some leading merchants and manufacturers".[80] The partial and inadequate
replies to his arguments and the exhibitions of bad temper
and poor taste in denouncing them formed but a poor offset
to the brilliancy and persuasiveness of *Progress and
Poverty.*

Henry George's ideas had surely been receiving all the
attention that any social reformer could desire. Professor

[80] James Taylor, American Political Philosophy: An Inquiry as to
the Remedies for Social and Political Evils proposed by Henry George
and Others, Columbus, Ohio, July, 1883, p. 23. See too M. L. Scudder,
The Labor Value Fallacy, Chicago, 1884, pp. 6, 7.

Hadley, reviewing *Social Problems* for the New York *Independent,* said: "Henry George exercises a strong influence over a vast number of people. We must face the fact squarely, whether we like it or not. His books are sold and read in America and England as no other books are sold and read; the sales are numbered by the hundred thousand, the readers by the million."[81]

[81] New York Independent, May 1, 1884, p. 11.

CHAPTER V

HENRY GEORGE AND LABOR POLITICS, 1881-1886

With Henry George's campaign for the mayoralty of New York City in 1886 begins a new phase of the single tax movement. The author of *Progress and Poverty,* regarded theretofore mainly as a doctrinaire, a propagandist of suggestive ideas, a brilliant writer who directed attention forcibly to grave and unsolved social problems, but whose theories were of little more than academic interest, becomes the leader of dissatisfied laborers, the champion of the masses and, in the eye of the public, a politician. Most men had believed that the wide distribution of land ownership and the presence of a supposedly limitless western expanse of land would preclude the practical consideration of George's theories in "free America", whatever their chance of becoming an immediate issue in countries such as Ireland and England which had an extreme concentration of land holding.[1] But George himself, with unfaltering faith in the sufficiency and final triumph of his remedy for poverty and social injustice, together with those who believed him to be the revealer of a new economic dispensa-

---

[1] The New York Times, June 6, 1880, said: "In the meantime, we have one complete security against any schemes which assail property in land. The American farmer holds doctrines about the exclusive individual ownership of land which an Irish landlord would never dream of asserting."

Also Horace White, reviewing Progress and Poverty in The Nation, Aug. 12, 1880, remarks that George's ideas are not liable to be popular "in a country where the ownership of land is widely distributed."

tion, awaited with confidence and hope the day when his
ideas should become an issue in American politics.

"Progress and Poverty's" appeal to the masses

Even before *Progress and Poverty* appeared, many
workingmen in the United States were interested in the land
question. The agrarian movement of the first part of the
nineteenth century had not ceased with the passage of the
Homestead Act of 1862.[2] In the sixties and seventies land-
grabbing abuses, coupled with the extravagant grants which
Congress gave to railways, aroused protest. In 1874 the
Industrial Brotherhood adopted as the fifth demand of its
preamble a declaration that the public lands, the heritage
of the people, should be reserved for actual settlers rather
than be allowed to fall into the hands of speculators or be
given to railroads.[3] Four years later, the first General Assembly of the Knights of Labor endorsed and adopted this
declaration.[4] Terence V. Powderly, Grand Master Work-
man of the Knights of Labor, said in his address at the
General Assembly of 1882 that in his opinion the land
question was "the main all-absorbing question of the
hour".[5] At the convention of 1884, the Knights of Labor
reaffirmed this same declaration and added a clause demand-
ing that "all lands now held for speculative purposes be
taxed to their full value".[6]

Progress and Poverty had appealed in a remarkable way
to the masses of the people. In 1885 Professor Ely wrote:

[2] For an account of this early agrarian movement see Commons,
Documentary History of American Industrial Society, vol.'s 7 and
8 (part 3).
[3] See Powderly, Thirty Years of Labor, p. 335.
[4] Ibid., pp. 335-36; see also Kirk, National Labor Federations in the
United States (Johns Hopkins University Studies, Series 24, 1906),
pp. 20-21.
[5] Powderly, Thirty Years of Labor, pp. 337-38.
[6] Ibid., p. 343.

"Tens of thousands of laborers have read *Progress and Poverty,* who never before looked between the two covers of an economic book, and its conclusions are widely accepted articles in the workingman's creed".[7] There were several reasons for this. Henry George was himself a workingman, and workingmen would trust him much more implicitly because he had come from their own ranks. As an editor in the California days he had championed the cause of the workers, favoring the eight hour day, the organization of labor, and other of the workingmen's aims.[8] Also the subjects of which he wrote and spoke so eloquently —poverty and misery—were facts "everpresent in the lives of so many of his readers".[9] Furthermore, as George Gunton wrote: "Unlike the ordinary treatises on political economy, Mr. George's book is to the laborer the unmistakable voice of a friend. He cannot read a single chapter of it without feeling that, whether Mr. George is right or wrong, in him the laborers have a friend in court."[10]

The conditions of the times bred discontent.[11] A deep-set feeling prevailed among workingmen that they did not receive justice in the distribution of wealth, that they did

[7] Ely, Recent American Socialism (Johns Hopkins University Studies, Series 3, 1885), p. 19.

[8] For George's early interest in the affairs of workingmen, see The Life of Henry George, p. 159.

[9] A. T. Hadley, reviewing George's Social Problem in the New York Independent, May 1, 1884.

[10] The Forum, Mar., 1887, p. 15.

[11] T. V. Powderly, the chief of the Knights of Labor, wrote in 1885: "That a deep-rooted feeling of discontent pervades the masses, none can deny; that there is a just cause for it must be admitted. The old cry: 'These agitators are stirring up a feeling of dissatisfaction among workingmen, and they should be suppressed', will not avail now. Every thinking person knows that the agitator did not throw two millions of men out of employment. . . . That the army of the discontented is gathering fresh recruits day by day is true." North American Review, vol. 140, p. 371 (1885).

not get what they "produced". George E. McNeill in *The Labor Problem* quotes as the diagnosis of the laborers' complaint in 1886 his diagnosis of their complaint in 1877: "We complain, that whereas labor produces all the wealth of the world, the laborer receives only as much as will keep him in the poorest condition of life to which he can be crowded down, for the shortest number of years; . . . that, whereas he is the most important factor he is treated as the least".[12]   So Henry George did not fail of a hearing among workingmen when he undertook to explain why "the working class means the poor class", putting forward a plan which purported to secure to the laborer the whole produce of his labor.   As W. H. Mallock said, the enormous sale of cheap editions of George's books bore testimony to the fact that the laboring classes were anxious to be assured on the basis of a definite economic theory that a radical change of some sort would be practicable and efficacious.[13]   Many hailed Henry George as a new and better Adam Smith, to whom it was reserved to explain "the nature and causes of the poverty of nations".[14]

Henry George and the New York workingmen, 1881-1885

The serial republication of *Progress and Poverty,* as in the New York daily *Truth* beginning in October, 1881, made it even more directly available to workingmen.[15] Samuel Gompers has described how the men read and discussed the book in their workshops.[16]   That Henry George's ideas quickly took hold upon the workingmen is plain

[12] McNeill, The Labor Problem, pp. 454-55.
[13] Mallock, Property and Progress, 1884, p. 91.
[14] Rae, Contemporary Socialism, 1901 ed., p. 441.
[15] See supra, ch. 4, also The Life of Henry George, pp. 355 and 356, note.   Progress and Poverty was also printed serially in the Chicago Express.
[16] In a talk at the 1914 Fels Fund Conference, Washington, D. C. Gompers was an early convert of Henry George.

from the reception accorded him on the occasion of his
return from his first English trip, in October, 1882. The
members of the Central Labor Union of New York received him with cheers and read an address to him which
declared that his name "had become a household word to
millions who recognized in him a leader whose teachings
would yet lead labor out of the house of bondage in which
it had so long sojourned".[17] Robert Blissert, president of
the Central Labor Union, said that this organization was
based upon the principles of Henry George's book, which
the New York workingmen regarded as "the holiest Bible
they ever received". The first plank in the platform of that
association, he said, was the nationalization of the land.[18]
Edward King, of the Type Founders' Union, said that
George had demonstrated that the possession of land was
the great regulator that determines how much or how little
the producers shall get of the wealth they call into existence.[19] The closing words of George's speech were a
significant appeal to the laborers and were enthusiastically
received: "Every man who desires to labor should be permitted to receive that which he produces. . . . The labor
question must be brought into politics. It is not charity,
but justice that is wanted. Move forward for that".[20]

The labor day demonstration of the next year, 1883, an
occasion which Professor Ely has said was probably the
first when large bodies of American laborers acted publicly
with outspoken socialists and marched under revolutionary
banners,[21] showed clearly Henry George's growing influence in the labor movement. Some of the legends on
banners carried in parade gave evidence of this. One in-

[17] New York Times, Oct. 21, 1882.
[18] New York Herald, and Sun, Oct. 21, 1882.
[19] New York Herald, Oct. 21, 1882.
[20] Idem.
[21] Ely, Recent American Socialism, (1885), p. 20.

genious device represented "Capital" flying a kite labeled "Rent", with a tail made up of balloons labeled "Coal", "Flour", "Meat", and "Prices", indicating that all were high. Some of the banners bore the motto "Down with Rent".[22] On George's return from England in April, 1884, he was welcomed at historic Cooper Union by a throng of workingmen which packed the building long in advance of the hour for opening. Enthusiastic speakers eulogized him as "the man who was considered by all true Americans as the greatest of living Americans".[23]

Not only were George's ideas working their way through the ranks of the trades-unionists, but they were opening a way for even more radical measures by reason of their influence with the socialists.[24] Professor Ely wrote in 1885: "Socialists very generally accept the 'no-rent' theory as a chief article in their creed, and one of the first to be realized. If they often reject Henry George's statement of his propositions, it is to their form rather than to their substantial purport they object."[25] Also he cites from a socialist paper the following "economic law":

"Warning! Landowners look out! There are breakers ahead! This is the new law governing the price of land in both city and country. The price of land is determined by the sale of Henry George's 'Progress and Poverty', falling as it rises, and rising as it falls. It is now past its hundredth edition, and it is going faster than ever. In ten years from now, town lots will not be worth more than the taxes! Private property and land is doomed!"[26]

[22] See accounts in the New York Herald, and Times, Sept. 6, 1883.
[23] New York Herald, April 30, 1884.
[24] On this point see Professor Ely's valuable monograph, Recent American Socialism (1885), ch. 2, Henry George and the Beginnings of Revolutionary Socialism in the United States.
[25] Ibid., p. 19.
[26] Ibid., p. 20.

Henry George's nomination for the New York
mayoralty, 1886[27]

The Central Labor Union of New York City, which
nominated Henry George for the mayoralty in 1886, grew
out of a Cooper Union mass meeting which the trades-
unionists held in the winter of 1881-82 to express their
sympathy with the Irish peasants in their uprising against
the landlords.[28] At that time Irish leaders were influential
in the New York labor movement. But the interest of the
laborers in the land question was not the immediate cause
of Henry George's being nominated for the New York
mayoralty in 1886. The entrance of the Central Labor
Union into politics was due rather to the dissatisfaction of
the workingmen with the administration of justice and the
attitude of the courts on labor matters. They hoped
through political action to make a showing which would
secure for them better treatment before the law, and
George's name came to the minds of the great majority as
the man best fitted to run for mayor.[29] "I was nominated",
said Henry George shortly after the election, "because it
was believed that I best represented the protest against unjust social conditions and the best means of remedying
them".[30]

The nomination was made in a remarkable manner.
When Henry George was asked whether he would accept

[27] The fullest account of George's New York mayoralty campaign
of 1886 is Post and Leubuscher, The George-Hewitt Campaign, New
York, 1887. The New York City Library and the Library of Princeton University have copies of this booklet. Other accounts are those
of Henry George, Jr. in The Life of Henry George, pp. 459-83, and
of F. C. Leubuscher in the Single Tax Review, Nov.-Dec., 1913.

[28] The Central Labor Union; its Formation and Growth, New York
Tribune, Oct. 26, 1890, p. 22. See also Leubuscher, op. cit., p. 21.

[29] Leubuscher, op. cit., pp. 21-22.

[30] Interview in New York Herald, Nov. 14, 1886, p. 8.

the nomination, he replied in a letter of August 26, 1886, that, while he had no dread of finding himself in a minority, a failure would injure the very cause he wished to help. In order to secure the united backing of the workingmen of the city, he made the unusual stipulation that he would become their candidate if nominated by the petition of thirty thousand men.[31] Some were skeptical as to whether this condition would be met, believing that Henry George presumed too much upon his popularity with the workingmen.   But, difficult as was this condition, it was promptly complied with, and, a month later, the campaign was in full swing.[32] The platform, adopted at Clarendon Hall, September 23, attacked monopolies and political corruption and urged as measures of reform Henry George's land tax and ballot reform.[33]

Henry George was never an office seeker; his real motive in going into politics was to advertise his theories and promote their discussion. When in one of his campaign meetings a man asked how his election would help their progress he replied: "My election will forward those theories simply by increasing the discussion of them. They cannot be carried into effect until the great majority of the people wish them to be carried into effect, and the great majority of the people will never wish them to be carried into effect until they have thoroughly discussed and considered them".[34] In a letter of September 10, he wrote to his friend Dr. Taylor that if he went into the fight his campaign would "bring the land question into practical politics and do more to popularize its discussion than years of writing would do".[35]

[31] Post and Leubuscher, op. cit., pp. 7-11.
[32] Ibid., p. 12.
[33] Ibid., pp. 13-15; also Single Tax Review, Nov.-Dec., 1913, pp. 24-25.
[34] Post and Leubuscher, op. cit., p. 88.
[35] The Life of Henry George, pp. 463-64.

Henry George's candidacy secured at once a great deal of public attention throughout the United States. *Public Opinion,* October 23, 1886, remarked at the head of a group of collected newspaper opinions that "few events of the year have excited so general and profound an interest as the candidacy of Henry George for the mayoralty of New York".[36] These newspaper citations reflected various attitudes toward him. Some called it an encouraging sign of the times that a philosopher should be taken up by the masses of the people as their champion. Others spoke of his sincerity, but termed him a visionary, "a rather high type of crank". Still other comments were to the effect that while, as mayor, he could not carry out his theories, his election would give an impulse to socialistic schemes which the bulwarks of society could not but view with alarm. But the labor unions of the country showed another sort of interest in his candidacy. "'Henry George and Labor' will be the battle cry for all enslaved toilers from the Atlantic to the Pacific", read a telegram to the New York Labor Convention from the Central Labor Union of St. Louis.[37]

All agreed that the man who had "written a book on economic science, which has been translated into a dozen languages, and which has had, in a few years, a larger sale than any book written by any American writer",[38] was not a candidate of the usual sort. It was quite generally recognized that his candidacy involved a great deal more than the question whether or not he possessed administrative ability; that the commitment of thirty thousand voters in the city of New York to such a declaration of principles was a striking sign of the times; and that, although as mayor he could do very little directly to forward his aims,

[36] Public Opinion, Oct. 23, 1886, p. 21.
[37] New York Herald, Sept. 24, 1886, p. 3.
[38] Public Opinion, Oct. 16, 1886, p. 19.

the fact of his election "would not be uninfluential upon public opinion".[39]

The campaign

The campaign was short, spectacular, and hot. The politicians, puzzled as to the possible strength of what was generally denominated "the Henry George movement", were at first disposed to belittle it, but the manifest earnestness of the forces of labor and the ease with which the thirty thousand signatures were secured in a little over two weeks threw a scare into the ranks of the then disunited Democratic organization. Smothering their quarrels, the factions joined in nominating for the mayoralty Abram S. Hewitt, while the Republicans chose Theodore Roosevelt. The real issues of the campaign were thoroughout between Hewitt and George, Roosevelt being, as a comment of December, 1886, has it, "not only with respect to his vote, but also with respect to the importance of his candidacy, only a third party candidate".[40]

Hewitt defined the issues at the outset in his letter of acceptance.[41] He believed that George's success would have "consequences . . . pernicious, if not disastrous, to the interests of the country and the stability of our institutions", and that the aim of George's campaign was "to substitute the ideas of anarchists, nihilists, communists, socialists, and mere theorists for the democratic principle of individual liberty". He charged George with attempting to array class against class, and, in his speeches, accused him of

[39] Ibid., Oct. 2, 1886, p. 483.

[40] Post and Leubuscher, op. cit., preface.

"Very few opinions were heard regarding the Roosevelt campaign; the Republican mayoralty candidate seemed to be disregarded, and all interest appeared to be centered on Hewitt and George as the giants in the field." New York Herald, Oct. 22, 1886, p. 2.

[41] This letter is reprinted in Post and Leubuscher, op. cit., pp. 32-37.

"preaching to one class of the community the doctrine of hate".[42] He reiterated such statements as: "I am here only for one purpose. I am a candidate for mayor only for one purpose. I regard the election of Henry George as mayor of New York as the greatest possible calamity that could menace its prosperity and its future hopes".[43] Such was the stress which Hewitt laid upon this idea that the *Times,* which supported Roosevelt, could say that "absolutely the only blessing which Mr. Hewitt promises to confer upon the city of New York through his election as mayor is the defeat of Henry George".[44]

Henry George accepted the gage of battle as thrown down to him. He forced the fighting, challenging Hewitt in an open letter to meet him in public debate to defend the charges he had made in his letter of acceptance, and to discuss the issues, which George declared to be clean elections and pure government. Hewitt declined the invitation to debate and replied in another open letter. A further exchange of open letters followed, forming one of the unusual features of this campaign; a reading of these letters brings out clearly the contrast between George's radicalism and Hewitt's conservatism.[45]

George, who was without newspaper backing except for the *Leader,* a campaign paper, and the socialist *Volkszeitung,*[46] made a most energetic campaign. His supporters spoke nightly from "cart-tails" in all parts of the city, while he himself made over a hundred speeches—on one occasion as many as eleven in a single evening.[47] Always an im-

[42] New York Herald, Oct. 30, 1886, p. 3.
[43] Ibid., Oct. 31, 1886, p. 9.
[44] New York Times, Nov. 1, 1886, p. 4.
[45] These letters are given in full in Post and Leubuscher, op. cit., and in the New York press, Oct. 18 to 25, 1886.
[46] See The Life of Henry George, p. 474.
[47] Post and Leubuscher, op. cit., p. 106. This work contains accounts of George's meetings together with reports of his speeches.

pressive speaker, Henry George was then in the prime of life and spoke powerfully. He invited questions from his audiences and was always ready with quick, and at times brilliant, answers.

The issues were clear cut. George spoke out for clean government and for the economic theories of *Progress and Poverty,* appealing directly to the masses and the radicals. Hewitt sought the support of the conservative elements, charging that "the George movement" was revolutionary and purely a class movement. Much was made of this latter charge. Tammany, in its formal letter of notification to Hewitt, complained that George was "a candidate for mayor who has not been named by a convention composed of delegates representing any distinct political opinions, but by a body claiming to represent certain trades and occupations." Tammany "observed with great regret and serious disquiet this attempt to create a political class in this country".[48]

To this charge Henry George replied that it was a case of "the masses against the classes". He claimed to find his backing not alone among hand workers but among all classes of men who earned their living by the exertion of hand or brain. The only class not represented among his supporters, he said, was "that class who live by appropriating the proceeds of the toil of others".[49]

Nevertheless it was true that the real bulk of George's support came from the trades-unionists, who made a most active canvass for votes. The New York *Tribune* reports that between the 1st of September and the 23d of October nearly seven thousand men were naturalized in New York, most of them in order to vote, and estimates that seventenths of these became citizens in order to vote for the

[48] New York Herald, Oct. 14, 1886, p. 3.
[49] Ibid., Oct. 19, 1886, p. 3.

labor candidate. The story was told of a certain German who was asked to take the oath of allegiance. He was told to place his hand on the Bible and the clerk began: "You do solemnly swear to support the constitution of the United States — ". "No! No!", shouted the German, "I supports Mr. George for mayor!"[50]

The hostile press was filled with editorial demolitions of Henry George's land theory, together with denunciations of the Labor Party and its leader. They attacked George as "an illogical, unpractical and dangerous fanatic", a "mischievous demagogue", who preached "dangerous socialistic, communial teachings". A considerable vote for him, it was said, would "immensely encourage and inflame the disorderly and anarchical element which he represents".[51] The New York *Nation* went so far as to say that "nothing has occurred in the history of New York threatening its welfare so seriously as what is called 'the George movement' ". The *Nation* feared that this movement was giving "an enormous stimulus to anarchical and anti-social ideas among a considerable portion of the population".[52]

This denunciation and abuse, however, was not taken at its face value. The following election day statement of the New York *Herald* is significant in this connection: "The mayoralty contest has been on the whole extremely satisfactory. . . . Nobody has taken much stock in the assertions of the different sides:—that Mr. Hewitt is a cruel and heartless despot and oppressor of labor, that Mr. George will be the savior or the destroyer of our social system, or that Mr. Roosevelt is a young man of incomparable ability". The *Herald* believed that the campaign had stirred the blood of the citizens in an entirely wholesome way.[53]

[50] New York Tribune, Oct. 24, 1886, p. 2.
[51] New York Evening Post, Oct. 25, 1886, p. 2.
[52] New York Nation, Oct. 28, 1886, p. 340.
[53] New York Herald, Nov. 2, 1886, p. 6.

The campaign on behalf of the workingmen closed on the Saturday evening before election with a parade which, in spite of a pouring rain, was large and enthusiastic. For two hours a procession of twenty-five thousand men marched past the reviewing stand cheering Henry George. They kept time to such cries as "Hi! Ho! The leeches—must—go!"; "George, George. Hen—ry George!"; and "Vote—Vote—Vote—for—George!".[54] But, in spite of the enthusiasm of the trades-unionists, the forces arrayed against George were too strong, and the official result of the balloting was: Hewitt, 90,552; George, 68,110; Roosevelt, 60,435.[55]

The meaning of George's big vote

That a man without experience in the arts of politics should enter the field against the most perfect political organizations in the country and after a few days' campaigning so nearly carry off the prize, was an event without precedent. The extent to which George's unexpectedly large vote signified the approval of his theories occasioned a wide-spread discussion, as did the possible political future of the Labor Party and its leader.[56]

George's surprisingly big vote represented much more than the wide-spread indorsement of his theories. It was, in the first place, a sign of political discontent. The old

[54] New York Tribune, Oct. 31, 1886, p. 2, and Post and Leubuscher, op. cit., p. 154.

[55] Henry George believed that he had really been elected but had been counted out. See The Life of Henry George, p. 481. There is much reason to believe that the vote counted did not represent the vote actually cast. For a description of the political methods then in vogue in New York, see Levey, An Election in New York, in the North American Review, vol. 145, p. 679 (1887).

To some extent Roosevelt was "knifed" in favor of Hewitt. Figures in the New York Evening Post, Nov. 3, 1886, p. 2, show that his vote was less than that of other Republicans on the ticket.

[56] See Public Opinion, Nov. 13, 1886, pp. 81-82.

party machinery had altogether failed to secure good municipal government for New York, and George's candidacy gathered support from many thousands who probably had no more definite purpose than a general protest against things as they were.[57]   And in the second place, it indicated the strength of the disaffected masses who saw in him a leader and friend.   Many who had little or no comprehension of his theory of social reform and to whom his notions of rent and interest were as unintelligible as Sanscrit, were attracted to him by his vivid portrayal of one class of the community living in ease at the expense of the exploited toilers.   To thousands of his supporters, Henry George was merely their champion in the "conflict between capital and labor".   The subject of comment now was rather Henry George the labor leader than Henry George the author of *Progress and Poverty*.   The burden of many comments was that by means of his campaign the laborers had succeeded in bringing their grievances to the attention of the community, and that these grievances should be considered more seriously than ever before.[58]

There was difference of opinion as to what the future of the Land and Labor Party might be.   As one comment had it, "There are politicians who call it a crackling of thorns under a pot; a blazing of dead leaves and dry stubble, which cannot last.   Others reckon that it will spread like a prairie fire".[59]   Prominent among the latter were Henry

[57] "That Mr. George, a candidate not long or intimately known to the people of New York, received the votes of nearly seventy thousand of its citizens is large and sufficient proof that a considerable part of our population believe themselves to have reason for dissatisfaction with the administration of the municipal government." New York Herald, Nov. 3, 1886, p. 6.

[58] See the New York Herald, Nov. 5, 1886, p. 4, also comments in Public Opinion, Nov. 13, 1886, pp. 81-82.

[59] Lessons of the New York City election: The Republican view, North American Review, Dec. 1886, p. 568.

George and his followers, who believed that they had won a great victory in that the Labor Party's vote was nearly a third of the total and greater than that of the Republican candidate. "I did not want the office; I did want the fight", said George at an enthusiastic "congratulation meeting" on the 6th of November.[60] He believed that the campaign marked the beginning of a new political era in which the doctrines of *Progress and Poverty* would become the vital issue.[61]

Hopes for the future ran high. Henry George and many of his followers believed that they were on the high road to immediate success. They anticipated that discussions and campaigns would continue without ceasing until his theories were embodied in law. This same "congratulation meeting" adopted a resolution calling for the organization throughout the United States of associations "for the purpose of carrying on the work of propagating truth by means of lectures, discussions, and the dissemination of literature, so that the way may be prepared for political action in their various localities, and for the formal organization at the proper time of a National Party". The meeting adjourned with cheers for "Henry George, our next Governor", and "Henry George, the next President".[62] And elsewhere his name was frequently mentioned as a possible Labor candidate for the presidency.[63]

[60] Post and Leubuscher, op. cit., p. 171.

[61] See the interviews in the New York Herald, Nov. 3, 1886, p. 10, and Nov. 4, 1886, p. 3. See also McGlynn, Lessons of the New York City election: the Labor Party view, North American Review, Dec. 1886, p. 576.

[62] New York Herald, Nov. 7, 1886.

[63] See comments in Public Opinion, Nov. 6, 1886, pp. 61-62; Nov. 13, 1886, "As to Mr. George and '88", p. 86.

The effect of the campaign on the furtherance of George's ideas

The problem which every radical movement must face—whether the better policy is political action or propaganda through education—has long agitated George's followers. Opinions have differed as to the effect of political methods in general and of this campaign of 1886 in particular upon the furtherance of his ideas. One view is that represented by C. B. Fillebrown, that "the political method as a means of putting the single tax on the statute books has been abundantly tried and found wanting", and that, in 1886, "the failure to receive a majority of votes did not represent all of Mr. George's loss. He lost infinitely more through campaign misrepresentation, vituperation and distortion of his doctrine by ignorant but well meaning friends as well as by foes. It must be a bold historian who would venture to say that Henry George and his cause stood any higher with the world after than before this bitter campaign".[64]

The contrary opinion is represented by F. C. Leubuscher, one of George's supporters in this campaign, who believes that George's campaign and the great vote he polled "have made single taxers of hundreds of thousands who might otherwise have lived and died without ever having learned that the 'earth belongs in usufruct to the living' ".[65] This was the opinion of Henry George himself. On the night of the election he said: "We have done in this campaign more for popular education, more to purify politics, more toward the emancipation of labor from industrial slavery, than could have been accomplished in twenty years of ordinary agitation".[66]

The great majority of single taxers would take issue with

[64] C. B. Fillebrown, Thirty Years of Henry George, pp. 12 and 10.
[65] Single Tax Review, Nov.-Dec., 1913, p. 32.
[66] Post and Leubuscher, op. cit., p. 170.

Mr. Fillebrown's view that this campaign hindered rather than helped the advance of Henry George's ideas. But an exact determination is not possible. There is plenty of evidence that much discussion during and after this, as nearly every political campaign, was on the plane of misrepresentation and abuse. Indeed the New York *Tribune* said editorially that when George was nominated for the mayoralty there began at once a studied effort to belittle and ridicule the movement, the man, and his doctrines.[67] As a somewhat extreme example, we may cite the words of one rather venomous commentator who went so far as to say that, when the returns showed that George had come so close to being elected, "many faces turned pale, many hands trembled, many thought seriously of selling their possessions and returning to Europe, where bayonet and bullet are always ready to suppress any socialistic movement"![68]

But it is certain that Henry George was correct in stating that his campaign for the mayoralty brought his theories most prominently to the fore. After the election, and mainly as a result of the interest aroused by the campaign, discussion of them became very active. When New York City elects a mayor the entire country looks on, and George's prominence in the campaign of 1886 kindled an interest in the doctrines of *Progress and Poverty* which extended from Maine to California.[69] It became a question of the

[67] New York Tribune, Aug. 21, 1887, p. 4.

[68] Rabbi Gottheil in his Thanksgiving day address, cited in the New York Tribune, Nov. 26, 1886, p. 2.

[69] Cf. the following two letters from single taxers to The Standard:—

"The late mayoralty campaign in New York has brought the land question to the front and made it the burning issue of the hour." (P. J. Kennedy's letter from San Francisco to The Standard, Feb. 26, 1887, p. 7.)

"I am . . . well enough acquainted throughout the State [Colorado] to know that great interest is being taken in this question, an interest largely occasioned by Mr. George's candidacy in New York." (J. W. Bucklin's letter in The Standard, Jan. 8, 1887, p. 3.)

hour "whether the people shall pay rent to private parties and taxes to the state, or rent to the state and no taxes".[70]

Although we cannot disregard that crystallization of ideas and closing of minds which follows the making of any matter a political issue, the evidence indicates that there was a net gain in this mayoralty campaign in focusing public attention upon Henry George. The sort of abuse hurled at him is subject to general discount. Moreover the fact that his opponents made him the object of so much mud-slinging merely testifies to the prominence of his candidacy. Had his place before the public eye been less conspicuous, he might have escaped this unpleasant attention, but, however, at the price of being ignored. The campaign could not but have furthered the sale of his books and caused increased activity on the part of his disciples. Many of those since most prominent in the single tax movement date their conversion from 1886.

[70] F. P. Powers, in Lippincott's Magazine, Mar., 1887, p. 491.

CHAPTER VI

THE EVENTS OF 1887

The year 1887 is an important year in the history of the single tax movement. The significant happenings of that year with which we are here concerned are: the founding of *The Standard,* Henry George's weekly organ; the origin of the distinctive use of the term "single tax"; the controversy arising out of Father McGlynn's break with the authorities of the Roman Church on account of his adherence to the doctrines of *Progress and Poverty;* the establishment of the Anti-Poverty Society; Henry George's candidacy for Secretary of State of New York on the Labor ticket; his quarrel with the socialists, resulting in their secession from the United Labor party; and the defeat and break-up of the United Labor party.

As a result of these events, single taxers proper achieved a greater degree of solidarity. In the mayoralty campaign of 1886, a heterogeneous group of trades-unionists, socialists, anarchists, and liberals of various stripes in addition to single taxers, had worked together under Henry George's leadership. But the outcome of the occurrences of this crowded year was the separation of George's disciples from the incongruous elements which had followed his leadership in 1886, and their becoming, in their distinctive ideas and propaganda, a well-defined group, not very numerous indeed, but active and energetic. The roots of the single tax movement as we know it today are found in these events of 1887.

"The Standard"

Henry George issued the first number of *The Standard* January 8, 1887.[1] Through the six years of its life this well-edited weekly served to unite his followers. It became an inspired commentary on all political and economic questions and an authoritative expositor of *Progress and Poverty,* which resolved the difficulties of the elect and strengthened their faith. *The Standard* gained at once an extensive circulation and had a great influence in the furtherance of the single tax cause.

The origin of the name "single tax"

The use of the term "single tax" as distinctive of the movement founded by Henry George originated in 1887. This phrase, incidentally a literal translation of the phrase *impôt unique* of the Physiocrats, occurs in a noteworthy passage in *Progress and Poverty* in which Henry George refers to "the effect of substituting for the manifold taxes now imposed a single tax on the value of land".[2] It is met elsewhere too in the literature discussing Henry George's theories, but nowhere as distinctively applied to the movement or its program. Previous to 1887 it was usual to speak of "the Henry George movement" and "Georgeism", or of "Georgeites" and "Henry George men", and, with respect to the political movement, of the "Labor Party", or the "Land and Labor Party".

But Henry George's followers, particularly after discussion had entered the arena of politics, came to feel the lack of a name suggestive of their aim or method. Early in

---

[1] Complete files of The Standard may be found in the New York City Public Library, the Library of Columbia University, and the John Crerar Library, Chicago. The Standard suspended publication in August, 1892.

[2] Progress and Poverty, bk. 8, ch. 4, pp. 424-25.

1887 correspondents in *The Standard* discussed this matter, urging that it was becoming vitally necessary to find a distinctive name.   Among the titles suggested we find "National Party", "Free Soil Party", "Free Land Party", and "Anti-Poverty Party", but none of these gained any acceptance.

No one was able to devise a fitting title until Thomas G. Shearman of New York suggested to Henry George the name "single tax".[3]   Under that caption Henry George published an article by Shearman in *The Standard,* May 28, 1887.   That the name satisfied a real want in the movement appears from the remarkable rapidity with which it was accepted.   It was used quite frequently in the columns of *The Standard* during the next few months, and by the fall of 1887 had become the commonly used designation of the movement and its program.

Henry George, Jr., says in *The Life of Henry George* that his father did not regard the term as descriptive of his philosophy, but rather as indicating the method he would take to apply it.[4]   In an editorial in *The Standard,* March 2, 1889, George gave an explanation of his attitude toward the name "single tax" which is worthy of being quoted at length.

"The term single tax does not really express all that a perfect name would convey.   It only suggests the fiscal side of our aims.   And in reality the single tax is not a tax at all. But it is a tax in form, and the term is useful as suggesting method.   Before we adopted this name, people, even intelligent people, insisted on believing that we proposed to divide land up: and many a time have I met a man who after informing me that he had read 'Progress and Poverty' and was familiar with my ideas, would continue: 'But what I don't understand is, how, after you have once divided land up

---

[3] See The Life of Henry George, p. 496, note, and Post, The Taxation of Land Values (1915), pp. 88-89.

[4] The Life of Henry George, p. 496, note.   See also George's views as expressed in an editorial in The Standard, Nov. 16, 1889.

equally, you propose to keep it divided.' Since we have used the term single tax this sort of misrepresentation seems to have almost entirely disappeared, and I think no little of the great progress we have made is owing to the fact that in our name we have kept before the public the idea that the practical measures we proposed consisted simply of a reform in taxation.

"Not only is single tax to my mind preferable to the term land rent tax as linking us to those great Frenchmen, ahead of their time, who, over a century ago, proposed the 'impôt unique' as the great means for solving social problems and doing away with poverty, but that it far more fully expresses our aim. What we want to do is not merely to impose a certain kind of a tax, but to get rid of other taxes. Our proper name, if it would not seem too high flown, would be 'freedom men', or 'liberty men', or 'natural order men', for it is on establishing liberty, on removing restrictions, on giving natural order full play, and not on any mere fiscal change that we base our hopes of social reconstruction. . . .

"This idea is more fully expressed in the term single tax than it would be in land rent tax or any other such phrase. We want as few taxes as possible, as little restraint as is conformable to that perfect law of liberty which will allow each individual to do what he pleases without infringement of equal rights of others."

Father McGlynn and Henry George[5]

During 1887 Father Edward McGlynn, priest of St. Stephen's Catholic Church, New York, came to occupy in the single tax movement a position nearly as conspicuous as that of Henry George himself. His connection with

[5] For accounts of Father McGlynn's relations with the Catholic Church authorities, see, for the George side: The Life of Henry George, index, sub nomine; the first half dozen issues of The Standard; and McGlynn's address, The Cross of a New Crusade, which has an introduction reviewing the McGlynn case (a pamphlet in the New York Public Library). For the Roman Catholic view, see the contemporary numbers of The Catholic World, vols. 44, p. 810; 45, p. 116; 46, pp. 94 and 588; 47, p. 51; and Preuss, The Fallacy of Socialism, St. Louis, 1908. For general comments, see Public Opinion, vols. 2 and 3, index, sub nomine. An excellent account of the whole affair is that of W. T. Croasdale, The Story of Dr. McGlynn, in the New York Independent, Aug. 4, 1887.

the movement brought it before the public eye more prominently than ever.

Father McGlynn had early been attracted to Henry
George through their common interest in the Irish land
question. During the mayoralty campaign of 1886 his advocacy of the doctrines of *Progress and Poverty* had got
him in difficulty with the Roman hierarchy and had led to
his temporary suspension. This suspension was extended
for the balance of the year 1886 as the result of McGlynn's
interview favoring George's doctrines which appeared in
the New York *Tribune,* November 26, 1886. But in spite
of the suspension he remained firm in his belief that his
adherence to George was not in conflict with the obligations
of his religion. Braving Rome's disapproval, he stayed
with the George party. "I have taught and I shall continue
to teach in speeches and writings as long as I live", said he,
"that land is rightfully the property of the people in common, and that private ownership of land is against natural
justice, no matter by what civil or ecclesiastical laws it may
be sanctioned; and I would bring about instantly, if I
could, such change of laws all the world over as would
confiscate private property in land, without one penny of
compensation to the miscalled owners".[6]

In January, 1887, Archbishop Corrigan removed Dr.
McGlynn from his pastorate at St. Stephen's. But the latter refused to accept the right of his ecclesiastical superiors
to control his utterances on political and economic questions.
"In becoming a priest I did not evade the duties nor sur-
render the rights of a man and a citizen", said Father
McGlynn. He denied the right of bishop or pope to punish
him for economic opinions or political actions which were
not "clearly contrary to the teachings of the Christian re-

[6] Father McGlynn's letter to Archbishop Corrigan, Dec. 20, 1886.
Printed in The Standard, Feb. 5, 1887, p. 1, and cited in The Life of
Henry George, pp. 486-87.

ligion". The priest's vow of obedience, said Father Mc-
Glynn, was "simply a promise to obey the church authorities in matters concerning the priests' duties of religion".[7]

Father McGlynn continued his active work for the Henry
George party in spite of his suspension. In March at a big
meeting in the New York Academy of Music he reiterated
his beliefs in a remarkably powerful address on the subject
"The Cross of the New Crusade".[8] And on Sunday evening the first of May, he delivered a most eloquent address
at the first public meeting of the Anti-Poverty Society.

This struggle between the independent priest and his
ecclesiastical superiors excited the greatest public interest.
When in January Archbishop Corrigan removed Father
McGlynn from the pastorate of the big Fifth Avenue
church, a hot discussion was precipitated which became nation wide. Henry George took it up as the leading matter
in the first issues of *The Standard,* attacking with great
vigor the position of the authorities of the Roman Church.

"Are we, or are we not, to have in this country a power
which can coerce a most important and influential body of
citizens into such political action as it may choose to dictate—
a power responsible only to a foreign authority, and which
sets up for itself the claim of being beyond even criticism or
remonstrance? The land question important as it may be, cuts
no figure in this case. . . .
"Is it not true that American Catholics, for the sake of
themselves, for the sake of the priests they love, and to avoid
scandal to their religion, should plant themselves on the same
ground taken by the great Irish liberator, *'as much religion
from Rome as you please, but no politics!' "*[9]

This last phrase of Daniel O'Connell was taken up widely
and became a slogan in the controversy.

[7] McGlynn's statement of his position in The Standard, Feb. 5, 1887,
p. 1.
[8] For an account of this meeting, see the New York Sun, Mar. 31,
1887, p. 2.
[9] The Standard, Jan. 8 and 15, 1887, p. 1.

Henry George's attack upon the Roman Church created
a profound sensation. The newspapers of the country gave
it a prominent place and discussed it editorially. It likewise
formed a subject of hot controversy in religious and secular
periodicals. Big demonstrations for McGlynn—protest
meetings and parades—were held, composed largely of
Catholic trades-unionists and members of St. Stephen's,
most of whom were loyal to their priest.[10] From the first
of January until after Dr. McGlynn's excommunication six
months later, a great number followed his case with the
keenest interest. Such indeed was the attention which it
secured for the doctrines of Henry George that in the view
of some of his followers the matter was a "heaven-inspired"
means for bringing them into the foreground throughout
the entire United States.

"The Anti-Poverty Society"[11]

Such then was the situation when a group of leading
single taxers organized the Anti-Poverty Society in New
York City. Father McGlynn was chosen president and
Henry George vice-president. The aim and spirit of this
remarkable organization can perhaps best be set forth by
quoting its platform:

"The time having come for an active warfare against the
conditions that, in spite of the advance in the powers of production, condemn so many to degrading poverty, and foster
vice, crime, and greed, the Anti-Poverty Society has been
formed. The object of the society is to spread, by such peace-
able and lawful means as may be found most desirable and
efficient, a knowledge of the truth that God has made ample

[10] See the New York Tribune, Jan. 31, 1887, p. 1, for an account of
one of these demonstrations.

[11] There is an account of the Anti-Poverty Society in The Life of
Henry George, pp. 491-95. The best contemporary account of the
Anti-Poverty phase of the single tax movement is a valuable article
by G. M. Grant, Progress and Poverty, in the Presbyterian Review,
Apr., 1888, p. 177.

provision for the need of all men during their residence upon
earth, and that involuntary poverty is the result of the human
laws that allow individuals to claim as private property that
which the Creator has provided for the use of all".[12]

The first public meeting of the society was held in
Chickering Hall on Sunday evening the first of May, 1887.
Dr. McGlynn's address was the main feature of the meeting. So tremendous was the crowd of those eager to attend
that many hundreds were unable to gain admittance. The
meeting took the form of a most enthusiastic demonstration
for the deposed priest.

The Anti-Poverty meetings became a regular Sunday evening event. And extraordinary meetings they were. The
earnest and eloquent addresses of Father McGlynn and
Henry George, the hymns and stirring choruses set to
popular airs and led by St. Stephen's choir, who had with-
drawn from the service of the church when their beloved
priest was deposed, moved profoundly such gatherings as
the largest auditoriums of New York were unable to ac-
commodate.[13] Religious fervor characterized the Anti-
Poverty Society. Its members used biblical language to
denote the work in which they were engaged; they were
taking "the cross of a new crusade", and "spreading the
gospel". They employed, too, such methods of propaganda
as have been used by the most ardent sections of the church,
engaging in "personal work", circulating tracts by hand or
folding them into their letters, and distributing *The Standard* gratuitously.[14] The Anti-Poverty Society gave to the
Henry George movement at this time a religious tone,
bringing about that confusion of the realms of religion and
political economy which is to the detriment of each. For

[12] Cited from The Life of Henry George, pp. 491-92, note.
[13] For a good detailed account of one of these meetings, see The
Standard, Dec. 31, 1887, p. 6. See also the accounts in the New York
daily press of May 2, 1887, and succeeding Mondays.
[14] See Grant, op. cit., pp. 178-79.

example, *The Standard* reports that the "Henry George
Club" of Columbus, Ohio, unanimously resolved that the
clergy of the city "be respectfully requested to discourse
from their pulpits at their earliest convenience upon the
subject, 'The land doctrines advocated by Henry George
the solution of the labor problem' "![15]   And Father Mc-
Glynn, in spite of his insistence that his adherence to the
cause of Henry George was outside the sphere of his relig-
ous accountability, appealed to the Anti-Poverty Society
in the name of Christian justice to further the program of
socializing land values by means of taxation.[16]

Word went out in May that Dr. McGlynn would be excommunicated unless he should present himself at Rome
within forty days.   He declined to go and accordingly,
early in July, Archbishop Corrigan pronounced the excommunication.   This caused no falling off in the enthusiastic
crowds which gathered for Anti-Poverty meetings, but
rather made them even greater than before.   Dr. McGlynn
himself was undisturbed, believing that "an unjust excommunication will never stand".[17]   His followers in St.
Stephen's and the Anti-Poverty Society remained loyal to
him, as did many Catholic trades-unionists and the leaders
of the Central Labor Union, for political activity in behalf
of which he had got himself in trouble with his ecclesiastical
superiors.   On the 18th of June, as a protest against the im-
pending excommunication, there was a parade of New York
workingmen in which, according to the New York *Tribune,*
thirty or forty thousand men participated.[18]

[15] See The Standard, Apr. 2, 1887, p. 5.
[16] "It is our purpose simply to preach to all men who will hear us
that great truth which is for us not only a truth of political economy,
of wisest statesmanship, but so radical and fundamental that we believe it to be the very essence and the core of all religion." Father
McGlynn's Anti-Poverty address, cited in The Standard, Dec. 17,
1887, p. 2.
[17] New York Tribune, July 11, 1887, p. 5.
[18] Ibid., June 19, 1887, p. 5.

In exciting wide public interest the cumulative effect of
Henry George's mayoralty campaign, the McGlynn affair,
and the doings of the Anti-Poverty Society was very great.
The latter in particular attracted the public eye, since its
crowds and enthusiasm invested the Henry George movement with that touch of the spectacular which always claims
attention. It drew the fire of the contemporary press and
became the butt of their ridicule and criticism.[19] Some
made much of the "collections" of the society and hinted
that it would justify its name by keeping poverty far away
from the estimable gentlemen who presided over its destiny.
But the burden of most comments was to the effect that
the aims of the society were over-ambitious and Utopian,
since the fundamental cause of poverty lay in human nature; that as long as the conditions of prosperity in this
world were industry and frugality, Anti-Poverty methods
would not encourage the cultivation of these virtues; and
that a course of history would be an excellent prescription
for the self-confident reformers who hoped to eliminate by
law the shadow of poverty which has so long followed the
race.

The following comment of *The Standard,* July 9, 1887,
bears testimony to the volume of discussion.

"Pick up any journal, religious, secular or comic, no matter where published, and in its pages you will surely find some
reference to the anti-poverty crusade—a sneer, a jest, a
labored argument, a studied falsehood, an advocacy of some
other remedy than ours. Read the utterances of men in public life—their Fourth of July orations, their after-dinner
speeches—and see how few of them are able to avoid taking
a little fling at anti-poverty. The preachers are discussing the
matter, the college forums are debating it, the little children
talk about it. There is no mistaking the signs of the times.

[19] See collected comments in Public Opinion, vol. 3, pp. 171-72. See
also the New York Nation, May 5, 1887, p. 380; New York Herald,
May 3, 1887, p. 6; Times, May 5, p. 4; and Tribune, May 8, p. 4.

The anti-poverty cause is gaining.   The pro-poverty folks are scared."

The enthusiastic activity of Henry George's followers in this period evidences the deep hold which his teachings had taken upon them.   It evidences their deep-felt conviction that they were the possessors of truth which would immensely benefit their fellows, the knowledge of which should be spread abroad.   Such sacrifices as that of Dr. McGlynn, his willingness to be excommunicated rather than renounce what he believed to be truth, were indicative of the spirit of many disciples of the new prophet.

The United Labor Party and the socialists[20]

The United Labor Party laid its plans confidently for the New York State campaign of 1887, with the presidential struggle of the following year in view as a possible future field of action.   There had been substantial agreement among George's backers during the mayoralty campaign, but all was not now harmonious.   The socialists disputed with Henry George and his followers the control of the United Labor Party.

Before the campaign of 1886, labor parties had played but a small part in the politics of New York City.   The Central Labor Union had participated in the elections of 1882 and 1883 as an independent organization, polling about 10,000 votes each time.[21]   Both socialists and followers of Henry George had been influential in the affairs of the organization in the years before 1886.   But in the course of the rapid growth of the United Labor Party during George's mayoralty campaign, it had naturally acquired

[20] For an excellent account of the events discussed in the remainder of this chapter, see Louis F. Post, Recollections, Twenty-five Years Afterwards, of the Political Party Out of Which Socialism and the Single Tax Came into American Politics, The Public, Nov. 3, 10, 17, and 24, 1911.

[21] Hillquit, History of Socialism in the United States, pp. 284-85.

a strong leaning toward single tax principles. Its campaign platform, adopted at Clarendon Hall, September 23, 1886, was strictly a single tax platform.[22]

The socialists had accepted George's leadership in this campaign and had backed him strongly.[23] But they worked in the movement only because they believed it to be a movement of labor against capital—"not on account of his single tax theory, but in spite of it", as the socialist *Volkszeitung* said.[24] Early in 1887, they began to contest the leadership with Henry George, and according to him "made the most persistent efforts to force socialistic doctrines upon us".[25] They insisted "that the burning social question is not a land tax, but *the abolition of all private property in instruments of production*".[26]

The matter came up for settlement in the Labor Party convention, which met at Syracuse in August. It was evident in the light of George's pronounced opposition to socialism that the socialist minority could not be seated in the convention. When the convention met, the expected happened; each of the contesting socialist delegates was given a hearing and after a long and heated struggle all were refused seats.[27] The reason given was that the constitution of the United Labor Party required its members to sever their connection with other political parties, and that the socialists wished to participate actively in the affairs of

[22] This platform is reprinted in the Single Tax Review, Nov.-Dec., 1913, p. 24.
[23] See in the New York Herald, Nov. 11, 1886, p. 8, an account of a big Cooper Union mass meeting of the socialists to celebrate George's big vote.
[24] Cited in Hillquit, History of Socialism in the United States, p. 277.
[25] See a letter of Henry George, cited in The Life of Henry George, p. 501.
[26] The socialist contention is cited in The Standard, Aug. 13, 1887, p. 1.
[27] For a full account of the proceedings of the convention, see the New York Herald, Aug. 16 to 22, 1887.

the Labor Party, while retaining their membership in the Socialist Labor Party.[28]

In justifying the expulsion of the socialists Henry George said just after the convention that "the united labor party is not and never has been a socialistic party, and we should be false to our principles if we allowed them to be given a socialistic color".[29] The socialists could say in reply that before the campaign of 1886 the party had not been a single tax party, but was captured by Henry George and his followers. Had a socialist leader of George's caliber arisen in his place in 1886, it is within the range of possibility that the party might have been socialistic, and shown a strength comparable to that shown by it under George. But the party actually was a Henry George party, the socialists were a minority, and as *The Standard* said editorially, August 27, 1887, "they were excluded because they were socialists, organized outside the united labor party to accomplish a purpose different from that which the convention desired". The question was simply a question of the wish and power of the majority.[30]

The socialists greatly resented their exclusion. On their return from Syracuse they held a protest meeting at which they denounced the Labor Party as a party of "office

[28] Hillquit says regarding this matter in his History of Socialism in the United States (p. 278) : "On a previous occasion the New York County executive committee had decided that the section [requiring members to sever their connection with other political parties] had no application to the Socialist Labor Party, since the latter was not a political party in the accepted sense of the term; but when the County general committee met on August 4, 1887, the point was raised again, and the previous decision was reversed, thus virtually expelling the members of the Socialist Labor Party."

[29] Interview in the New York Herald, Aug. 21, 1887, p. 9.

[30] For the single tax view of this controversy, see The Life of Henry George, pp. 496-98, and the Single Tax Rev., Nov.-Dec., 1913, pp. 32-33. For the socialist view, see Hillquit, History of Socialism in the United States, pp. 272-81.

seekers, free traders, and deadheads," and at which they adopted the following resolution: "Resolved that we, workingmen of this city, in mass meeting assembled, repudiate Henry George, his platform and his personal political machine; that we denounce his pandering to the hatreds and prejudice of the capitalistic class in attempting to cast odium upon that earnest body of wage-workers and advanced thinkers who for fifty years have fought the battles of humanity and progress on two continents".[31] On the occasion of the Labor Day parade in September, the socialist sections vented their spite by hissing as they passed Henry George's reviewing stand.[32] They organized the Progressive Labor Party in opposition to the United Labor Party.

The New York State campaign of 1887

We recur now to the Syracuse convention and its doings after the expulsion of the socialists. It adopted a platform similar to that on which Henry George had run in 1886, and nominated a full list of candidates for state offices. Henry George headed the ticket as candidate for Secretary of State. At a big ratification meeting held in New York September 17, Henry George said in his address: "Now we take one step forward from the city to the arena of State politics, as next year, please God, we shall take one step forward into the arena of national politics".[33]

The campaign was energetic and enthusiastic. During the two months preceding the election, the Labor Party prosecuted what *The Standard* characterized as "the most rapid and wonderful work of propaganda, that the world has ever seen".[34] Henry George, Dr. McGlynn, and others

[31] New York Herald, Aug. 23, 1887, p. 2.
[32] Ibid., Sept. 6, 1887, p. 3.
[33] New York Herald, Sept. 18, 1887, p. 11.
[34] The Standard, Oct. 29, 1887, p. 4.

stumped the entire state; for a month each speaker spoke
nearly every night to audiences eager to learn about the
doctrines of *Progress and Poverty*.   More than a million
tracts on the land question were distributed.[35]   Henry
George's disciples in all parts of the state arranged meetings and organized Land and Labor or Henry George Clubs.

The hopes of the Labor Party were high.   At the close of
the campaign George said that he had found everywhere a
surprising readiness to hear his doctrines.   He believed that
the movement had taken a good hold in the interior of the
state, and was confident that the vote of New York City
would at least reach the figure attained in the mayoralty
election.   He believed too that the cause had been strengthened rather than weakened by the conflicts resulting from
his support of Father McGlynn, and from the Labor Party's
break with the socialists.   While not expecting to win, believing that the corrupt methods of his opponents made
victory impossible, he was confident that "the vote to be
received by our party will again astonish the politicians".[36]

But the Labor Party leaders were doomed to disappointment.   In this case those politicians who predicted at the
time of the Syracuse convention that the Labor Party would
not get "in all the State a vote so large as Mr. George received in this city alone when he ran for Mayor last Fall"[37]
was more nearly correct.   The count of votes for Secretary
of State showed:[38]

Cook (Democrat)	480,355
Grant (Republican)	459,503
George (United Labor)	72,781
Huntington (Prohibitionist)	41,897

[35] The Life of Henry George, p. 499.

[36] Interview, New York Tribune, Nov. 9, 1887, p. 9.

[37] New York Times, Aug. 20, 1887, p. 4. See also in this connection
an editorial, "Prospects of the Labor Party", Times, Sept. 20, 1887,
p. 4; New York Nation, Sept. 8 (p. 186) and Sept. 22 (p. 222), 1887;
and especially the New York Sun, Sept. 18, 1887, p. 6.

[38] New York Herald, Nov. 10, 1887.

A little over one half of George's vote was in New York City, and 15,000 of the remainder in Brooklyn.

The Progressive Labor Party played but an insignificant part in the campaign, polling a total of about 5,000 votes.[39] But the campaign of this party (which was but the Socialist Labor Party under another name, with a socialist platform and candidates) was the first in which the socialists "stood out openly as an uncompromising socialist party in American politics".[40] Since 1887 the socialists, with the Socialist Labor Party and the newer and stronger Socialist Party, have participated continuously in politics in the United States.[41]

Out of the United Labor Party have come into American politics the two leading rival programs of social reform, socialism and the single tax. But in strikingly different ways. The socialists have persistently maintained their political organization independent of the regular parties, while the single taxers have maintained no permanent independent political organization. In politics they have worked with the Democrats mainly,[42] and what sporadic independent political activity they have manifested has been not often in behalf of their candidates but rather in behalf of special single tax measures.

[39] See Hillquit, History of Socialism in the United States, pp. 280-81.

[40] Louis F. Post, in The Public, Nov. 24, 1911, p. 1199.

[41] The Socialist Labor Party named a presidential candidate for the first time in 1892, and has done so at each subsequent election. Its maximum vote, attained in 1900, was 49,699.

In 1900 the Socialist Party entered the arena of politics. It was composed of dissatisfied elements of the Socialist Labor Party, and new elements, mainly from the West. The newer party has grown rapidly, most of the members of the Socialist Labor Party being merged with it, and it received its maximum vote, 901,873, in 1912. See Post, op. cit., p. 1199.

[42] Infra, ch. 12.

The significance of the result of the election of 1887

There were several reasons why George's vote in New York State at this time was but 5,000 larger than his New York City vote in the previous election. The loss of the aid of the socialists, together with the open hostility of some of their leaders, alienated many who had supported the Labor Party in 1886. But a much more potent factor was the opposition of the great political power of Romanism, whose antagonism was aroused by George's spirited defense of McGlynn and his fearless attacks upon those who were disciplining the resolute priest.[43] The influential *Irish World,* which has supported George in 1886, now sided with the Catholic authorities against him, in spite of the fact that Patrick Ford, its editor, had been intimately associated with him. Likewise the *Leader,* now in the hands of the socialists, and the *Volkszeitung* turned against him, leaving the United Labor Party entirely without newspaper support except from *The Standard.* Still another factor of some importance was the return to the Democratic fold of the Irving Hall faction, which had supported Henry George for mayor.

There were also important differences in the circumstances of the two campaigns. As candidate for the office of Secretary of State Henry George was less spectacular and much more prosaic than as reform candidate for the mayoralty at a time when his candidacy embodied the fervent protest of laborers aroused against corrupt municipal government and inequality before the law. Moreover the

---

[43] "Many of the George-McGlynn adherents . . . were driven from the United Labor colors by fear of the wrath of the Catholic Church. This was an important element in the campaign just closed. Catholic ecclesiastics and fervent Catholics generally were determined to show that the George party would no longer be formidable after Dr. Mc-Glynn had been put out of the church doors." New York Tribune, Nov. 10, 1887, p. 1.

campaign of 1886 was a municipal campaign, while that of 1887 was significant for national party politics. Voters would be less likely to chance "throwing away their votes" in an election keenly contested by the older parties, each of which coveted the control of the New York State administration the year before a presidential campaign.[44]

Viewed in the light of these circumstances, a vote of 73,000 under the unfavorable conditions of 1887 was not the utter defeat which many considered it. Henry George well said, writing in *The Standard,* November 12, 1887:

"We begin the new campaign with a body of men of whose principles and motives there can be no doubt—a small, but compact and determined army from whose ranks the holiday soldiers, the camp followers and the incongruous elements have all been swept away. . . .

"In all the history of great reforms, what great reform is there that could in such a time make such a showing? Who, two years ago, would have dared to predict that in 1887, under such circumstances and against such odds, over 38,000 votes would be cast in New York city, and over 70,000 in the state at large, for a platform on which the single tax on land values was the cardinal feature?

"No, we may be disappointed, but we are not disheartened."

Henry George said rightly that it was a "new campaign" which began at this time. But it was a new campaign in a fuller sense than single taxers realized at the time. The real significance of the falling off in the vote consisted in the fact that during the year of dissension and discussion which intervened between the two elections a development of very great importance had gotten well under way. In a manner at the time unrecognized by its leaders, *the Henry George movement had become the single tax movement.* The loss in numbers marked a gain in solidarity.

Just how far George's big vote in the election of 1886 represented the acceptance of his theory of social reform is,

[44] The Tribune (Nov. 10, 1887, p. 1) believed that corruption thinned the ranks of the United Labor Party.

we have seen, impossible to say.[45]   In the main it represented a protest against corrupt municipal government and
the discontent of the aroused workingmen of New York
City.   Likewise, indeed, in 1887 we have no way to determine how much of the Labor Party's vote of 73,000 was
a "labor" vote, and how much was polled by those properly
classed as single taxers.   But it is certain that during the
eventful year between the two elections many of the incongruous elements—socialists, anarchists, and non-single
tax trades-unionists—deserted George's standard, as the
Labor Party became under his leadership a single tax workingmen's party.

The defeat of 1887 was, however, more than a sign of
the loss of the incongruous elements.   It was an event which
had the effect of shaking from adherence to George the remainder of those who were neither interested in nor com-
prehended his teachings.   Only those who accepted the
views of *Progress and Poverty* remained.   The transition
was indeed not completed for some months after the election.   The final fate of the United Labor Party and the
break-up of the Anti-Poverty Society, causing the loss of
that element in it which was purely the personal following
of McGlynn, is a part of the subject of the next chapter.
But with the Labor Party on the rocks, single taxers faced
the necessity of developing a line of advance to take the
place of activity in labor politics.

With the close of the political activity of 1886 and 1887
comes the close of a phase later characterized by single
taxers as "the howling dervish stage of emotional insanity".
Since that time, though ideas stressed by single taxers have
undergone important changes, their methods and activities
have been similar to those of today.

[45] Supra, ch. 5.

CHAPTER VII

WORKING OUT A SINGLE TAX PROGRAM, 1888-1890

Henry George's big vote in the New York mayoralty campaign of 1886 had led single taxers to believe that they were on the high road to immediate success. But the defeat of 1887 had shattered their optimistic hopes of success through independent political action, and had brought that discouragement which follows the failure of a program which had promised much. It placed squarely before single tax leaders the problem of a method of advance.

The split on the question of political action

There were two alternatives before the single taxers: continuance of independent political action, or working with one of the older parties. The former policy appealed to many who had a sincere desire to keep the movement "pure", believing that any association with the corruption of the older political parties would be morally wrong.[1] It appealed also to some who wanted to "stand up and be counted", believing that the formation of a national single tax party would unify the movement, and that the party would become a greater power by "going straight ahead". The advocates of the policy of working with one of the older parties believed, however, that any independent single tax party would be too weak to be influential. Numerous

---

[1] "I would sooner be dead than voluntarily vote to indorse the crime and corruption represented by both of the old parties", wrote a correspondent in The Standard, Dec. 3, 1887, p. 8.

correspondents discussed the matter at length in the columns of *The Standard* during November and December, 1887, the letters of the advocates of a national party being perhaps in the majority.

This was the situation when, in an editorial in *The Standard,* Henry George declared his conviction that the duty of single taxers was to support the Democratic Party if it should make a fight on the issue of tariff reform.[2] Grover Cleveland's notable tariff message had indicated such a probability. "Should this prove to be the case", said George, "our entrance into the presidential field might put us in the position of voting against a candidate pledged to measures of reform, which though small in themselves are in the line of our principles, and which would be among the first we ourselves should adopt if we obtained the power".[3]

Henry George's declaration precipitated at once a hot controversy between the advocates of an opportunistic policy and those extremists who favored a national campaign on the Syracuse platform,[4] a platform which contained no declaration on the tariff issue. Henry George carried with him the more substantial leaders and the great majority of the rank and file of single taxers throughout the country. The opposition came chiefly from Father McGlynn and a few of the labor leaders of New York. In the Anti-Poverty meeting of January first, 1888, McGlynn declared his belief that the United Labor party should go straight ahead without a declaration regarding the tariff, working through independent political action for the principles of the Anti-Poverty Society and the Syracuse platform.[5] In a letter to George he declared that he would "feel recreant to a clear duty" if he should work through

[2] The Standard, Dec. 17, 1887, p. 1.
[3] Idem.
[4] For this platform, see the New York Herald, Aug. 20, 1887, p. 2.
[5] See The Standard, Jan. 7, 1888, p. 3.

any means other than a separate national party.[6] On the other hand certain of the leaders of the United Labor party, led by John McMackin and Gaybert Barnes, advocated, from motives which, in the light of subsequent events, appear to have been decidedly less lofty,[7] this policy of entering upon a tariff campaign ignoring the main issue.

Henry George outlined his position with more detail in a series of editorials in *The Standard* during January and February, 1888. He saw in the raising of the tariff issue "a means of bringing the whole subject of taxation, and, through it, the whole social question, into the fullest discussion".[8] He urged that the single tax movement was primarily an "abolition movement" which aimed to get rid of indirect taxes, one of the most burdensome of, which was the tariff; that the Democrats, in attempting to reduce this burden, were moving in the direction of free trade; and that free trade was a step toward the single tax, which George believed to be the logical consequence of giving up the policy of "taxing labor". He asked those advocates of a national single tax campaign who had at heart the best interests of the cause to consider that its progress must come through gradual steps, in the accomplishment of which it would be necessary to "rely upon the aid of those who are not with us in ultimate aim, but are, for the moment, at least, only willing to take the immediate step".[9]

But with those who had the idea of a national single tax party which should enter a campaign ignoring an issue so fundamental to it as the tariff, George had less patience. "The proposition to ignore the tariff question arises from the desire to have a party, not from the desire to advance a principle", he wrote in *The Standard*.[10] He saw clearly

[6] Ibid., Jan. 14, 1888, p. 5.
[7] Infra, pp. 131-32.
[8] The Standard, Feb. 18, 1888, p. 3.
[9] Ibid., Jan. 14, 1888, p. 1.
[10] Ibid., Feb. 18, 1888, p. 1.

the position in which such a party would find itself. Since the single taxers of whom it would be composed would be in the main free traders, it would play into the hands of the Republicans inasmuch as the vote of such a party could represent little more than so many votes which the Democrats did not get. Under such circumstances the stigma of the suspicion of a "deal" with the Republicans would be ruinous to the single tax cause, apart from the detriment to the cause of tariff reform.

The break-up of the Anti-Poverty Society

The first result of the disagreement between George and McGlynn was a split in the ranks of the Anti-Poverty Society. McGlynn attacked Henry George for deserting the United Labor Party, saying that if he should wish to come back, he would "have to take a much humbler position in the ranks than he has heretofore held".[11] In order to prevent a censure from the executive committee of the society on account of this statement, McGlynn made an attempt to pack the committee, whereupon a majority of the committee withdrew, including such well-known single taxers as Louis F. Post, W. T. Croasdale, E. J. Shriver, Hugh Pentecost, T. L. McCready, J. W. Sullivan, J. O. S. Huntington, and Tom L. Johnson.[12] A contest for the control of the society threatened and some of the leaders on George's side sought to enjoin the McGlynn faction from employing the title "Anti-Poverty Society". But George, wishing to avoid a fuss and harmful publicity, counseled that the society be surrendered without a fight, and this was done.[13] McGlynn

[11] Cited in The Standard, Feb. 18, 1888, p. 3. For McGlynn's explanation of his position, see The Standard, Mar. 17, 1888, p. 6.

[12] See The Standard, Feb. 18, 1888, pp. 2 and 3, also the signed statements of Messrs. Post, Croasdale, Sullivan, McCready, and Urner in this same issue of The Standard, pp. 4 and 5, reviewing the controversy and showing McGlynn's alleged high-handed methods.

[13] See The Standard, Feb. 25, 1888, p. 1, and Mar. 24, 1888, p. 3.

took undisputed possession and maintained the Sunday evening meetings for a considerable time. But they became rather his own personal forum and were really outside the pale of the single tax movement.

Single taxers in the national campaign of 1888

The single taxers entered actively into the national campaign of 1888. They organized Free Trade Clubs to back Cleveland and worked vigorously for his success. George, Shearman, Post, and others made numerous free trade speeches in behalf of the Democrats. *The Standard* practically became a Democratic weekly, and carried on an able discussion of questions of public policy, particularly the tariff, the labor question, and ballot reform. But the single taxers were disappointed in their political hopes for the third time in as many years, and although Cleveland's popular vote exceeded that of Harrison he went down to defeat.

The United Labor party played an inglorious part in the campaign. Its convention, held at Cincinnati in May, nominated Robert H. Cowdray of Illinois and W. H. T. Wakefield of Kansas for president and vice-president.[14] But the influence of McGlynn and the other leaders was cast for the protectionist side. "Before the election came, the thin disguise of running a candidate was thrown off, and Dr. McGlynn advised his followers to vote for Harrison".[15] A further commentary on the situation was the appointment, in the summer of 1889, of the chairman of the party's executive committee for New York to a position in the custom house.[16] Cowdray and Wakefield received 2,668 votes, most of them in New York and Brooklyn,[17] in the pivotal

[14] See The Standard, May 26, 1888, p. 4.
[15] Henry George's statement in The Standard, Oct. 5, 1889, p. 2.
[16] See The Standard, Aug. 24, 1889, p. 2.
[17] Ibid., Nov. 10, 1888, p. 1. The total popular vote of Cowdray and Wakefield was 2,808.

state whose vote went to Harrison by only 13,000. It was generally believed that this result, and consequently Grover Cleveland's defeat, were due to the famous "Harrison and Hill" deal for vote-trading.

The problem of a program again

"Now, without any practical politics to hamper us, what we have to do is to press on the work of education and propaganda", wrote Henry George in *The Standard* shortly after the election.[18] The question of a program again faced the single taxers, and two rival plans were proposed.

The first was to concentrate all efforts upon a single state in order to secure the single tax there if possible. It was believed that the adoption of the single tax in any community would provide such an evident demonstration of its benefits that its rapid spread would follow. Many believed that the best line of advance lay in making an "invasion" of New Jersey.[19] Henry George was at first somewhat favorably inclined towards such a proposal, although he believed that "it would hardly be wise to 'invade' New Jersey or any other state. The best way would be to answer the Macedonian cry, 'come over and help us' ".[20] This notion of making a special effort to capture a state and furnish the opportunity for a trial of the single tax, although not accepted at that time, persisted among single taxers until it bore fruit in the notable Delaware campaign of 1895-96.[21]

[18] Ibid., Nov. 17, 1888, p. 2.

[19] On this matter of an attempt to capture a single state for the single tax, see The Standard, Dec. 1, 1888, p. 2; Dec. 8, p. 2; Dec. 22, p. 2; Jan. 5, 1889, p. 1; Jan. 12, p. 4. States mentioned other than New Jersey were Massachusetts and Rhode Island.

[20] The Standard, Jan. 5, 1889, p. 1. The dangers of "invasion" have been exemplified recently in the attempts made by single taxers to capture the states of Oregon and Missouri with the financial aid of the Joseph Fels Fund. See infra, ch.'s 9 and 10.

[21] Infra, ch. 8.

The second proposal, for the centering of the efforts of single taxers upon the circulating of a national petition and state petitions, gradually grew in favor. This plan had been tried out by single taxers in several places during 1888, notably in Texas, in Minnesota, and in the District of Columbia, where a petition for the exemption from taxation of real estate improvements had secured several thousand signatures.[22] During the Cleveland campaign of 1888, the single tax Cleveland and Thurman committee of New York had in a similar manner secured the enrolment of eleven thousand free trade single tax Democrats.[23]

These two plans—the concentrating of efforts upon a single state, and the pushing of the circulation of a petition—were not at first rival in the sense that each was urged to the exclusion of the other. But the concensus of single tax opinion soon came to favor the petition idea as the main line of work. It was believed that the concentration of effort upon a single state might mean the giving up of promising work which was going on in many parts of the country.[24] So the idea of a national petition was taken up with much enthusiasm.

The single tax national petition

The petition prayed Congress for the appointment of a special committee "for the purpose of making a full inquiry into and report upon the expediency of raising all public revenues by a single tax upon the value of land, irrespective of improvements, to the exclusion of all other taxes,

[22] See The Standard, June 9, 1888, p. 2; July 28, pp. 1-3; Aug. 4, pp. 3, 5; Aug. 18, p. 2. The plan had also been used in Michigan, Ohio and New York.

[23] These signatures were those of "persons supporting Mr. Cleveland for President on the ground that his tariff policy was in the direction of free trade and [who] . . . were free traders because they were single taxers." Louis F. Post in The Public, Nov. 22, 1912, p. 1110.

[24] See The Standard, Jan. 19, 1889, p. 3.

whether in the form of tariffs upon imports, taxes upon internal productions, or otherwise".[25]   The Single Tax Enrolment Committee, organized about December first, 1888, had charge of the petition.[26]   William T. Croasdale was the Committee's chairman, and the success in securing signatures to the petition was due largely to his efforts.   The wording of the petition was purposely made broad enough to secure the signatures of any who were willing to have the single tax investigated by Congress.   The method of filing signed petitions was devised with a view to keeping a record of the signers; each petition was on a separate slip of paper, and the Enrolment Committee classified these slips geographically.

Single taxers in every section of the United States at once took up the forwarding of the ·petition with the greatest enthusiasm.   Signatures poured into the Enrolment Committee's office for several weeks at a rate of more than five hundred a day.   At the end of a few weeks *The Standard* was able to report that the Enrolment Committee "has practically organized machinery in every state and territory save one (Mississippi), through which, during the coming year, popular interest in our doctrines may be steadily extended".[27]   Two months of work saw the total number of signatures reach 24,000; the 50,000 mark, which had been originally set for the first year's work, was attained in the first five months; and at the end of the first year, 70,000 names were on file.   Signatures continued to come in, though more slowly, during 1890 and 1891, and by March, 1892, the petition, now having 115,503 signatures, was adjudged ready for presentation to Congress.[28]

[25] Ibid., Mar. 30, 1892, p. 2.
[26] See the statement of this committee in The Standard, Jan. 19, 1889, p. 3.
[27] The Standard, Feb. 9, 1889, p. 3.
[28] Ibid., Feb. 9, 1889, p. 3; Apr. 27, 1889, p. 7; Nov. 23, 1889, p. 2; Mar. 30, 1892, p. 5.

The petition was presented to Congress in a unique form. The separate sheets were bound in books, filed, and indexed by states in a cabinet on the sloping top of which, beneath a piece of plate glass, was mounted a photographic enlargement of the petition as signed by Henry George, containing beneath the signature the words "and one hundred and fifteen thousand five hundred and two others".[29] But the elaborate form of the petition did not induce Congress to undertake the desired investigation.

It is most difficult to estimate the significance of the number of signers to this petition as an index of the strength of the single tax movement at that time. In themselves, signatures to a petition may or may not be significant, since "it's a pretty mean man who won't sign a petition". We have the story of a small town of the Middle West where, under the initiative law, an enterprising citizen desirous of testing the ease of signature-getting, obtained a considerable number of signers for a petition urging that a roof be erected over the sun dial in the public square! Many would no doubt sign a petition for a Congressional investigation of the single tax who were in no way favorable to Henry George's program, not to mention those who would sign to get rid of importunate seekers after signatures.

However, the significance of the petition to the single tax movement is not measured by numbers but by a consideration of the ends which it was designed to effect. These ends, which were propaganda and the organization of the movement, it accomplished admirably. For propaganda purposes it afforded an opportunity for single taxers to approach men on the subject of the single tax. It offered an excuse for approaching strangers in trains, clubs, hotels, and other public places. It resulted in the

[29] Ibid., Mar. 30, 1892, p. 5.

conversion of many and the interesting of still others in the single tax.[30]   The securing of names put the Enrolment Committee in touch with single tax workers and sympathizers throughout the entire United States, and gave at headquarters a list of those who could be "followed up" with single tax literature.   Altogether the petition was an effective means of propaganda.

The organization of the single tax movement

To understand the significance of the national petition as a means of organizing the movement throughout the United States, we must consider what had been done in that line prior to 1889.   A beginning was made in George's mayoralty campaign of 1886.   The "congratulation meeting" of November 6, 1886, had called upon the followers of George's standard to form organizations which, it was believed, would "provide in each locality a nucleus around which earnest men who believe in the general principles of the Clarendon Hall platform may gather in preparation for future political activity".[31]   To help with the work of organization this meeting had appointed a temporary central committee.

The work of organization proceeded both rapidly and extensively at that time.   These organizations were known generally as Land and Labor or Henry George Clubs. *The Standard* in January, 1887, reported that Land and Labor Clubs were organizing at the rate of about thirty a week, and that the correspondence of the committee included every state in the Union.[32]   Besides the Land and

---

[30] The Standard, Mar. 30, 1892, p. 2, comments that the petition "has furnished many an opportunity for explaining the single tax to men who did not understand it, and whose interest was first excited by a request to sign; and thousands of conversions can be traced to the work it has in this way already done."

[31] The Standard, Jan. 8, 1887, p. 7.

[32] The Standard, Jan. 8, 1887, p. 7, and Jan. 15, p. 3.   Particularly

Labor Clubs, a number of local Anti-Poverty Societies were formed in various parts of the country between the time of the organization of the New York Society, May first, 1887, and the occurrence of the split between George and Mc-Glynn early in 1888.[33]

This organizing movement, though considerable, proved to have little permanent significance. The Land and Labor and Henry George Clubs were little more than a passing phase of the labor movement, induced by George's spectacular fight for the New York mayoralty as the champion of labor. With the defeat of the United Labor party in November, 1887, most of these organizations dropped out of sight as rapidly as they had appeared. Their influence outside the sphere of the New York political movement was at no time very great. The branch Anti-Poverty Societies were unable long to survive the disruption of the parent organization. Only in a few instances did organizations established at this time become the nuclei of more permanent single tax societies.

At the time when the petition plan was devised "the organized single tax movement was languishing and apparently falling to pieces", wrote W. T. Croasdale in *The Standard*, a little more than a year after the inception of the petition.[34] It was devised, he continued, "not so much with a view to its effect on congress, as because of the opportunity it would offer for finding our friends and bringing them together." As Henry George said, it was de-

active in the matter of organization were the states of Ohio, Minnesota, Louisiana, and California. See The Standard, Feb. 26, 1887, p. 1; March 26, p. 5; July 2, p. 4; July 9, p. 7; and Aug. 6, p. 6.

[33] See The Standard, July 9, 1887, p. 7, and Dec. 10, 1887, p. 8.

[34] Ibid., Feb. 19, 1890, p. 1. The report of the Single Tax Enrolment Committee (in The Standard, Oct. 5, 1889, p. 6) says that the Committee "was organized shortly after the last presidential campaign at a time when there was a general feeling of depression among our friends."

signed to provide the means for prosecuting "a campaign that will go on and on, that will not wait until election times when the brass bands begin to play and the bonfires are burning".[35]

The circulation of the petition proved a most successful means for bringing single taxers together and inducing the formation of single tax societies. "At the time this work began there were not twenty living single tax organizations in the whole country. Our people were scattered and unknown one to another, and many of them were filled with despair".[36] By means of the listing at headquarters of the names of single tax workers in each section, and the bringing of them into closer touch with one another through the columns of *The Standard,* single taxers were helped to find one another out, and the result was a considerable organizing movement during 1889. *The Standard* at the close of 1889 listed 131 single tax organizations in the United States.[37] These were widely distributed; New York had 22, Ohio 14, Pennsylvania 13, Massachusetts 12, New Jersey 9, Indiana 6, California, Colorado, Illinois, and Iowa 5 each, there were 12 in the South, and the remaining 23 were scattering. A further index of the wide distribution of single tax work is the fact that in March, 1890, when the petition had 77,000 signatures, only 5,000 were from New York City, which had been the headquarters of the movement from the beginning.[38] Through the influence of *Progress and Poverty,* the speaking tours of Henry George and others, George's political activity, and the work of *The Standard,* converts had been won for the cause in every section of the Union.

[35] Ibid., Nov. 17, 1888, p. 2.
[36] Ibid., Sept. 3, 1890, p. 1.
[37] Ibid., Dec. 28, 1889, pp. 14, 15.
[38] Ibid., Mar. 12, 1890, p. 13.

The first National Single Tax Conference, 1890

In September, 1890, a National Conference of single taxers convened in New York City.[39]   Five hundred delegates from more than thirty states were present.   The purpose of the conference was to bring together workers from all parts of the country in order to consult, to exchange experiences, and to consider plans for promoting the cause.   The conference formed a national organization, "The Single Tax League of the United States", with a national committee composed of one member from each state and an executive committee of which William T. Croasdale was the first chairman.[40]   One of the acts of the Conference was to welcome home the chief of single taxers, Henry George, now returning from a trip around the world, a trip whose incidents bore testimony to the wide influence and extensive acceptance of the teachings of *Progress and Poverty.*[41]

A decade had now passed since George had first come east to commence the wider spreading of his economic gospel.   His book had first made a big stir in the intellectual world, challenging boldly the older economic ideas.   Then his doctrine had become an issue in the heated class struggle of 1886, had been embroiled in Father McGlynn's

[39] For a full account of this conference, see The Standard, Sept. 10, 1890, and an article by Louis F. Post in The Public, Sept. 1, 1911, pp. 903-14.

[40] In May, 1888, the "Single Tax League" had been organized.   The method of action proposed for this organization was stated as follows in its constitution: "Its method of work consists chiefly in the formation of small neighborhood groups, which carry on the work of the league by such means as they deem best.   The purposes of the league are purely educational, and its participation, or the use of its name, in political action is prohibited." (The Standard, May 5, 1888, p. 2). The organization of 1890 proved to be mainly an organization on paper.

[41] See The Life of Henry George, pp. 522-41.

controversy with the Catholic Church authorities, and had been associated with the spectacular history of the Anti-Poverty Society. From these entanglements it emerged with enemies prejudiced and bitter, but at the same time with firmer and more numerous friends. The two years following the break-up of the Anti-Poverty Society had seen an increasing respect for Henry George's ideas. Henry George's policy of opportunism, of following the line of least resistance, and of working in the company of the less radical, who strove for reforms not inconsistent with the single tax principle, had been successful in securing a more courteous and favorable hearing, as well as placing the movement on a more lasting basis of influence and dignity.

The "Henry George movement", of 1886-87, with its incongruous elements—socialists, trades-unionists who were not single taxers, the personal followers of McGlynn, and others—had now completed its evolution into the single tax movement. It had become unified and had achieved a high degree of solidarity. It was indeed less noisy and less sensational, but it had a stronger support in the group of enthusiastic disciples having a reasonable comprehension of Henry George's economic and political philosophy. By 1890, the end of the first decade after the publication of *Progress and Poverty*, the movement had taken a form and adopted a method of activity which, in the main, it retains today.

CHAPTER VIII

THE SINGLE TAX MOVEMENT, 1890-1907

The aim of this and succeeding chapters is to give an account of the activities of single taxers since 1890. These activities have included both propaganda of a purely educational sort and the prosecution of political campaigns.[1] The educational work through the instrumentality of single tax organizations, the personal proselyting work of individuals, the spread of literature, and the publication of single tax periodicals, have been important factors in the discussion of the problems of public finance and social reform. But the educational propaganda of single taxers has aimed generally to prepare the way for political action at some future time, hence the most prominent place in the history of the movement is occupied by the various efforts which single taxers have made to place upon the statute books laws in line with single tax principles.

Single taxers and federal finance

For several years from the time when Henry George entered the presidential campaign of 1888 to work for free trade, the interest of single taxers centered rather upon national than upon state or local politics. In the tariff discussion which was so prominent from 1888 to the passage of the Wilson tariff in 1894 single taxers took an active part. George's *Protection or Free Trade,* published in

---

[1] An account of the Fairhope, Ala., single tax colony, which chronologically is within the field of the present chapter, is given under the head of Single Tax Tactics in ch. 12, infra.

141

1886, had circulated widely and exerted considerable influence.

But in 1892 a small group of single taxers in the House of Representatives, led by Tom L. Johnson of Ohio, conceived a plan for giving the book a yet wider circulation. This plan was none other than that Johnson and the five other single tax congressmen—William J. Stone of Kentucky, Joseph E. Washington of Tennessee, Thomas Bowman of Iowa, George W. Fithian of Illinois, and Jerry Simpson of Kansas—should insert the entire book in the Congressional Record as a part of their remarks on the tariff question. The actual cost of printing had indeed to be met by those who wished to circulate the book, but under the "franking" privilege it could be mailed without cost to the single taxers into any part of the United States. Accordingly, in April, 1892, these six congressmen introduced the book into the Congressional Record as an extension of their remarks under the leave to print privilege.[2]

Incensed at this abuse of the franking privilege, the Republican minority, led by Congressman Burrows of Michigan, attempted to have the book expunged from the Record. But the motion to expunge was lost. Therupon the Republicans, not to be outdone, introduced a pamphlet on protection and some other material, which was likewise printed in the Record.[3] The *Protection or Free Trade* incident attracted considerable attention, and this gave the single taxers the opportunity they desired to circulate extensively what came to be known in the House as "St. George". Large and small gifts from single taxers formed a fund to meet the expense of printing a tremendous edition at a cost

[2] There is an account of this incident in The Life of Henry George, pp. 571-74.
[3] For the discussion of the motion to expunge and the vote, see the Congressional Record, April 14, 1892, pp. 3299-3306. See also the New York Times, Apr. 17, 1892, p. 2.

of less than one cent per copy. Copies were sent broadcast into all parts of the country. Henry George, Jr. estimates that more than a million two hundred thousand copies of this edition were circulated in this manner.[4] More recently single taxers have circulated additional copies of this work under the frank of Henry George, Jr.[5]

Another episode deserving of mention occurred when the income tax of 1894 was under discussion. James G. Maguire of California, Henry George's old friend, moved an amendment for an annual direct tax of $31,311,125, to be levied upon land values, the tax to be apportioned according to population. The proposal was defeated, 180 to 6.[6] Judge Maguire believed that the introduction of his amendment marked a new era in the tax reform movement of the United States.

None of the recent developments in the tax system of the American federal government, however, have been along single tax lines.[7] This is in striking contrast to the most significant of recent developments in English and German national finance—the land taxes of the famous Lloyd George budget of 1909, and the German Imperial land increment tax of 1911. In the United States, since real estate has long been the chief object of state and local taxation, discussions of the problems of federal finance

<hr/>

[4] The Life of Henry George, p. 574. For a description of the sending out of these copies, see The Standard, May 25, 1892, pp. 5-6.

[5] See Report of Proceedings of the Second Annual Single Tax Conference, Chicago, 1911, pp. 24-25, regarding this point, also regarding a proposal to introduce Progress and Poverty into the Congressional Record. In 1912 Daniel Kiefer, Chairman of the Joseph Fels Fund Commission, was indicted for misuse of the mails in circulating copies of the Congressional edition of Protection or Free Trade, but the indictment was dismissed. See The Public, Jan. 24, 1913, p. 80.

[6] Congressional Record, Jan. 31, 1894, p. 1739.

[7] Unless we regard the tariff reduction of 1913 as a reform in line with the general single tax program of lessening the burden of indirect taxation.

have given practically no consideration to land taxation; they have turned rather on the questions of the income tax and the tariff.

For the reduction of the tariff single taxers have worked earnestly and persistently. But they have been generally hostile to the income tax. They oppose it because it is based upon the ability rather than the benefit theory of taxation—as "taking from the individual in proportion to what he has, irrespective of how he gets it, not in proportion to what service he receives from government or what privilege he may enjoy".[8] They regard the income tax as only slightly better than indirect taxes, and accept it only in so far as it taxes incomes derived from land. They oppose it on the ground that it taxes "earned" and "unearned" incomes alike, distinguishing the two sorts of income on the basis of their assumption that land incomes are coincident with "unearned" incomes, while other incomes of whatever nature are "labor" incomes and therefore "earned". They oppose it too because, according to their extreme individualistic political philosophy, the state has not a "natural right" to deprive a man of any part of the produce of (his?) labor, i.e., of income gained in any way other than from ownership of land.

Single tax principles, then, have not played an important part in discussions of American national finance, and there seems little likelihood that they will do so. In the past single taxers have worked mainly in the fields of local and state finance, and this is undoubtedly their most promising field for future activity.

[8] E. J. Shriver, The Income Tax, in Single Tax Rev., Jan.-Feb., 1914, p. 40. See also J. D. Miller, The Income Tax, ibid., Mar.-Apr., 1908, pp. 8-16; J. Harrington, The Demand for an Income Tax, ibid., May-June, 1908, p. 5; Bolton Hall, The Federal Income Tax, ibid., Jan.-Feb., 1910, pp. 15-17.

The single tax experiment at Hyattsville, Md.

In the early nineties the little town of Hyattsville, in the state of Maryland just over the District of Columbia line, attempted an experiment along single tax lines. In the summer of 1892 its Board of Commissioners, a majority of whom were single taxers, decided to tax land alone for local purposes. Jackson S. Ralston, now a member of the Joseph Fels Fund Commission, was the leader in the movement.[9]

Single taxers had begun an agitation several years prior to this step, as a result of which the local taxation of personal property had been abandoned.[10] Also they had introduced the separate assessment of land and improvements, land being assessed at a relatively greater percentage of its value than improvements, a practise similar to that which has attracted some attention lately as carried out by Pastoriza in Houston, Texas.[11] The single taxers secured from the Maryland Legislature of 1892 a charter empowering the Board of Commissioners "with a view for the government and benefit of the community, to make such deductions or exceptions from or additions to the assessment made by the Assessors as they may deem just".[12] Thereupon the Board proceeded to exempt improvements from taxation and to impose all of the town's taxes upon

[9] J. H. Ralston gives an account of this episode in the Single Tax Rev., Oct. 15, 1904, pp. 5-8. There is also a review of it in the New York Times, Mar. 16, 1893, p. 1, and in the National Single Taxer, Jan., 1900, p. 23.
[10] See the Standard, May 28, 1890, p. 6; July 23, p. 5; Aug. 27, p. 5. The assessment figures are given thus in The Standard, Aug. 27, p. 5:

	1889	1890
Land value	$123,053	$314,204
Improvement value	120,855	135,685
Personal property	15,533	

[11] Infra, ch. 10.
[12] Cited in the New York Times, Mar. 16, 1893, p. 1.

land values, raising the rate from fifteen to twenty-five cents per hundred dollars.

Immediately the opponents of this innovation bestirred themselves. The little town became a single tax debating forum, each side holding meetings, and considerable bitterness of feeling developed. The complainants appealed to the Circuit Court of Prince George's county for a writ of mandamus, directing the Commissioners to include personal property and improvements in their assessment and restraining the collection of taxes already levied.[13] But the Court denied the writ and upheld as lawful the action of the single taxers. The case then was taken before the Maryland Court of Appeals. That Court denied the appeal on the ground that the action of the petitioners was wrongfully brought, that they should have proceeded by way of injunction and not by mandamus, but declared *obiter* that the action of the single taxers was in violation of the Maryland Constitution and would be so held by the Court.[14] Thereupon the single taxers, seeing that to continue would invite their defeat, gave up their experiment.

Single taxers have claimed that even this brief experience of Hyattsville with the single tax, from July, 1892, to March, 1893, greatly increased the town's prosperity, that coincident with the adverse decision of the Maryland Court of Appeals building came to a standstill and the erection of projected improvements was abandoned, and that twice as much building took place during these months as in the two and a half years succeeding.[15] On the other hand it was declared by their opponents that the "cranks

---

[13] Ralston, op. cit., p. 6.

[14] 77 Maryland 125. Cited in National Single Taxer, Jan., 1900, p. 23.

[15] See Why? (a single tax paper published at Cedar Rapids, Ia.), Jan., 1902, p. 13, also a letter from J. H. Ralston to Justice (Philadelphia, and Wilmington, Del.), Aug. 31, 1895, p. 4.

were ruining the town".[16]   The New York *Times* stated
that sentiment in the town was about equally divided, with
most of the property owners opposed to the single taxers.[17]

The single tax "invasion" of Delaware

Even after the Democratic defeat in the elections of November, 1894, some single taxers felt that the most promising field for activity was still in national politics, working
for free trade and direct taxation with the radical wing of
the Democrats.[18]   But many single taxers were not content
thus to confine political action to the national field.   They
felt that the result of several years of effort in national
politics, outside of the general educational effects, was very
small.   Besides, they believed that, inasmuch as the increasing prominence of the money question had relegated
the tariff question to the rear, a further agitation for free
trade was not along the line of least resistance.   They felt
that attempts to introduce the single tax as a state or local
expedient were more promising of success, since it is a
lesser task to convert a local community or carry a state
than to convince the majority of the voters of a nation.[19]
So in 1895 they decided to center their efforts upon a single
state, and Delaware was the state chosen.

The project of concentrating forces upon a single state
had been broached as early as 1887.   However at that time
single taxers had rejected it in favor of the furtherance of
the national petition.[20]   But in 1895 the proposal met with
a ready acceptance.   Single taxers felt that such a campaign
would have considerable advertising value in directing pub-

---

[16] New York Times, Mar. 16, 1893, p. 1.

[17] Idem.

[18] See statement of the National Executive Committee of the Single
Tax League in Justice, Jan. 19, 1895, p. 1.

[19] See letters in Justice, May 18, 1895, p. 1, and June 15, p. 1.

[20] Supra,

lic attention to the single tax and would also kindle new
fires of enthusiasm among single taxers throughout the
United States. Also it was believed that should one state
adopt the system, its working would so demonstrate its
virtues as to lead to its general adoption by the rest of the
states and ultimately by the federal government.[21] The
attempt to make Delaware the first single tax state was,
then, in the eyes of single taxers, more than a local matter.
It was to mark the next step in advance in the progress of
the cause. "If it wins it will mark the greatest turning
point in the political, industrial and economic development
of this country, perhaps of the civilized world".[22]

There were several reasons for selecting Delaware.[23] It
was a small state, having only about 40,000 voters, a third
of whom were in the city of Wilmington and thus easily
reached; the Legislature consisted of only twenty-one members in the House and nine in the Senate; the state was
evenly balanced politically; there were no constitutional
obstacles to the single tax; already single taxers had done
considerable work in and around Wilmington; and moreover the state was within easy reach of several cities which
had strong single tax organizations. Altogether conditions were believed to be exceptionally favorable. With
only 40,000 voters to convert, and eighteen months in which
to prosecute the work of education, the carrying of the
state seemed "not a work of such terrible magnitude, when
the strength of our arguments is considered".[24] The single
taxers undertook to secure, in the autumn of 1896, the elec-

---

[21] Cf. in this connection statements made about 1912 by single taxers
regarding the land value tax systems of western Canada, that competing communities in the United States would be forced to some
similar system in order to retain their prosperity.

[22] Justice, Jan. 25, 1896, p. 3.

[23] Ibid., July 20, 1895, p. 1.

[24] Ibid., Aug. 3, 1895, p. 2.

tion of a Legislature which should provide the single tax as the method for raising revenue for the state.

This, the most varied and spectacular campaign which single taxers have waged, was inaugurated on the afternoon of Saturday, June 15, 1895, when a group of a dozen uniformed single tax men, the vanguard of the invasion of Delaware, advanced over the frontiers of the Diamond State.[25] These emissaries of the Philadelphia Single Tax Society were bent on the first of a series of week-end expeditions from the Quaker City. Their coming was the prelude to an influx of speakers and workers from all over the country. Leading single taxers, including Henry George, Louis F. Post, Lawson Purdy, J. G. Maguire, Edward McGlynn, Thomas G. Shearman and William Lloyd Garrison, addressed mass meetings. Speakers of less prominence addressed smaller meetings. In the first four months of campaigning and a full year before the election, single taxers reported the holding of 469 meetings, at which 76 speakers had made 1,060 addresses, the attendance being estimated at more than 90,000.[26] Sinews of war came from single tax enthusiasts from Maine to California. There was a weekly newspaper, *Justice,* of which from eight to ten thousand copies were distributed weekly; a single tax tent with stereopticon and spell-binders; single tax songs, stickers, flags and sandwich signs. A small army of uniformed propagandists with knapsacks of literature tramped, bicycled, or drove unweariedly from one end of the little state to the other. They argued with farmers at the plow, and on reaching a town sent around a boy with

[25] The files of Justice, published in Philadelphia and Wilmington during this campaign, contain a complete account of it. Justice, 1895-98, is in the Princeton University Library. There is a good account of the campaign, written by Harold Sudell, in the Single Tax Rev., Oct. 15, 1904, pp. 8-11.

[26] Justice, Oct. 26, 1895, p. 2.

a bell and hand bills to gather in the public square or a hired hall an audience for them to harangue. " 'As goes Delaware so goes the Union', is the cry of the sanguine single taxer as he mounts his bicycle on Saturday morning, tightens his knapsack and wheels along a road in Delaware towards some centre of population where he can raise his persuasive and denunciatory voice to give vent to the faith that is in him. . . . On Sunday night, weary but hopeful, he returns to Philadelphia and whispers to his colleagues, 'Courage, friends, Delaware is almost ours. And after Delaware the deluge!' ".[27]

A free speech fight supplied a sensational element. From the beginning certain town officers had interfered with single tax meetings. But the climax came in the spring and summer of 1896, when more than a score of single tax speakers were thrown into jail.[28] At one time the "Dover Jail Single Tax Club" had as many as fifteen members. The issues in this, as in other free speech fights, centered around the rights of freedom of speech and of assemblage, and the manner of exercise of these rights. One single tax speaker was arrested, as the officer told the court, "for obstructing the highway and preaching the single tax".[29]

In September, 1896, "The Single Tax Party" was formed in Delaware with a state and county organization. It nominated a full state ticket, with Dr. Lewis N. Slaughter as candidate for governor. The party chose "The Earth" as its symbol and device, and adopted a straight single tax platform which endorsed Bryan and Sewall.[30] The draft

[27] New York World, cited in Justice, Aug. 3, 1895, p. 3.

[28] For accounts of this phase of the campaign, see Justice, June 6; July 25; Aug. 1, 22, 29; Dec. 5, 1896.

[29] Ibid., June 6, 1896, p. 1.

[30] The bulk of the single taxers supported the Democrats here as in most of the other national campaigns. Bryan's declaration that "free government will not long survive when a few own the land and means of support, while the many are tenants at will", was much quoted by single taxers. See Justice, Oct. 17, 1896, p. 2.

The platform of the Single Tax Party is in Justice, Sept. 19, 1896.

of a single tax bill to be presented to the Legislature provided that only land should be taxed.[31] All land and lots were to be assessed for taxation at their "just and true rental value in money, excluding from the basis of such assessment all buildings, fences, orchards and other improvements and products of industry incorporated with the land." The bill made willful and knowing under-assessment of the rental value a misdemeanor. It indeed retained the poll tax for constitutional reasons, but the single tax platform proposed its reduction to the lowest possible point, some proposing to make it one cent.

Single taxers looked to the election with high hopes. They expected to secure a plurality of votes in New Castle county, in which the city of Wilmington is located, and counted on making a good showing in the remainder of the state.[32] But their hopes were as usual over-sanguine. In the excitement of the national campaign of 1896, with the money question strongly to the fore, they had counted too much on attracting voters from the standards of the older parties. Of a total vote of about 38,000 in the state they polled 1,173, or a little over three per cent.[33]

The result was a great disappointment to single taxers, since it did not seem commensurate with the effort expended. Nevertheless they seriously considered continuing the campaign. But their opponents soon put a damper upon whatever hopes of success remained. Not satisfied with having beaten the single tax at the polls, they desired to prevent the "eternal turmoil and confusion" caused by the single taxers. Accordingly, at the constitutional convention of 1897, they placed in the constitution, by a vote of fifteen to two, Section 7 of Article VIII, which, according to

[31] Justice, July 4, 1896.
[32] Ibid., Oct. 24, 1896, p. 1.
[33] Ibid., Nov. 20, 1896, p. 2.

its sponsor, was designed to prevent the legislature from putting in force "a system of taxation the object of which is the confiscation of land".[34] "Let us speak in such positive terms in this convention as will protect this little garden spot, as we will term it, against the ravages of those who entertain these new fancies, and want to make their tests here, for the rest of the people of the United States".[35] Accordingly, when "We, the people" of Delaware adopted this constitution "in convention" (the convention not condescending to submit it to the electorate), this provision was embodied in Delaware's organic law.

Henry George's New York mayoralty campaign of 1897[36]

When, in 1886, Henry entered the mayoralty campaign of New York City as the candidate of the trades-unionists, his motive was to focus public attention upon his doctrines and to gain for them a wider audience. Eleven years later similar motives impelled him again to become a candidate for this office at the time when Greater New York was electing its first mayor. This was the first election after the constitutional separation of municipal from state and national elections.[37]

In 1897 Henry George was in his fifty-eighth year. But he had not then the physical strength which had carried him through the strenuous days of 1886. He was weakened, not only from his great exertions in propagating the single tax movement in the United States and abroad, but

[34] Ibid., Mar. 27, 1897, p. 1; also Mar. 13, 1897, p. 1.
[35] Ibid., Mar. 27, 1897, p. 3.
[36] For accounts of this campaign, see: The Life of Henry George, pp. 593-611; James Bryce, The Mayoralty Election in New York, Contemporary Rev., vol. 72, pp. 751-60 (1897); Delos F. Wilcox, The First Municipal Campaign of Greater New York, Municipal Affairs, vol. 2, pp. 207-20, (1898); E. M. Shepard, The political inauguration of the Greater New York, Atlantic Mo., vol. 81, pp. 104-20 (1898).
[37] Bryce, op. cit., p. 753.

by a stroke of aphasia which had stricken him a few years previous. In 1897 he was at work upon *The Science of Political Economy*, which he hoped would summarize his economic and political philosophy. But when the possibility of his becoming a candidate for the mayoralty of Greater New York was mentioned, he saw in it an opportunity to further the single tax cause, and was convinced that, notwithstanding his weakened condition, it was his plain duty to enter the campaign. So he became a candidate in spite of the deterring efforts of his friends and the opinion of his medical advisors that such action would in all probability cost him his life.[38]

When George entered the field there were already three candidates. Two of these stood for the spoils system and for the principle of partisanship in municipal affairs—Judge Robert A. Van Wyck, the Tammany nominee, and General Benjamin F. Tracy, candidate of the Republican machine. The third candidate was Seth Low, nominee of the Citizens' Union.

The latter organization had been formed early in 1897 by men of the old parties as a protest against the rotten politics which these parties represented.[39] The chief plank in its platform was non-partisanship in municipal affairs. For several months this organization carried on a campaign of education. Seth Low, who had served with distinction as president of Columbia University and as mayor of Brooklyn, became the Citizens' Union candidate for mayor, accepting the nomination after a memorial urging it had received in the course of the summer nearly 130,000 signatures.[40]

The presence of Seth Low in the field would seem to have rendered superfluous the candidacy of Henry George

[38] The Life of Henry George, p. 593, et seq.
[39] Wilcox, op. cit., p. 212, et seq.
[40] Ibid., p. 213.

as an additional "independent" on a reform platform. But within the Democratic organization all was not harmonious. Many of the rank and file desired the endorsement of Bryan and the Chicago platform of 1896, and when Boss Croker and his henchmen decided not to take such action and announced municipal issues, they alienated thereby a considerable number of Democrats. Before the Tammany convention met on September 30th, the United Democracy and the Democratic Alliance had offered the mayoralty nomination to George, and, on the eve of October 5th, at an enthusiastic mass meeting in Cooper Union, he accepted the nomination of several political organizations which represented the radical and anti-Tammany Democrats and the Labor elements.[41]   These banded themselves together under the name of "The Democracy of Thomas Jefferson", and endorsed Bryan and the Chicago platform, denounced Tammany, protested against government by injunction, and demanded cheaper gas, municipal ownership, municipal home rule, and tax reform.

The four-cornered campaign was full of excitement. Henry George entered into it enthusiastically, notwithstanding his weakened physical condition. Forgetting a resolve made at the outset that he would make but a few speeches, he spoke at three, four, and five meetings daily.[42]   He threatened that, if elected mayor, he would bring Bosses Croker and Platt before the grand jury.[43]   He justified his presence in the campaign as a reformer in addition to Low, who was so well qualified for executive work, by his Jeffersonian political theories. "He is a Republican and is fighting the machine, which is all very good as far as it goes. But he is an aristocratic reformer; I am a demo-

[41] Ibid., p. 218.
[42] The Life of Henry George, p. 601.
[43] Wilcox, op. cit., p. 219.

cratic reformer. He would help the people; I would help the people to help themselves".[44]

The tragic culmination came early on Friday morning, the 29th of October, five days before election. On Thursday evening, wearied by having spoken four times, Henry George had gone with his party to the Union Square Hotel. Early the next morning, while the city slept, a stroke of apoplexy fell, and he died without regaining consciousness.

His death stirred the city to its depths. Opponents, respecting his ability and sincerity, did him honor. To quote a New York newspaper of another faction:

"He was a tribune of the people, poor for their sake when he might have been rich by mere compromising; without official position for their sake when he might have had high offices by merely yielding a part of his convictions to expediency. All his life long he spoke, and wrote, and thought, and prayed, and dreamed of one thing only—the cause of the plain people against corruption and despotism. And he died with his armor on, with his sword flashing, in the front of the battle, scaling the breastworks of intrenched corruption and despotism. He died as he lived. He died a hero's death. He died as he would have wished to die—on the battlefield, spending his last strength in a blow at the enemies of the people. Fearless, honest, unsullied, uncompromising Henry George!"[45]

Seldom have there been greater public griefs. All day Sunday the body lay in state in the Grand Central Palace, while a hundred thousand persons passed beside his bier and a like number were prevented from doing so only by reason of the press of the crowd.[46] At night more thousands silently followed the catafalque from the Grand Central Palace to the Brooklyn City Hall. From every part of the world came messages.

Henry George's oldest son and namesake was selected to take his place on the ballot. But the death of the leader had

[44] The Life of Henry George, p. 606. See also pp. 595-96.
[45] Ibid., p. 608.
[46] Ibid., p. 609.

broken the strength of the forces he led, and the twenty thousand votes which the younger George received were no indication of the vote his father might have had.

The result of the election was decisive. "To Hell with Reform!" triumphed over "Down with the Bosses!",[47] and the Tammany candidate received 228,000 votes; Low received 148,000; and Tracy, 101,000.[48]

The single tax agitation in Colorado, 1899-1902

The Senate of Colorado, March 27, 1899, adopted a resolution appointing a commission to investigate Colorado's state and local revenue laws and "so far as possible, discover their defects and a just, wise, and complete remedy therefor".[49]   The commission was furthermore "particularly instructed to investigate the tax laws of New Zealand and the Australian colonies and the effect of such laws", and to report the results of their investigation together with recommendations for systematizing, revising or amending the revenue provisions of the law of Colorado.[50] In pursuance of this resolution the chairman of the commission, James W. Bucklin, visited Australasia in the winter and spring of 1899 and 1900. Bucklin, a single taxer, had been agitating the single tax question for some time in Colorado. He had been particularly active in endeavoring to secure the passage of a constitutional amendment permitting home rule in taxation.

The report, most of which Bucklin wrote, is substantially a single tax document, and has been widely circulated by single taxers for propagandist purposes. It condemns the general property tax, inheritance tax, income tax, and oc-

[47] Wilcox, op. cit., p. 220.
[48] New York Herald, Nov. 4, 1897, p. 5.
[49] Report of the Commission, p. 1. This report was reprinted as Senate Doc. 209, 56th Cong., 2d Sess., vol. 15.
[50] Idem.

cupation taxes, and presents "as a substitute for unjust and
unwise tax plundering the existing Australasian land-value
tax system".[51]   The report makes a distinction which has
not always been made so clearly, between the single tax and
land value taxation when it says: "The single tax would
abolish all other forms of taxation and raise all public revenue from one source; while the Australasian land tax is
only one of many kinds of taxes. . . . [It] does not abolish
private property in land, and only converts into the public
treasury a small proportion of the rent of land.   In short,
it contains only a small part of the single tax ideas".[52]   The
commission recommended the submission to the people of
a constitutional amendment permitting home rule in taxation and allowing "the gradual adoption of the Australasian land-value tax system or any part thereof".[53]

The legislature, by a vote of twenty-six to six in the
Senate and fifty to eleven in the House, recommended the
submission to the voters at the general election of November 4, 1902, of an amendment to Article X of the Colorado
constitution.[54]   This amendment embodied the recommendations of the commission, modified however by omitting
its recommendation that the legislature have power to exempt personal property and improvements and not land,
and by adding to Section 11 a clause limiting the additional
rate which might be levied upon land and the value of franchises to two mills on each dollar of assessed valuation.
The amendments as proposed authorized, in short, county
option in taxation, limited, however, by a proviso that
neither the whole nor any part of the full cash value of
land or franchises should ever be exempted, and the classi-

[51] Ibid., p. 2.
[52] Ibid., p. 13.
[53] Ibid., p. 34.
[54] The recommendations of the Commission and the text of the
amendment are on pages 34-36 of the Report.

fication of property for state taxation so as to permit heavier taxation of the value of land and franchises. Section 11 of the proposed amendment read as follows:

"The rate of taxation on property for State purposes shall never exceed four mills on each dollar of valuation; but the provisions of this section shall not apply to rights of way, franchises in public ways, or land, the full cash value of which may be taxed at such additional rate, not exceeding two mills on each dollar of assessed valuation, as shall be provided by law, after exempting all personal property and improvements thereon from such additional rate of taxation."

The single taxers prosecuted an active campaign for this amendment "to establish in Colorado a 'city of refuge', to which the tax-burdened labor and capital of the world can flee".[55] Public interest was considerably augmented by an unsuccessful attempt to prevent a vote on the measure, the governor convening a special session of the legislature whose chief end was the recall of the amendment.[56] The usual features of a single tax campaign appeared: debates, speeches, literature distribution, and press hostility. The "Anti-Bucklin Amendment League", with the motto "The Bucklin Amendment means the single tax, confiscation, confusion, panic," fought the measure, and the commercial organizations of Denver adopted hostile resolutions, asserting that the amendment meant the confiscation of real estate, the confusion of the tax system, the disturbing of business, and the driving away of capital.[57] Professor Le Rossignol's *Taxation in Colorado,* published in Denver during the campaign, had a chapter devoted to an argument against the measure. One of his objections, drawn from peculiar local conditions, was that in Colorado, where so much of the value of land was due to the building of costly

---

[55] James W. Bucklin, in the Single Tax Rev., Oct. 15, 1901, p. 14.
[56] Single Tax Rev., Apr. 15, 1902, pp. 51-52.
[57] E. O. Bailey, The Movement in Colorado, ibid., Oct. 15, 1902, pp. 14-17.

irrigation works and other improvements, the assessors would find it impossible to distinguish between the value of the land and of the improvements.[58] The trades-unions, in this as in most other single tax campaigns, backed the single taxers.[59] The Republican party condemned the measure, while the Democrats gave it no mention in their platform. The outcome of the election was the defeat of the amendments by a narrow margin.[60]

After this Colorado campaign single taxers raised the question of the wisdom of urging their proposals under some name other than that of single tax. While the opponents of the Bucklin amendments had fought them as single tax measures, the single taxers had emphasized rather the feature of local option in taxation. Of course the aim of the single taxers was to secure the support of the conservative by urging a more moderate measure which was but a very short step in the direction of the single tax. But some single taxers felt that in dodging the accusations that the single tax was the end coveted they placed themselves in the position of appearing afraid of it, and thereby aroused suspicion in the minds of the very ones whom they hoped to attract by a show of moderation. They felt that the educational advantages of a radical campaign had been largely lost as the result of the sort of fight made in this campaign in Colorado.[61]

"Irenic Propaganda" in Massachusetts

In striking contrast to the boisterous agitation of the political campaigns waged by single taxers is the campaign of education which the Massachusetts Single Tax League

[58] Le Rossignol, Taxation in Colorado, p. 57.

[59] Single Tax Rev., July 15, 1901, p. 39.

[60] The single taxers made the charge of fraud, claiming to have "won at the polls and lost in the count". Single Tax Rev., Jan. 15, 1903, p. 55.

[61] See an article by E. O. Bailey, Ibid., Apr. 15, 1903, p. 36.

has carried on since 1896. Charles B. Fillebrown of Boston, whom Joseph Dana Miller, editor of the Single Tax Review, so rightly characterises as "easily the most successful propagandist of the movement",[62] is the man whose influence has given the tone to this work. Fillebrown was treasurer of the League in 1892, and its president 1899 to 1909, and its unique plan of propaganda was conceived by him and carried on largely through his efforts.[63]

Of the many ways in which single taxers have striven to gain a hearing for their views, none, it is safe to say, has more successfully accomplished its purpose than the banquet campaign which the Massachusetts Single Tax League inaugurated in 1896. This series of nineteen banquets covered the period from 1896 to 1907. For each occasion the single taxers chose an after-dinner speaker who could best present their argument to the particular group of guests. Following the paper of the evening it was the usual custom to have a free discussion in which the guests were invited to participate, the points raised being taken up either by the speaker or Fillebrown. The tactful manner in which the affairs were managed had the happy result of putting both single taxers and their guests in a more reasonable frame of mind, and of bringing to each a better comprehension of the viewpoint of the other.

The list of organizations to which the banquets were given is worthy of citation as indicating the sort of game which Fillebrown and his associates hunted: The Patrons of Husbandry; The Association of Massachusetts Assessors; Massachusetts Labor Organizations; Massachusetts Woman's Suffrage Association; New England Free Trade League; Massachusetts Clergy; Young Men's Christian As-

<hr />

[62] Reviewing Fillebrown's The A-B-C of Taxation, in the Single Tax Rev., May-June, 1909, p. 50.

[63] See Fillebrown, The Single Tax Movement. This booklet is an account of the "irenic propaganda", as Fillebrown termed it.

sociation; Boards of Charities and Corrections; Representative Taxationists; Representative Business Men; Twentieth Century Club; Real Estate Men; Catholic Clergy; Members of the Boston Merchants' Association; Political Economists; Landlords of Boston; and The Economic Club of Boston. Among the prominent single tax speakers besides Fillebrown at these occasions were Thomas G. Shearman, Father Edward McGlynn, Tom L. Johnson, G. Frank Stevens, and J. O. S. Huntington. At the two dinners given in 1902 to professional economists, Professors Charles J. Bullock, F. S. Baldwin, W. M. Burke, G. S. Callender, T. N. Carver, Willard C. Fisher, C. W. Mixter, C. C. Plehn, and E. R. A. Seligman read papers or took part in the discussion.[64]

These banquets aroused considerable interest in Massachusetts. The press of Boston were friendly and liberal both in news reports and editorial comment. Fillebrown's presentation of "Boston Object Lessons in Taxation" in particular attracted attention. The press comments collected in Fillebrown's *The Single Tax Movement*, an account of this banquet campaign, bear testimony to its educational influence in relation to the problems of taxation. The press complimented Fillebrown and his associates for the spirit of good fellowship and reasonableness in which they carried on a radical movement.

Fillebrown's methods have been at variance with those of most other single taxers almost from the start. He is a conservative, a "single taxer limited", who believes that the limit of revenue under the single tax should be "the same as under any other system of taxation, the cost of government economically administered".[65] But the members of the radical wing had recognized from the beginning and do

[64] Fillebrown, The Single Tax Movement, pp. 6-11.
[65] Fillebrown, A 1915 Single Tax Catechism, Q. 16.

recognize his valuable services to the cause. In the first year of the banquet campaign, when the disappointments of the Delaware failure were still fresh, a writer to the *National Single Taxer* remarked that "the Massachusetts plan of capturing generals has already demonstrated its superiority over the Delaware method of trying to enlist privates—voters—first".[66]   Fillebrown's fellow single taxers give him credit for accomplishing what so many of them have been unable to accomplish—inducing the hostile mind to listen without antagonizing it.[67]

[66] National Single Taxer, June 23, 1897, p. 6.
[67] Joseph Dana Miller, editor of the Single Tax Rev., said at the 1907 National Single Tax Conference: "The progress we have made under the marvelously tactful leadership of Mr. C. B. Fillebrown, president of the Massachusetts League, is evidenced in the friendly attitude of the Boston press. . . . Numbers of eminent converts have been made in that State—converts at least to the first step we would take, who are perhaps more efficient influences than they would be were they to be designated as single taxers, or as accepting our doctrines in their fulness". Single Tax Rev., Jan.-Feb., 1908, p. 8.

CHAPTER IX

THE FELS FUND AND THE ATTEMPT TO CAPTURE OREGON, 1908-1914

During the half dozen years following the Colorado single tax defeat of 1902 the single tax was not an issue in American politics nor was it prominently before the public eye. But beginning with the Oregon campaign of 1908 there ensued what we may term a single tax revival. The chief instrumentality in making this revival effective and influential has been the Joseph Fels Fund of America.

The Joseph Fels Fund of America

Early in 1909 Joseph Fels, manufacturer of Fels-Naptha soap, promised to contribute the sum of $25,000 a year for five years for the promotion of the single tax movement in the United States.[1] He promised a like sum in support of the British movement for the taxation of land values, and varying sums to the single tax organizations of Germany, Denmark, Hungary, Australasia, and Canada. The terms of these gifts were that the single taxers of each of these countries should raise equal amounts. Fels agreed to "match every dollar" up to the sum stipulated. In fact, he was even more munificent than his promise. The balance sheet of the Joseph Fels Fund of America for the six years 1909-10 to 1915 inclusive states that during that period Fels and (since his death in February, 1914) his

[1] See the Single Tax Rev., Jan.-Feb., 1909, pp. 40-41; Sept.-Oct., 1909, pp. 52-55. See also the circular letter of the Joseph Fels Fund Commission, "To the friends of a great cause", May 1, 1909.

widow, Mrs. Mary Fels, have given $173,000.[2]   During
this same period other single taxers have given $119,788.45.

Fels entrusted the administration of the fund to a com-
mission, whose chairman from the beginning has been
Daniel Kiefer and whose first treasurer was the late Tom L.
Johnson.   The present (1915) treasurer is A. B. DuPont
and the other members are George A. Briggs, Frederic C.
Howe, Charles H. Ingersoll, Jackson H. Ralston, Lincoln
Steffens, and Mrs. Carrie Chapman Catt.   The headquarters
of the commission are in Cincinnati.

The aim of Fels and the commission was "to put the
single tax into effect somewhere in the United States within
five years".[3]   To this end it was believed that a concentration of effort to secure the prestige of substantial victories
was preferable to using the fund for general and promiscu-
ous educational propaganda of the usual sort.   Acting on
the theory that "one demonstration will save a hundred
arguments",[4] the commission in its first circular, issued
May 1st, 1909, proposed the centering of effort in localities
which it regarded as offering promising opportunities, particularly, Oregon, Missouri, and Rhode Island.   Other
items in the program suggested in this same circular were:
to establish a headquarters which should keep a list of single
taxers and act as an organizing center for the movement;
to maintain press bureaus and a depot for the distribution
of literature; the support of the *Single Tax Review;* and
the arranging of conventions of single taxers which should
bring about closer relations among them and thereby
strengthen the movement.   In short, the commission offered itself as a central supervisory agency for the American single tax movement.

[2] Report of Receipts and Disbursements, Jan. 1 to Dec. 31, 1914, supplemented by statement in The Public, Sept. 3, 1915, p. 855.
[3] Fels Fund Commission Circular, "Is it worth while?".
[4] Daniel Kiefer, in the Single Tax Review, Sept.-Oct., 1909, p. 53.

The policy of the Joseph Fels Fund Commission was not uncriticised by other single taxers. Some charged that it was a self-appointed, autocratic body which, instead of stimulating the work of the various local organizations, had attempted to supersede them.[5] But the commission met this criticism in good part and readily convinced the body of single taxers that its aim was to work out the plans best calculated to serve the movement and not in any way to supersede the work of others. It should be said, too, that at no time did the thought arise that Joseph Fels was trying to force his views upon the single taxers of the country; his sole purpose in contributing was to promote the adoption of the single tax in some part of the United States at the earliest possible time. The criticism that educational propaganda by means of speeches, the distribution of single tax literature, and the like, is a more effective means of furthering the cause than political action, was met with the answer that the Joseph Fels Fund was not established to propagandize the country but to secure the single tax somewhere in the United States within five years.[6]

One important criticism of the first few months' work of the commission was that it was too much concerned with direct legislation and in danger of being side-tracked from straight single tax work.[7] The November, 1910, report of the commission showed that it had expended $19,089.93 for land value taxation and $5,331.07 "in the effort to put the initiative and referendum into state constitutions so that the people may have the power and opportunity to initiate

[5] See the Single Tax Review, May-June, 1910, p. 47; Sept.-Oct., 1910, pp. 49-50; Nov.-Dec., 1910, pp. 20-21 and 25-26.
[6] See the Report of the Single Tax Conference held in New York City November 19-20, 1910, under the auspices of the Joseph Fels Fund Commission, Cincinnati, 1911, p. 10.
[7] Ibid., Index, under "Direct Legislation". See also the letter of A. C. Pleydell (Single Tax Review, Sept.-Oct., 1910, pp. 49-50).

and vote upon the question of taxation independently of the wishes and prejudices of legislatures controlled by special privileges".[8] In justifying its course the commission argued that, since constitutional amendments must precede the consideration of single tax measures in most states, and since these amendments can best be secured where the people have the initiative, the furtherance of direct legislation was calculated to lead most quickly to practical results in states where there was a considerable sentiment favorable to the taxation of land values. The commission urged that the initiative had made possible Oregon's adoption of county option in taxation in 1910, and that without it the submission of any kind of land value tax amendment in Oregon or Missouri in 1912 would be impossible.[9] Although many felt that since conditions were favorable for single tax campaigns in several states already having the initiative and referendum, the funds should not be diverted to the support of direct legislation campaigns in other states,[10] the sentiment was, "Let them do their job in the five years that they have, and then report what they have done".[11]

The work which the Joseph Fels Fund Commission has done has followed quite closely the program mapped out in its first circular of 1909.[12] It has financed the most of the Oregon, Missouri, Rhode Island, Colorado, and California

[8] Fels Fund Conference Report, 1910, p. 4.
[9] Ibid., pp. 5, 6, 9, 10.
[10] The Fels Fund Commission had spent more than $3,000 for the initiative and referendum in Ohio in 1909. Ibid., p. 4.
[11] See also the criticisms of New York City single taxers, given in the Report of the Second Annual Single Tax Conference, 1911, Cincinnati, 1912, pp. 9-10.
[12] For detailed accounts of the work of the Joseph Fels Fund Commission see the Reports of the First (1910) and Second (1911) Annual Single Tax Conferences (Cincinnati, 1911 and 1912), and the files of the Joseph Fels Fund Bulletin, published monthly since 1913 at Cincinnati.

campaigns, and has contributed to single tax work elsewhere; it has worked for direct legislation in New Mexico,
Arizona, Colorado, Arkansas, Minnesota, and Ohio; has
made up the large deficits in running expenses of the *Single
Tax Review* and *The Public;* has supported a press bureau
under the name of the "American Economic League" which
has sent out single tax matter regularly to several hundred
newspapers; has published a four page monthly, the *Joseph
Fels Fund Bulletin;* has distributed through various chan-
nels a large amount of propaganda literature; and has
fathered several national conferences which have resulted
in the gathering together for consultation and mutual en-
couragement of single taxers from every section of the
United States. Altogether the Joseph Fels Fund has accomplished the greatest and most efficient single tax activity
in the history of the movement.

The policy of the commission has had the approval of
the great body of single taxers throughout the country.
The National Advisory Conference of Single Taxers which
met at Boston, November, 1912, pursuant to the invitation
of the commission, expressed the following opinion in a
resolution:

"It is the opinion of this Conference that the work of the
Commission has been gratifying in very high degree, and successful beyond reasonable expectations. Its expenditure of
funds deserves the hearty approval of the more than 3,000
contributors and of all other single taxers.

"When this Commission was organized, in 1909, there was
no general discussion of the single tax in the United States.
Apart from the sporadic work of a few public speakers and
clubs, a limited distribution of literature, and occasional indirect and obscure efforts at securing favorable consideration
from legislative bodies, the movement appeared to have but
little life in this country. To those within it the future seemed
dark; by those without, the subject was generally regarded
as one of mere academic interest, in so far as it was generally
considered at all. This condition changed with the advent of
the Commission.

. . . "On the whole, we regard the administration of the Commission as having been intelligent, conscientious and effective".[13]

On February 22nd, 1914, in the fifth year of the Joseph Fels Fund Commission, its generous founder died. But his death did not put a stop to the work of the commission, since his widow, Mrs. Mary Fels, has taken up the work he began where he laid it down.[14]

It is too early to appraise the reorganization of the single tax movement which Joseph Fels' gifts, backed by the energy of his personality, have brought about. It remains for the future to show whether the revival of interest in the single tax which has taken place since 1909 is only a revival artificially stimulated by a fund of generous money, or whether it is significant of a more lasting and broader growth of public interest in the ideas of Henry George.

The Joseph Fels Fund Commission and the opportunity in Oregon

When, in 1909, the Joseph Fels Fund was established, the most promising opportunity confronting its managers was in the state of Oregon. In the election of 1908 a state-wide single tax measure had received thirty-four and one half per cent of the vote upon it, while in Multnomah County, which contains the city of Portland, it had failed of passage by only a few hundred votes. It was with high hopes that the Joseph Fels Fund Commission undertook as practically its first task the pushing of the Oregon campaign. The single tax political propaganda in Oregon con-

---

[13] The Public, Dec. 6, 1912, p. 1162.

[14] See Mrs. Fels' letter to the Commission, Single Tax Rev., May-June, 1914, pp. 41-42. The Report of Receipts and Disbursements of the Joseph Fels Fund Commission of America for the year 1914 (issued in the spring of 1915), states in a note that "Mrs. Fels hopes to be able (and to be called upon by our contributors) to match them up to $36,000 this year".

stitutes the most elaborately planned effort which single taxers have made.

The Oregon election of 1908

On January 28th, 1908, the single taxers filed with the Secretary of State of Oregon an initiative petition proposing a constitutional amendment to be voted upon at the election in June. The proposed amendment was as follows:

"The Legislative Assembly shall provide by law for uniform and equal rate of assessment and taxation; and shall prescribe such regulations as shall secure a just valuation for taxation of all property, both real and personal, excepting that all dwelling houses, barns, sheds, outhouses, and all other appurtenances thereto, all machinery and buildings used exclusively for manufacturing purposes, and the appurtenances thereto, all fences, farm machinery, and appliances used as such, all fruit trees, vines, shrubs, and all other improvements on farms, all live stock, all household furniture in use, and all tools owned by workmen and in use, shall be exempt from taxation; excepting also such property for municipal, educational, literary, scientific, religious or charitable purposes, as may be specially exempted by law".[15]

This amendment was peculiar in that it did not, like most of the single tax proposals, provide in general terms for the exemption of personal property and improvements. The list of objects to be exempted from taxation discriminated in a manner hardly consistent with the single tax philosophy in not providing for the exemption of intangible personalty and of the improvements and fixtures of businesses other than manufactures. The single taxers in this campaign placed considerable emphasis upon the desirability of attracting manufactures to Oregon through

[15] Galloway, Taxation Developments in Oregon, Proceedings of National Tax Ass'n., 1911, p. 245. This article by a member of the Oregon State Tax Commission gives a good brief account of the single tax campaigns of 1908 and 1910. Another good account of these campaigns is that of F. G. Young, The Single Tax Movement in Oregon, American Economic Rev., Sept., 1911, pp. 643-48.

tax exemption.[16]   Indeed, an Oregon single taxer stated to the writer that manufacturers had been induced to contribute several hundred dollars to the single tax war fund before it was generally known that the measure was a single tax proposal.

The single taxers, working under the name of "The Oregon Tax Reform Association", waged a straight single tax campaign.   In the voters' textbook containing copies of the measures voted upon, the single tax argument states:

"The proposed amendment is a step in the direction of the single tax.   If adopted it would exempt most personal property and improvements from taxation, and the argument submitted has in view that all such property will ultimately be exempted.   It does not exempt business buildings, merchandise, cash, improvements of public service corporations, and a few other articles of personalty and improvements".[17]

No argument opposing the measure appeared in the voters' textbook.   But during the four months prior to the election, June 1st, 1908, the press gave considerable space to discussion of the single tax.[18]   The result of the ballot was the defeat of the measure, 32,066 to 60,871.[19]   But in Multnomah County the single tax was defeated by only 483 votes, the ballot being, 10,828 for, and 11,311 against.[20]

The Oregon election of 1910

The single taxers, by initiative petition, submitted to the voters of Oregon at the election of 1910 the following amendment:

"No poll or head tax shall be levied or collected in Oregon; no bill regulating taxation or exemption throughout the State shall become a law until approved by the people of the State

[16] Young, op. cit., p. 645.
[17] Quoted by Galloway, op. cit., p. 246.
[18] Young, op. cit., p. 645.
[19] Oregon Blue Book, 1913-14, p. 124.
[20] Secretary of State of Oregon, Abstract of Votes cast at the 1908 election.

at a regular general election; none of the restrictions of the Constitution shall apply to measures approved by the people declaring what shall be subject to taxation and exemption and how it shall be taxed or exempted whether proposed by the Legislative Assembly or by initiative petition; but the people of the several counties are hereby empowered and authorized to regulate taxation and exemptions within their several counties, subject to any general law which may be hereafter enacted".[21]

The three outstanding features of this proposal were: the abolition of the poll tax, the tying of the hands of the legislature so as to deprive it of the right to enact laws regulating taxation or exemption, and the granting of local option in taxation.[22]

In 1908 the single taxers had advocated their measure as "a step in the direction of the single tax". But in 1910 their tactics were less direct. The argument in the voters' pamphlet made no reference to the single tax, and was submitted, not by a single tax organization, but by the Oregon State Federation of Labor and the Central Labor Council of Portland and Vicinity.[23] As one writer put it, the single taxers "allowed the labor organizations to pull out of the fire some no-poll-tax chestnuts, which are found to have a strong single tax flavor".[24]

Professor F. G. Young of the University of Oregon, in his account of the campaign, stated that, "The single tax or rental value taxation was not by its advocates, during

[21] See the 1911 Report of the Board of State Tax Commissioners, p. 22, for the text of the amendment. This report contains an excellent discussion of the merits of local option in taxation.

[22] In addition to the single tax measure there were submitted, by the Legislature, two amendments designed to permit the classification of objects of taxation and the separation of the sources of state and local revenue. Both were rejected by narrow margins. See the 1911 Report of the Board of State Tax Commissioners, p. 19, et seq.

[23] Galloway, op. cit., p. 248.

[24] Haynes, People's Rule in Oregon, Political Science Quart., vol. 26, p. 55 (1911).

the progress of the campaign, very openly declared to be
the aim of the county option amendment".[25]   A 128-page
booklet, *People's Power and Public Taxation,* which the
single taxers mailed to every voter in the state, did not
employ the term single tax in referring to the measure.[26]
It explained that the booklet was prepared and distributed
at the expense of the Joseph Fels Fund (which spent $16,-
775 in this campaign[27]), and stated that the purpose of that
Fund was "to get the people of the United States to study
and apply the science of just taxation in support of their
government".[28]   "Just taxation" it defined further on as
"collection of all taxes from the special privilege and
natural resource values that are created by the presence of
industry of all the useful workers who labor in all the
trades";[29] but it did not employ the term single tax.

But although the ulterior object of the amendment did
not receive direct mention in the voters' textbook, it was

[25] American Economic Rev., Sept., 1911, p. 647.

Cf. the following comment of W. S. U'Ren in the Report of the
1910 Fels Fund Conference: "We did. not make a single tax fight
this year, because that was not the kind of a fight to make. We rely
upon the printed word, and we discuss and advocate the questions
actually before the people to be voted on; but we do not go outside
the record and advocate measures upon which no vote is to be
taken." (p. 23).

[26] This booklet contained calculations purporting to show how the
interests of various classes in each county would be affected by the
substitution of land value taxation for the general property tax.
(p. 34, et seq.). This booklet was designed as an appeal to self-
interest, since the figures promised lower taxes to the majority under
the single tax régime. Professor Seligman has pointed out (Essays in
Taxation, 1913 ed.) that the validity of the figures there given is
based upon the assumption (which he deems fallacious) that the
"raw land value" of cultivated land can be measured and that it is
the same as that of adjacent land which is unimproved. (p. 91, n. 4).

[27] Report of 1910 Fels Fund Conference, p. 3.

[28] People's Power and Public Taxation, pp. 125-26.

[29] Ibid., p. 126.

"well known and generally recognized . . . [that] it was,
to make possible the adoption of the 'single tax', piecemeal,
by the several counties".[30] The real end of the measure
was so brought out in the press and on the stump that the
voters had plenty of opportunity to understand it.[31]

It has been charged that the opening sentence of the
amendment—"No poll or head tax shall be levied or collected in Oregon"—and its attractive ballot title—"For constitutional amendment providing for the people of each
county to regulate taxation and exemptions within the
county, regardless of constitutional restrictions or state
statutes, and abolishing poll or head tax"—had considerable
influence in gaining a favorable vote.[32] Especially has it
been charged that the opening clause, which abolished the
poll tax, involved a misrepresentation because of "the
curious fact . . . that the state poll or head tax in Oregon
had already been abolished",[33] and that "it was apparently
resurrected in this title merely as a bogie, to distract the
voter's attention".[34]

The situation was as follows. The legislature of 1907
had done away with the state poll tax of one dollar. But
most of the counties were levying a three dollar per capita
road tax in 1910. The statement that the state poll tax had
been abolished is technically correct, but it fails to take
account of the fact that the road poll tax was still very
much alive.[35]

[30] Haynes, op. cit., p. 55.
[31] Cf. L. B. Shippee's letter to the Atlantic Mo., vol. 109, p. 431
(1912).
[32] Galloway, op. cit., pp. 247-48.
[33] Shields, Single Tax Exposed, (1912), p. 13.
[34] Haynes, op. cit., p. 55. See also A. H. Eaton, The Oregon System
(1912), pp. 22, 32-37, 134 et seq.
[35] Young, op. cit., p. 646. See also the single tax booklet, Clackamas
County assessments and taxes in 1910 showing the difference between
assessments and taxes under the general property tax system and
the land value or single tax and exemption system, pp. v-vii.

Considering the close vote on the amendment—44,171 for it, and 42,127 against[36]—and the fact that about a thousand votes would have turned the scale, there is warrant for the conclusion that the prominence given to the abolition of the poll tax in the opening sentence of the measure and in the argument in the voter's textbook turned enough votes in its favor to insure its adoption when an amendment providing for local option alone would have failed.

The Oregon election of 1912

The campaign of 1912 on the single tax issue began in reality when it was known that the anti-poll-tax-local-option amendment had carried. Its passage evoked a storm of protest from its opponents, who declared that the voters had been fooled into adopting it. On the other hand the jubilant followers of Henry George claimed that "this victory is clearly the greatest that has been won in the history of the movement for the taxation of land values",[37] and announced the single tax as the leading state issue for 1912. During the two years 1910-1912 the tax fight was fast and furious, and Oregon became "the critical battle field of the single tax propaganda in America".[38]

The single taxers, taking advantage of the local option amendment of 1910, submitted measures exempting personal property and improvements from taxation in three counties—Clackamas, Coos, and Multnomah, the latter containing the city of Portland. They also submitted a statewide measure, commonly known as the "Graduated Single Tax and Exemption Amendment", which bore the following description on the ballot:

[36] Oregon Blue Book, 1913-14, p. 124.
[37] Report of 1910 Fels Fund Conference, p. 8.
[38] Haynes, People's Rule on Trial, Political Science Quart., vol. 28, p. 20, (1913).

"For amendment of Section 2, Article IX, of the Constitution of Oregon providing for specific graduated taxes, in addition to other taxes, upon all franchises and rights-of-way, lands and other natural resources in excess of $10,000 under one ownership and assessing water powers in the counties where situate; exempting from taxation all personal property of every kind, and improvements on, in and under land, except a county may enact a county law to tax the same".[39]

This amendment is probably the most extraordinary measure which single taxers have ever submitted. It departs from the accepted single tax theory in admitting progressive taxation. The scale was elaborately worked out. The amendment provided for a graduated tax, in addition to taxes levied at the ordinary rate, on individual or corporation holdings of land or franchises within each county of value in excess of $10,000. The rate rose from $2.50 per $1,000 on holdings valued at from $10,000 to $20,000 till it reached $30 per $1,000 on holdings valued at more than $100,000, a maximum rate of three per cent, which, added to the regular tax rate, would have confiscated practically the entire value of holdings to which it applied. Section (i) established the single tax "limited"[40] throughout the state, but permitted the taxation of personal property and improvements by counties which should thereafter specially vote to tax them. Section (g) was aimed at the State Tax Commission, which has vigorously fought the single taxers; it abolished the offices of the two appointive members.

A description of the other tax proposals on the ballot at this election of 1912 is requisite to an understanding of the situation.[41] Besides the single tax measures there were no

[39] Pamphlet containing a copy of all measures . . . to be submitted to the legal voters of the State of Oregon . . . at the regular general election to be held on the fifth day of November, 1912, p. 226. For the text of the amendment, see pp. 226-29.

[40] For the history and meaning of this term, see infra, ch. 13.

[41] For the text of these proposals and a discussion of them see the 1913 Report of the Board of State Tax Commissioners, pp. 5-12.

less than seven amendments relating to taxation before the voters of Oregon. Of these, the legislature submitted three. One of them was designed to repeal the local option feature of the single tax measure of 1910, but retained the prohibition of the poll tax. The other two were designed to permit the classification of objects of taxation and the separation of the sources of state and local revenues. In addition to these measures, the Legislative Tax Committee, provided for by the legislature of 1911, consisting of five Senators and seven Representatives acting in conjunction with the Board of State Tax Commissioners, submitted four amendments. These were designed to make possible an income tax, to exempt household goods and personal effects, to exempt securities and most forms of credits, and to amend the inheritance tax law in the direction of the "model law" recommended by the National Tax Association. With eight (and, in three counties, nine) tax measures on the ballot, the electors of Oregon surely had ample opportunity to exercise their franchises upon the subject of taxation.

With the possible exception of the Missouri campaign of this same year, this Oregon campaign was the hottest ever waged on the single tax issue.[42] The single taxers, liberally supplied with sinews of war from the Fels Fund, organized a thorough campaign. They employed paid workers and sent speakers and literature into every part of the state. The Labor interests cooperated actively with the single taxers.

The argument upon which the single taxers laid the greatest stress was that their measure would add greatly to the tax burdens of land speculators and monopolists.

[42] For copies of the single tax literature used in this and the 1914 single tax campaigns, the writer is indebted to W. S. U'Ren, H. D. Wagnon, Charles V. Galloway of the Oregon State Tax Commission, and to the officials of the State Library of Oregon.

They compiled elaborate statistics purporting to show the graduated taxes which certain corporations and prominent land-holders would have to pay under the proposed amendment. As to its general effect, W. S. U'Ren, leader of the single taxers, said: "Under the graduated single tax and exemption amendment, about 2,500 monopolists and monopoly corporations of Oregon would have to pay more than two-thirds of all the state and local taxes. They would have to pay more than $5,000,000 of the graduated taxes, besides paying the usual county and district levies. . . . Under the present system the people pay about two-thirds and the monopolists about one-third".[43]

Single tax propaganda made much of the prosperity enjoyed by the Canadian West under a system of local option in taxation and the partial exemption of personal property and improvements. It was argued that, were Oregon to pursue a like policy, capital would flow to her from every quarter, whereas the existing system operated as a penalty upon the production of wealth. An illustrated pamphlet in rhyme, *The Tale of a Million Dollars and Why He Left Town*, represents Mr. Million Dollars as coming to Oregon and leaving for Vancouver where improvements were untaxed. The single taxers, citing the experience of rural districts in western Canada, made an especial effort to convince the farmers that the proposed amendments would be to their advantage. They compiled and mailed to each voter in Clackamas County a seven by eleven inch document of one hundred and fifty-nine pages purporting to show the taxes of each property owner in the county under the two systems respectively.[44] This was meant as an appeal

[43] The Single Tax Broacher, Portland, Sept., 1912 (vol. 1, no. 4), p. 5. This campaign paper was an effective piece of literature.

[44] W. S. U'Ren and W. G. Eggleston, Clackamas County assessments and taxes in 1910 showing the differences between assessments and taxes under the general property tax system and the land value or

to self interest, since the figures promised lower taxes to the great majority under the single tax régime.

Meanwhile the enemy were not idle. They found the single taxers vulnerable in that they were largely dependent for support upon foreign capital. Some of this feeling found expression in crude notions.[45] An idea which gained considerable spread was that Joseph Fels wished Oregon to adopt the single tax in order that it would so depress the price of farm land in the Willamette Valley that he could buy it up for a song; then he would have the single tax repealed and make big gains from the ensuing increase in land values. On general principles the voters of Oregon did not take kindly to an effort to "make Oregon the goat"; many felt that the single tax proposal was "a reckless attempt to try an experiment on Oregon, just to see whether the patient can survive".[46] On the other hand, single taxers pointed out that the leader of the opposition was imported from Seattle for the express purpose of fighting them, and, frankly acknowledging that the Fels Fund furnished the bulk of their support, inquired without receiving an answer regarding the source of his support.[47]

It was soon pointed out that the single tax state-wide amendment had several bad features. The graduated tax scheme, in providing that each parcel of land or franchise value worth more than $10,000 in a given county should be subject to the additional rate, would have worked much injustice as between individuals, not to mention the confiscatory nature of the progressive rates. If a man owned $100,000 worth of taxable property in a single county, his

single tax and exemption system. For a criticism of the validity of the method employed see note 26, supra.

[45] See the Joseph Fels Fund Bulletin, May, 1913, p. 4.

[46] Rational Tax Reform vs. Single Tax, issued by the Legislative Tax Committee, 1912, p. 16.

[47] U'Ren and Eggleston, op. cit., p. xiii, and The Public, Nov. 8, 1912, p. 1065.

total tax would have been $1,150; had his property been cut
in two by a county line, $500; if equally distributed in ten
counties, there would have been no tax at all.[48] The law
also contained a section which did away with the offices of
the two appointive members of the State Tax Commission,
a body which has striven earnestly for tax reform in Oregon. The single taxers had been vigorously opposed by the
Commission and, in turn, they opposed all the measures it
put forward, although some of these measures embodied
reforms such as single taxers in other states have earnestly
backed.

The opponents of the single tax made extensive use of
quotations from *Progress and Poverty* regarding the injustice of private property in land, e.g. "private property in
land is a bold, bare, enormous wrong, like that of chattel
slavery", and, "We must make land common property".[49]
These sentiments, together with the belief that the single
tax would add to the burden of farmers, counted heavily
against the amendments. It was argued, too, that the
single tax would exempt from taxation many who were well
able to pay. "Don't you see that your taxes will be increased if sky-scrapers and department stores, bank buildings and money, factories and railroad locomotives and
cars are exempt from taxes?"[50] It was denied that Vancouver had the single tax, or that what measure of land
value taxation it had was a contributing factor to its prosperity.[51] In fighting the single tax its opponents made a
thorough canvass, distributing a flood of literature and in-
serting big advertisements in the newspapers.

[48] Legislative Tax Committee, Rational Tax Reform vs. Single Tax,
pp. 12-13.
[49] Progress and Poverty, bk. 7, ch. 3, p. 356; bk. 6, ch. 2, p. 326.
[50] Cited in The Public, Nov. 22, 1912, p. 1114.
[51] See Shields, Single Tax Exposed (1912), pp. 85-89. This booklet,
which is an effective attack upon the single tax, has been given a
wide circulation in connection with recent single tax campaigns.

The election returns[52] showed that the "Graduated Single Tax and Exemption Amendment" was lost: 31,534 to 82,-015, the latter being with two exceptions the largest negative vote on any measure. The fate of the county amendments was:

	For	Against
Multnomah County	11,146	23,901
Clackamas County	1,827	3,787
Coos County	1,113	1,909

The vote on the other taxation amendments was:

	For	Against
Repeal of county tax option	63,881	47,150
Permitting different tax rates on classes of property	52,045	54,483
Divorce of local and state taxation	51,852	56,671
Income tax amendment	52,702	52,948
Tax exemption on household effects	60,357	51,826
Tax exemption on moneys and credit	42,491	66,540
Revising inheritance tax laws	38,609	63,839

Thus the only measures to carry were the repeal of county tax option, by a majority of 16,731, and the exemption of household effects, by 8,531. The total vote on the state-wide single tax proposal was greater than that on any one of the thirty-seven measures on the ballot excepting the woman's suffrage amendment, which carried at this election after three successive defeats.

The Oregon election of 1914

In 1914 the single taxers submitted two amendments.[53] One proposed "to exempt up to $1,500 all kinds of personal property and land improvements of all kinds", but not land. This amendment contained a clause directing the Secretary of State to re-submit the measure, if adopted in 1914, at

[52] The figures are from the Oregon Blue Book, 1913-14, p. 125.
[53] The text of these measures and the arguments pro and con are in the official pamphlet, . . . Measures . . . to be submitted to the electors of the state of Oregon at the general election, Tuesday, November 3, 1914, pp. 37-41, 60-64.

the regular elections of 1916 and 1918, an unfavorable vote at either of these elections to repeal it. The other proposed a graduated sur-tax on owners of "land and natural resources and interest therein" of value greater than $25,000.

Both amendments were defeated more than two to one— the former 65,495 to 136,193; the latter, 59,186 to 124,-943.[54] An amendment designed to make the adoption of tax measures more difficult by requiring a two-thirds vote was beaten three to one. Its sponsors claimed that it would kill the single tax.[55]

The Legislative Tax Committee continued its efforts to secure the classification of objects of taxation and the separation of sources of state and local revenue by submitting two amendments.[56] Both were beaten by majorities as big as those rolled up against the single tax amendments. Commenting on this defeat the State Tax Commission said, in its report of 1915:

"There have been so many tax measures proposed and so many schemes placed before the people of Oregon in recent years, that voters have naturally become suspicious of everything containing the words 'tax' or 'taxation'. . . .

"Again, the ballot titles under which the two classification amendments appeared were to their disadvantage. To say that a proposal is designed to abolish, or substitute something else for, the old time-honored (though impossible) rule of equality and uniformity in taxation, gives it a black eye right at the start. To one not trained in the fundamentals of taxation words and form are often of more influence than facts and substance".[57]

[54] Secretary of State of Oregon, Abstract of votes cast at the 1914 election.

[55] Voter's official pamphlet, election of Nov. 3, 1914, pp. 97-98.

[56] See the Legislative Tax Committee's pamphlet, Make real tax reform possible in Oregon, 1914, containing fifty-six letters from leading tax experts endorsing the measures the Committee submitted.

[57] Report of Oregon State Tax Commission, 1915, p. 15.

Conclusion

The Oregon single tax agitation has thus far brought no indication of results commensurate with the efforts expended. Analysis of the votes shows that the adoption of any part of the single tax program was no nearer in 1914 than in 1908. The measure of 1908 received 34.5 per cent of the votes; that of 1910, for local option, received 51.2 per cent (but was repealed in 1912); that of 1912 received 27.8 per cent; those of 1914 received 32.5 and 32.1 per cent respectively.

The managers of the Oregon campaigns were unfortunate in their tactics. The measures proposed do not compare favorably with the straight-forward proposals, providing for a gradual transition, which the single tax leaders in Washington, Missouri, Pennsylvania, and New York have urged.[58] The amendment of 1908 was not wholly consistent with single tax principles in that it did not exempt personal property, or improvements and fixtures used for other than "manufacturing purposes". The amendment which carried in 1910, besides being put through by equivocal methods, presented "the possibility of serious injury to the fiscal system of the State" by depriving the legislature of the right to enact laws regulating taxation or exemption.[59] The unjust features involved in the state-wide single tax proposal of 1912 we have already commented upon.

In many states single taxers and other tax reformers have found it possible to coöperate in pushing measures upon the desirability of which most students of taxation agree, such as loosening the constitutional restrictions surrounding the general property tax. But not so in Oregon. The single taxers have fought every proposal for tax re-

[58] Infra, ch.'s 10 and 11.
[59] Report of Oregon Board of State Tax Commissioners, 1911, p. 23.

form which the State Tax Commission and the Legislative Tax Committee have made, most of these proposals being of the sort which single taxers in other states have seen fit to support. One can hardly blame the Legislative Tax Committee for saying regarding the opposition of single taxers to a proposed amendment of 1912 abolishing the taxation of intangible personal property: "The agents of the Fels Fund Commission object to this bill. If enacted, it will deprive them of opportunity for one of their chief complaints against the present system of taxation".[60]

The result of six years of single tax campaigning in Oregon has been to close the minds of the people to tax reform of that or any other brand. The rejection at the 1914 election of several diverse tax proposals by about the same majorities is evidence that the voters have become suspicious of all tax measures alike.[61] Nevertheless, W. S. U'Ren, leader of the Oregon single taxers, believes that "the best work that can be done for the single tax movement hereafter, in Oregon at least, is to submit at every election a straight single tax measure".[62]

[60] Legislative Tax Committee, Rational Tax Reform vs. Single Tax, p. 10.

[61] Supra, pp. 180-81.

[62] The Public, Dec. 11, 1914, p. 1184. U'Ren offered the following prediction in a paper in the Annals of the American Academy of Political and Social Science, Mar., 1915, p. 227: "There may be two or more campaigns . . . without gaining much on the present percentage of the total vote, but we shall be gaining ground, nevertheless. Sometime from the third campaign to the fifth, that is, between six and ten years, our single tax measure will go with a rush, just as the prohibition and equal suffrage measures were adopted."

CHAPTER X

THE SINGLE TAX MOVEMENT IN OTHER WESTERN STATES

Single tax activity in Washington, 1897-1899

In 1897-99 the single tax was quite actively discussed in the state of Washington. In May, 1897, the courts declared unconstitutional a law by which the legislature had undertaken to exempt from taxation $500 of improvements and a like value of personal property.[1] The State Board of Equalization, in its report of 1897, favored the exemption of personal property and improvements.[2] The legislature submitted an amendment providing for local option in taxation which was voted upon in November, 1898, receiving 15,969 votes in a total vote of 49,835.[3] In this campaign the local option measure was favored by the fusion of Democrats, Populists, and Silver Republicans. The regular Republicans, however, were hostile, denouncing the measure as "a single tax amendment" and appealing to the farmer vote to defeat it. As Delaware had been the single tax storm center, 1895-96, so to a lesser degree single tax hopes were focused upon Washington in the two years following.

[1] National Single Taxer, June 9, 1897, p. 1. See also regarding this point an excellent article by C. L. Clemans, Washington's Constitution and the Single Tax, in The Public, Jan. 26, 1912, pp. 78-80. Clemans discusses this case of 1897 (State ex rel. Chamberlain vs. Daniel, 17 Wash., 111), and a later case which modified it (State ex rel. Wolfe vs. Parmenter, 50 Wash., 177).

[2] Cited at length in Justice (Wilmington, Del.), Nov. 20, 1897, p. 1.

[3] National Single Taxer, Sept. 29, 1897, p. 6; Jan., 1899, pp. 25-26.

The Everett, Washington, single tax episode

The state of Washington again entered the single tax limelight when, at the election of November, 1911, the city of Everett, with a population of 25,000, adopted an amendment to its charter which provided for the exemption of improvements from taxation. The amendment, adopted under the title "Single Tax", provided that "for the years 1912 and 1913 there shall be exempt from such taxation 25 per cent, and for the years 1914 and 1915, 50 per cent, and for the year 1916, 75 per cent and thereafter 100 per cent of the value of all buildings, structures and improvements, and other fixtures of whatsoever kind upon land within said city".[4] The amendment was carried by a majority of only ninety-eight votes.[5]

But the commissioners who had been chosen at this same election for the purpose of preparing a new charter for Everett decided to submit the single tax amendment at the special charter election of April 16, 1912, "to be voted on separately, without prejudice to other provisions" of the new charter.[6] At this referendum election the charter was adopted by a majority of fifty-eight, but the single tax clause lost by fifty-three votes.[7]

In November, 1912, Everett voted upon this measure for the third time. This time, however, the vote was decisive, and the amendment was adopted by a vote of 4,858 to 2,637, nearly two to one.[8] It carried in every precinct. Although the issue was squarely met on the single tax—the ballots

---

[4] Everett, Wash., Charter of 1912, art. XVII, sec. 154, pp. 50-51. The writer is indebted to Miss Elizabeth Payzant of Everett for a copy of the charter.

[5] The Public, Nov. 24, 1911, p. 1194.

[6] Charter of 1912, p. 51.

[7] Ibid., pp. 51-53. See also The Public, May 3, 1912, p. 422.

[8] There is an account of this election in The Public, Dec. 6, 1912, pp. 1156-57.

being marked "Single Tax; For, Against"—there was but little substantial opposition.   Indeed, the single tax campaign expenses were reported as amounting to only $27.65, excluding postage.[9]   The propaganda work consisted chiefly of the distribution of a few thousand pamphlets.   An important factor in this election was the coöperation with the single taxers of the socialists, who had considerable voting strength.

In this campaign, like the other recent single tax fights, western Canada's prosperity while enjoying home rule in taxation and the partial exemption of improvements was extensively invoked.   The proximity of Everett to the Canadian border made this argument more effective here than elsewhere.   The reasons for Everett's adoption of the amendment seem to have been similar to those which have induced cities of the Canadian West to exempt improvements from taxation, the fact that corporations or absentee owners held a considerable area of unimproved land within the city.[10]

The amendment, however, has never been permitted to take effect.   Shortly after the 1912 election the State Tax Commission ruled that it was unconstitutional, and instructed the local assessor to ignore it and proceed to assess property as usual.   Since the single taxers raised no contest, the matter has been dropped, and the amendment has become a dead letter.[11]

The two campaigns in Seattle

At two successive elections, March, 1912, and March, 1913, the voters of Seattle passed upon proposals to exempt

[9] Idem.

[10] Statement to the writer of R. J. Faussett of Everett.

[11] For this information the writer is indebted to R. J. Faussett and to T. D. Davies, Assessor of Snohomish Co., Wash., who is also (1915) the City Assessor of Everett.

personal property and improvements from municipal taxation.[12]

At the beginning of 1912 the City Council of Seattle, several of whom were single taxers, voted to submit to the electorate an amendment which provided for the total exemption of personal property and improvements after July 1st, 1912. An interesting feature of this (the Erickson) amendment was that it expressly permitted the retention of restrictive license taxes, and, while forbidding occupation taxes for purposes of revenue, allowed them when they had "the avowed purpose of limiting and discouraging the pursuit or object so taxed", this purpose to be stated in the ordinance. These clauses were evidently included to disarm possible opposition on the ground that the single tax would not allow the use of the taxing power for purposes of restriction and regulation. Another less radical amendment (the Griffiths), proposing the gradual exemption of improvements through a period of five years, was also on the ballot.

The single taxers waged a most aggressive campaign in behalf of their measures, using varied lines of appeal in their literature and propaganda.[13] They quoted Seattle's Port Commission to the effect that "industrial sites in Seattle are in the grip of a comparatively small number of real estate holders, whose power to extort tribute from every effort to upbuild the industries of the city is the greatest handicap upon its growth today", charging that the high speculative value of Seattle's lands had repelled desirable

[12] The writer is indebted to Thorwald Siegfried of Seattle for copies of the propaganda literature used by both sides in these campaigns.
[13] There are accounts of the campaign in the Single Tax Review Jan.-Feb., 1912, pp. 42-44; Mar.-Apr., 1912, pp. 52-53, 54; The Public, Feb. 23, 1912, pp. 169-70; Mar. 15, 1912, pp. 245-49; Mar. 29, 1912, pp. 295-96.

industries, and citing concrete cases where this was alleged
to have taken place.[14]   "If we stop taxing factories, more
factories will come and those now here will grow."   Appeal
to direct personal advantages was prominent, single taxers
using such slogans as "95% of Seattle homes will pay less
taxes under Amendment No. 2," and "30,000 homes will
pay less".   A widely circulated leaflet stated that "the
Erickson Amendment will shift taxes from residence property to business property", a statement not exactly consistent with the argument that the measure would be a
boon to business.   The single taxers made much of land
speculation, stating that "in Seattle seven lots out of every
nine are vacant".   They used telling statistics of the increase in Seattle's land values.

Canadian prosperity as an object lesson of the benefits
of a policy of exempting improvements from taxation
played an important part in this as in other recent single
tax campaigns.   The single taxers urged that if Portland
should adopt "municipal single tax" as had Vancouver,
prospective factory-builders and home-seekers would find
irresistible the attractions of Seattle's building-exempting
rivals, and her charms would exert their lure in vain.[15]

The Seattle press was almost solidly hostile to the amendments.   The anti-single taxers offered an active opposition.
They made a point of the fact that the amendment was of
doubtful constitutionality.   They urged the usual arguments that the measure would confiscate the value of land,
and that the exemption of improvements would permit
many rich tax-payers to be free from their tax burdens.
The "anti"s charged, too, that it would force the fore-
closure of many mortgages, and promised that the adoption
of the single tax would be a serious blow at the city's pros-

[14] Ibid., Mar. 15, 1912, p. 247.
[15] Ibid., Feb. 23, 1912, pp. 169-70.

perity. According to the Seattle *Post-Intelligencer,* the possibility of the passage of the single tax amendments depressed the price of real estate. "Already this threat, it seems, has caused a serious financial injury to a considerable class of people, who have borne a heavy tax burden without serious complaint, while without income from their taxable property to aid them in doing so".[16]

The vote was as follows:[17]

	For	Against
Erickson Amendment (immediate exemption)	12,191	28,180
Griffiths Amendment (gradual exemption)..	7,933	31,390

An amendment proposed by the Chamber of Commerce, providing for a ten-year exemption of factories, lost, 18,025 to 22,475. But, though the single tax measure was defeated, George F. Cotterill, single taxer, won the mayoralty from Hiram Gill.

Undaunted by the set-back, the single taxers proposed for the election of March 4th, 1913, another amendment which provided for spreading the total exemption of personal property and improvements over a period of four years, and which also expressly permitted restrictive taxes. The 1913 fight was in reality a continuation of that of 1912.[18]

An interesting feature of this second campaign was that each side published a propaganda newspaper, *The Seattle Spirit* oppugning *The Single Tax News.* Most of the unspecialized press was hostile, though a socialist sheet, the Seattle *Herald,* favored the amendment. The single taxers advertised their arguments in paid spaces in the newspapers and on the billboards of the city.

[16] Cited in The Public, Feb. 23, 1912, pp. 169-70.
[17] The figures of the vote were furnished to the writer by the city clerk of Seattle.
[18] For accounts of this campaign see the Single Tax Review, Jan.-Feb., 1913, p. 67; Mar.-Apr., 1913, p. 37; The Public, Feb. 21, 1913, pp. 176-78; and Mar. 14, 1913, pp. 244-45.

A more detailed description of a copy of *The Seattle Spirit* of date February 17th, 1913, sheds light upon the sort of arguments by which the single tax was defeated.[19] The first page is nearly half covered with a tall picture of Seattle's proudest possession, a forty-two story building, with the statement in large letters that "under single tax this mammoth structure would escape taxation". Under the caption "Single tax would exempt wealth of corporations" we find the following:

"Seattle banks pay $134,443 this year in taxes.
    Single Tax would exempt them.
"Four Seattle department stores pay $35,011 in taxes.
    Single Tax would exempt them.
"Who, then, must pay this tax?
    The lot owners of Seattle.
"Do you believe in exempting the rich man's automobile, his pictures, and his furniture?
    Single Tax does.
"Do you believe in exempting $2,500,000 of street railway equipment?
    Single Tax does.
"Do you believe the paving trust should be taxed?
    Single Tax does not."

The statement appears that Mr. Fels, in putting up money for the campaign, "is anxious to make Seattle the 'goat' ". It criticizes him for trying "to force the single tax doctrines of Henry George on the people of this city", and calls attention to the large Fels Fund expenditures in Oregon in 1912. The last page bears a cartoon representing single taxers as rodents literally "gnawing at the roots" of "private ownership of land", which is represented as the "source of national life, moral, social, and material advancement". Henry George's famous declaration in *Progress and Poverty*, that "private property in land is a bold, bare, enormous wrong, like that of chattel slavery",[20]

---

[19] C. H. Shields, who has played an active part in anti-single tax campaigns in the Northwest, was editor of The Seattle Spirit.

[20] Progress and Poverty, bk. 7, ch. 3, p. 356.

was used against the single taxers here, as in other campaigns, with powerful effect; the "anti"s charged that the aim of the single taxers was not a mere change in taxation, but the abolition of private property in land.[21] Thorwald Siegfried, who took a leading part in these two Seattle campaigns, wrote to *The Public* that "the fact is clear that the opposition places its greatest reliance for permanent security on the fact that ultimately the single tax will confiscate economic rent".[22]

Seattle again voted down the single tax in a decisive manner. The amendment received 10,578 votes, while 21,260 voted against it. The vote in 1913 was slightly more favorable to the single tax, a third of the total vote being for the measure, as compared with thirty per cent in 1912.

Missouri farmers and the single tax

The single taxers of Missouri, by initiative petition, submitted to the voters of the state at the election of November, 1912, a proposed constitutional amendment prescribing for the state a tax system embodying a considerable measure of the single tax.[23]

The transition to the proposed system was to be gradual. The amendment provided for the immediate exemption from taxation of bonds issued by the state of Missouri or its local units; for the exemption of personal property from

[21] The Seattle Spirit, Feb. 17, 1913, p. 3.
[22] The Public, Mar. 14, 1913, pp. 244-45.
[23] For accounts of this campaign see Prof. A. A. Young (then of Washington University, St. Louis), The Vote on the Single Tax in Missouri, American Economic Rev., Mar., 1913, pp. 203-06; also the Single Tax Rev., Jul.-Aug., 1912, pp. 52-54, 60; Nov.-Dec., 1912, pp. 33, 50-52; Mar.-Apr., 1913, pp. 34, 43-45. The writer is indebted to Dr. William Preston Hill, President of the Missouri single tax organization, for copies of the chief propaganda literature used by both sides in this campaign.

state and local taxation, the abolition of poll and license taxes (excepting licenses imposed for purposes of restriction or regulation), and the exemption from state and local taxation of improvements on homesteads to the value of $3,000, these provisions to take effect beginning with 1914; and for the exemption from all taxes, state and local, of one-fourth of the value of "all improvements in or on lands" in the years 1914 and 1915, one-half in 1916 and 1917, three-fourths in 1918 and 1919, and the whole in 1920 and thereafter. The amendment also provided specifically that land, with which was classed "all franchises for public service utilities", should never be exempt from taxation, and contained a proviso that "nothing in this Amendment shall be construed as limiting or denying the power of the State to tax any form of franchise, privilege or inheritance". Existing limitations upon the tax rate were to be repealed. Another amendment proposed the creation of a permanent tax commission of the type found in many other states.[24]

The single taxers prosecuted an active campaign for their amendments. But, as in the Oregon campaign of this same year, 1912, they did not advocate their proposed amendments as "a step toward the single tax", anticipating a less serious opposition by making the effort to keep the single tax proper out of the arena of discussion, and trying to have the measures considered on their merits, apart from the aims and theories of their backers. To this end the single tax organization which had charge of the campaign adopted the name of "The Equitable Taxation League", and sought

---

[24] For the text of the law, see The Public, Nov. 1, 1912, pp. 1035-36, and Jan. 3, 1913, p. 10. For an excellent discussion of the merits of the law, see the Report of the Municipal Finance and Taxation Committee of the Civic League of St. Louis on the Taxation Amendments to the State Constitution of Missouri to be submitted November, 1912. This report was written by A. A. Young and F. N. Judson.

to avoid mention of the single tax in its literature. But the opponents of the amendments refused to accept the gauntlet as thus thrown down, and organized "Anti-Single Tax League"s and a "Land Owners' Protective Association" to combat the measures. As the result, a great deal of the discussion centered around the Henry George single tax.

Here as in Oregon the single taxers attempted to attract votes by making a direct appeal to personal self-interest. They worked out elaborate computations of the tax burdens of property owners under the existing and proposed systems, and notified those who would be benefited of the favorable change in their tax bills.[25] These estimates included both city and rural districts. The single taxers attempted to show that the proposed change would be of economic advantage to both farmers and city business men: to the former because the bulk of land values is found in cities, and to the latter because the abolition of the repressive taxes upon "industry" and upon "the products of labor" would stimulate the production of wealth and attract capital from localities which continued the employment of such taxes.

Seldom has the proposal of a law stirred up such bitter opposition as did this single tax measure.[26] Its opponents formed several organizations to fight it. Of the opposition, Professor Allyn A. Young, then of the Washington University, St. Louis, wrote: "It is unfortunate that much of the active work against the proposed changes was done by men who were willing to defend the worst features of Missouri's present system of taxation, and who were willing to appeal to the crudest prejudices in order to gain

[25] A. A. Young, American Economic Review, Mar., 1913, pp. 203-04.
[26] Two of the chief pamphlets written to oppose the single tax in this campaign were: E. B. Silvers, Single Tax a Fallacy (Kansas City, 1912), and George Falloon, Single Tax Explained; Its Origin, Purpose, and Effect (Kansas City, 1912).

votes".[27] The platforms of the two older parties condemned the amendment, and the Progressive candidate for
governor declared against it. The State Federation of
Labor was practically the only non-single tax organization
to support it.[28]

But the real opposition came from the farmers. They
formed an organization and raised $50,000 at the first
meeting.[29] They believed thoroughly that the single tax
was a measure designed to lighten the taxes of the rich
city man by adding to those of the already heavily-burdened
agriculturalist. They resented, too, the fact that the campaign was largely supported from without the state by
means of the Fels Fund money.

The following description of the experiences of J. R.
Herman gives an idea of the difficulties of single tax mis-
sionary work in Missouri in 1912:

"I live in Denver, Colorado, and entered the campaign at
St. Joseph, Missouri, situated in the richest farming section
of the State. Francis Neilson, M. P., had delivered a speech
in favor of the measure the night before at the Court House.
That settled it with the farmers. Two foreigners, one from
a foreign state and another from a foreign country, dared to
presume to dictate to them how they should run their own
affairs. This was but a match to a powder magazine that had
been heated to explosion by misrepresentation so outlandish
as to be unbelievable, but that this Englishman, a representative of a monarchy, should tell freeborn American citizens
that they intended to take their land away from them, was the
limit, and the way those farmers went about to protect American institutions was a caution. No one can realize the serious-

[27] A. A. Young, op. cit., p. 205. Cf. this passage from a pamphlet
of the Taxpayers' Union, "What is Single Tax? Some Answers by
Single Taxers": "But IS the Single Tax a glorious thing? Under it
SOMEBODY must pay the taxes. It will not be the trusts, monopolies, big stores. It will not be the owners of stocks, bonds and
mortgages. Under Single Tax personal property is exempt. But
somebody must pay. How about the farmer—the home owner?"
[28] Single Tax Review, Nov.-Dec., 1912, p. 51; Mar.-Apr., 1913, p. 43.
[29] Ibid., Mar.-Apr., 1913, p. 43.

ness to which the state of feeling developed who did not take part in the campaign. My experience was common to other speakers and writers, and the reason we were not all killed can be attributed to some accident.

" . . . At first we found an occasional hero who dared to advertise a meeting, but two weeks from the election we could not find a man who dared to make a speech in his own neighborhood not for fear of being boycotted, but for fear of his life. . . . I was billed to debate at Marysville, and as I entered the Court House, a farmer stepped up to me and politely told me I ought to have a bullet put through me and that would put a stop to this damn foolishness. Then I was obliged to make my own dates. . . . At Marysville, the lights were cut off and I was left alone in the court room, and as I groped my way out of the building, I was told that a mob of sixty boys and men with eggs and rocks was coming in the other side, but I escaped it. . . . W. J. Flacy, a clothing merchant at Cameron, advertised a meeting to be held in the park on Saturday afternoon. I missed my train and did not get there until evening. We learned later that an organized committee of fifty men had intended to meet me at the depot. Soon after I began speaking, eggs began to fly at me and the audience, but eggs did not stop the speaking. Then a rough character stepped in front of the stand and tried to pick a quarrel with me. Failing in this, he started to pick a quarrel on the outside of the audience, and but for the quick action of the marshall, I would not be able to write this story. The plan, we afterwards learned, was to start a riot and in the mixup, I was to be strung up to a tree, but the marshall clubbed the leader over the head and put him in the lockup. The last I heard of Cameron, they were trying to punish this leader, and the city officially wrote me a letter of apology.

" . . . The farmers said if the cities outvoted them, they would resist by force,—that it was merely a scheme on the part of the cities to load all the taxes on the farmer."[30]

There was no doubt as to the decisiveness of the verdict of the Missouri electorate.[31] The amendment received 87,000 votes, fourteen and a half per cent of the total, while

[30] Ibid., pp. 43-45. See also The Public, Oct. 11, 1912, pp. 966-68, 972; Oct. 25, 1912, pp. 1018-19.
[31] The vote is tabulated by counties in The Public, Jan. 3, 1913, pp. 10-12.

508,000 were polled against it. Analysis of the vote brings out some interesting points. The city of St. Louis voted 48,000 for, and 65,000 against, and the counties including the cities of St. Louis, Kansas City, St. Joseph, and Springfield showed a favorable vote of thirty-seven per cent. But in the remaining one hundred and ten counties the total favoring vote was only 22,000, as opposed to a hostile vote of 400,000. The fate of the single tax measure was shared by the amendment which provided for a permanent state tax commission. The two measures were numbered, respectively, 6 and 7 on the ballot, and both alike met the displeasure of the "embattled farmers", who evidently believed that somehow No. 7 contained an insidious plot to smuggle in the single tax.

A sequel to the single tax fight was an attempt made in 1914 to secure an amendment to the constitution of Missouri which would prevent a popular vote upon any measure relating to taxation. It was proposed to amend that part of the constitution relating to the initiative and referendum (Section 57 of Article 4) by prohibiting the use of direct legislation "to pass a law or constitutional amendment authorizing any classification of property for the purpose of levying different rates of taxation thereupon, or of authorizing the levy of any single tax on land or land values or land sites at a higher rate or by a different rule than is, or may be, applied to improvements thereupon, or to personal property, or to authorize or confer local option or other local powers in matters of taxation in or upon any of the counties, municipalities, or political subdivisions of the state, or to repeal, amend or modify these provisions relating to taxation".[32]

[32] The text of the proposed amendment is given in the literature of the Missouri Popular Government League, which was organized to fight the amendment. This literature states clearly the case against it.

But the real purport of this proposed amendment (of which the above quotation is only a small part) was, according to ex-Governor Folk, to "destroy the effectiveness of the initiative and referendum". It contained jokers which, it was alleged, might, on technical grounds, prevent the appearance of such measures upon the ballot. By taking advantage of the unpopularity of the single tax in the rural districts and of prohibition, recently rejected, in the cities, enemies of direct legislation, according to ex-Governor Folk and Senator Owen, hoped to get the measure through.[33] However, the so-called "anti-single tax amendment" was beaten decisively, 138,000 votes being cast for it, and 334,000 against it.[34]

Extra-legal application of single tax principles in Houston, Texas

The city of Houston, Texas, has a place in an account of the single tax movement because of the activities of one man, J. J. Pastoriza, Houston's Finance and Tax Commissioner. Elected commissioner of this commission-governed city in April, 1911, he decided at once to go as far as he dared under the existing laws in applying single tax principles.

During his first year of office he introduced the separate valuation of land and improvements and the Somers system of assessment.[35] The franchises of public service corpora-

The case for it is argued in W. H. Wallace's paper, The Citizen (Kansas City). Wallace favors prohibition and woman suffrage, but opposes the single tax because he is convinced it will redound to the interests of "the brewers" and "the millionaire personal property owners". See especially The Citizen, September, 1914, p. 2.

[33] The citations of ex-Governor Folk and Senator Owen are from the literature of the Missouri Popular Government League.

[34] Fels Fund Bulletin, Dec. 1914, p. 1.

[35] Pastoriza's leaflet, To the Tax Payers of Houston, 1912, pp. 5-6. The writer is indebted to Mr. Pastoriza for literature relating to Houston's tax methods.

tions, which Houston had not previously taxed, he assessed at nearly $2,000,000.[36] Since the policy of assessment in Houston had been to underassess buildings relatively to land and to ignore most personal property, Pastoriza decided to go further in this direction. In July, 1912, he announced that "the city of Houston has decided to exempt from taxation all personal property in the hands of individuals, such as cash in banks, stocks, bonds and mortgages, and all household goods", and that "land will be assessed at 70% of its full value, and all improvements upon land at 25% of their value".[37] He also secured the repeal of the charge for building permits.[38]

In the 1914 *City Book* of Houston, Pastoriza thus described and justified "The Houston Plan of Taxation"—as it has come to be known among single taxers. "The Houston Plan recognizes the impossibility of assessing certain forms of personal property equitably, so under it such forms of personal property as cash, notes, mortgages, credits and other evidences of debt, as well as household furniture, are totally exempted from taxation. The franchises of public service corporations are taxed at their fair value. Lands, no matter by whom owned, are taxed equitably at their fair value, while improvements upon land are taxed 25 per cent of their value. This latter exemption being adopted because of the well known fact that improvements deteriorate with age, and the further fact that the exemption will stimulate the construction of more and modern buildings and in time have a tendency to reduce rents".[39]

[36] The Public, June 21, 1912, p. 578.
[37] Pastoriza's leaflet, To the Tax Payers of Houston, p. 8. Pastoriza stated, however, in his report in the 1915 Illustrated City Book of Houston that in 1912 buildings were assessed at 33⅓% of their value, and were not assessed on the 25% basis until 1913 and 1914. (Statistical table facing p. 104.)
[38] Pastoriza's leaflet, The effect of the partial exemption from taxation of personal property and improvements in Houston, Texas.
[39] Houston Illustrated City Book, 1914, p. 97.

Of the popular attitude to the system, Pastoriza wrote in his report of 1914: "The people have expressed themselves universally as being satisfied with the Houston Plan of Taxation, and I believe that if the matter was submitted to a vote of the people, over 90 per cent of them would vote in favor of it".[40] Pastoriza has twice been re-elected, his platform each time being "The Houston Plan of Taxation". In March, 1913, he received 4,913 votes, 1,225 more than were cast for any other candidate for commissioner.[41] In February, 1915, he received 5,659 votes, as against 1,963 for his opponent.[42]

Until early in 1915 no one took the legal steps within his power to compel an assessment more nearly in conformity to the law, although Pastoriza's course was by no means free from protest. But in January, 1915, the Harris County Taxpayers' Association took the matter to the courts asking the Texas State District Court at Houston for a mandamus directing the tax department to assess all property equally.[43] The decision of Judge Read, rendered March 3, 1915, declared Pastoriza's action illegal, and required him to assess personal property and improvements together with land by the same standard of valuation.[44]

Pastoriza had promised that, were action taken to compel him to follow the tax provisions of the law, he would undertake to enforce it to the letter by assessing all property,

[40] Idem.
[41] The Public, Mar. 14, 1913, pp. 249-50.
[42] Ibid., Feb. 26, 1915, p. 193.
[43] Ibid., Feb. 5, 1915, p. 130.
[44] J. W. Baker et al. vs. City of Houston et al., No. 65,847. The court declared that such a "fixed and established plan of discrimination and exemptions" as Pastoriza had "deliberately adopted" was plainly violative of the general property tax provisions of the Texas constitution. The court particularly enjoined Pastoriza from assessing lands at a higher proportion of full value than buildings. The defendants gave notice of appeal.

land, improvements, and personalty, at one hundred per cent valuation, and that he would make an effort to secure the completest possible list of all property in Houston by means of a careful inquisition regarding securities, money, and credits, and an inventory of household goods and merchandise.[45] The threat of such a strict enforcement of the general property tax undoubtedly postponed the taking of the matter to the courts. When the decision adverse to him was handed down he undertook to comply with it. In April, 1915, he said:

"In complying literally with this order of the court, the city has increased its assessment upon all the lands, buildings and other improvements upon land at a price which represents its true and full value in money. Some people call it 100 cents on the dollar of its value. We are also assessing forms of property which we never assessed under the Houston Plan, and are assessing them at their full and true value in money."[46]

But later developments indicate that Pastoriza may risk contempt of court by persisting in his ways. In a letter to the San Francisco Fels Fund Conference, August, 1915, he wrote:

"I have about decided, as chairman of the board of appraisement, to listen to the voice of the people rather than to the order of court, and when the assessments for 1915 are completed, I rather suspect that land will be assessed at its full value and buildings at from forty to fifty per cent of their value, and while we have made a great effort to assess all forms of personal property this year, I firmly believe that next year there will be no personal property assessed that was exempted under the Houston plan of taxation. This is the will of the people, and certainly coincides with my desire".[47]

Pastoriza's hope is that the constitutional application of

[45] See The Public, Mar. 19, 1915, pp. 285-86; May 28, 1915, p. 525; and June 11, 1915, p. 571.

[46] Cited from a leaflet, Address of J. J. Pastoriza before the Sixth Annual Convention of the Southern Commercial Congress, held at Muskogee, Okla., Apr. 26-30, 1915.

[47] Single Tax Rev., Sept.-Oct., 1915, pp. 273-74.

his plan will be possible both in Houston and in other Texas cities through the granting of local option, for which the single taxers have already moved.

Single taxers have acclaimed Pastoriza's method as opening up a whole new vista of single tax opportunity. Under the title, "More Pastorizas Wanted", the *Joseph Fels Fund Bulletin* said: "Single taxers must get busy at once and investigate the possibilities in their respective localities of 'Pastorizing' them".[48] But the decision adverse to this plan will no doubt put a damper upon such action.

Houston's prosperity in the period during which the "Houston Plan of Taxation" was in effect has formed a favorite theme for single tax propagandists.[49] Especially in connection with the New York City movement to tax buildings at a lower rate than land have they invoked Houston's experience. In Pastoriza's leaflet, "Why Houston, Texas, Grows", he stated that "the effect of the Houston Plan of Taxation which exempts certain personal property entirely, buildings, machinery and merchandise partially from taxation, has been magical"; that during the two years 1912-1913 building increased fifty-five per cent, rents fell, bank deposits increased $7,000,000, and population increased twenty-five per cent. He advertised that "a perpetual bonus to manufacturers and merchants is offered by the city of Houston, Texas, through its system of exemptions from taxation".[50]

The claims of Pastoriza and his fellow single taxers have not gone unchallenged. The most extensive attack upon them is a letter of Allan Robinson, president of The Allied

[48] Joseph Fels Fund Bulletin, May, 1913, p. 2. See also Single Tax Rev., May-June, 1913, pp. 32-33.

[49] Cf. an article by W. E. Walter, The growth of Houston, Texas, under partial application of the single tax principle, Single Tax Rev., May-June, 1915, pp. 150-56.

[50] Mailing card entitled, Houston, Texas, New Year gift to the business men of the United States, 1914.

Real Estate Interests of New York City, to the New York *Evening Post*, July 24, 1914. Robinson charged that Pastoriza's statistics of increase of population included Houston's suburbs; that his bank deposit figures for 1911, besides being for a date six months before his plan took effect, had omitted state bank deposits, while the 1913 figures had included them; that a large part of the increase in the value of building permits was the result of two disastrous fires of 1912; and that other Texas cities had grown as rapidly as had Houston.

It is beyond question that Houston has prospered. But that its tax system has been chief among the many important factors affecting prosperity is no more conclusively evidenced than in the case of the prosperity of western Canada under the partial exemption of improvements.[51]

Regarding Pastoriza's method, it is hardly necessary to comment that there are evident dangers in the use by assessors of such extreme discretionary powers as he has exercised in deciding upon the objects and methods of taxation in any locality.

The single tax movement in Colorado, 1913-1915[52]

The provisions of Section 6 of Article XX of the Colorado constitution grant extensive home rule powers to cities

[51] Cf. the discussion of this point in the Proceedings of the National Tax Ass'n, 1914, pp. 405-69.

Since this section was written there has appeared Dr. R. M. Haig's report, prepared for the Committee on Taxation of the City of New York, on the subject: The Exemption of Improvements from Taxation in Canada and the United States (New York, 1915). This report presents a careful analysis of the data bearing upon the effects of "The Houston Plan of Taxation" (pp. 241-52). The conclusion of Dr. Haig's investigation is: "The situation in Houston is very complicated and interesting but . . . there is little basis for drawing conclusions either in favor of or in opposition to the plan of exempting buildings from taxation" (p. 252).

[52] For information regarding these Colorado single tax campaigns

having the commission form of government. Under this Section the cities of Pueblo, Colorado Springs, and Denver voted on single tax measures in November, 1913, April, 1915, and May, 1915, respectively. The single taxers won at Pueblo, but lost decisively at Colorado Springs and Denver. The Pueblo single tax law, however, was repealed in November, 1915, before having a chance to take full effect.

The amendment adopted at Pueblo, which was submitted by initiative petition, provided that in 1914, fifty per cent, and in 1915, ninety-nine per cent of the value of improvements, should be exempt from municipal taxation. The one per cent was retained in order to forestall possible unfavorable action of the courts. The amendment prescribed the retention of a nominal tax upon personal property, not less than a fourth of a mill nor more than one mill, and expressly stated that liquor licenses should not be disturbed. The vote on the amendment was 2,711 for, and 2,171 against. The opposition did not wage as aggressive a campaign as the single taxers have usually been obliged to face.[53]

The law, however, was short lived. The taxes of 1914 were levied on the basis of a fifty per cent exemption of improvements, but before the ninety-nine per cent exemption prescribed for 1915 could go into effect the measure was repealed, 3,255 to 3,042.[54]

The Colorado Springs and Denver amendments, likewise submitted by initiative petition, met with most strenuous

the writer is indebted to George J. Knapp of Pueblo, Earnest Sinton of Colorado Springs, and Ben J. Salmon of Denver.

[53] For a description of the Pueblo campaign, see The Public, Oct. 3, 1913, p. 944, and the Joseph Fels Fund Bulletin, Oct., 1913, p. 2, and Nov., 1913, pp. 1-2. The text of the amendment is in the Joseph Fels Fund Bulletin, Nov., 1913, p. 2.

[54] See The Public, Nov. 19, 1915, p. 1123.

opposition. They were defeated, respectively, by votes of 7,241 to 944, and 27,125 to 7,988.[55] The Colorado Springs amendment provided for the total exemption of personal property and improvements from municipal taxation, this to take effect the first of January, 1916. The Denver amendment retained a merely nominal tax rate upon personal property and improvements, prescribing a rate of not less than one-fourth mill nor more than one mill per dollar. The amendment likewise was to take effect the first of January, 1916. Both amendments provided expressly for the retention of licenses pursuant to the police power. The Colorado Springs amendment declared: "The purpose of this amendment is to have installed and put into effect in the City of Colorado Springs what is known as the single tax for municipal purposes".[56]

Before the Colorado Springs and Denver campaigns were begun the single taxers of neither city were agreed as to the timeliness of political action. But the advocates of political action took the matter into their own hands by proceeding to initiate the measures. A critic of these campaigns wrote to *The Public* that more "deliberate, intensive and extensive propaganda and organization" should have preceded.[57]

In these campaigns single taxers offered the usual arguments that the single tax would add to the taxes of land speculators and the owners of valuable land sites in cities while exempting the owners of homes.[58] But the most

[55] For excellent accounts of these campaigns, see the articles of Earnest Sinton on the Colorado Springs campaign (Single Tax Rev., May-June, 1915, pp. 168-71), and of Louis Wallis on the Denver campaign (The Public, May 28, 1915, pp. 520-21).

[56] Single Tax Rev., May-June, 1915, p. 169.

[57] Louis Wallis, The Denver fight and its lessons, The Public, May 28, 1915, pp. 520-21.

[58] A favorite single tax proposition was the following: "$100 Reward to any person that can prove how many vacant lots, how much

striking feature of their propaganda was the appeal to self-interest which was its central idea. In the Oregon, Washington, and Missouri campaigns single taxers had made something of this idea, but never did they give it such stress as in the Colorado agitation.

The single taxers had gained Pueblo largely by such tactics. George J. Knapp, who managed that campaign, believed that the old single tax custom of throwing bricks at "landlords" and inveighing against private ownership of land had been a failure at vote-getting. Single taxers, he believed, should lay stress upon the prosperity of the Canadian West while enjoying the partial exemption of improvements from taxation; they should talk up their measures as a prosperity policy, seeking for them the backing of the business interests on that ground.

Accordingly, the managers of the Pueblo campaign urged that the policy of exempting improvements from taxation would boom the city and give it a considerable economic advantage over its rivals. They urged that factories would come and more homes would be built, were they exempt from taxes.

In the more recent single tax propaganda the idea is occasionally met that a modified application of the single tax would be to the interest of landowners, because the stimulus it would give to growth (*vide* Vancouver and Houston) would add to the value of their land.[59] Ortho-

idle coal land, how many unused agricultural acres . . . are necessary to make a community prosperous".

It was also argued that "The single tax . . . will lower the taxes of homeowners and merchants [and] enormously reduce rents and the cost of living". (Single tax leaflets).

[59] Cf. the following comment in a letter to The Public, July 18, 1913, p. 680: "This freer use of land, together with increasing population, intensifies the demand for land, and thus raises its price, with the result that the change is brought about without the dreaded loss to landholders. In fact, the values of land advance to such degree that the added tax becomes a negligible quantity."

dox single taxers have qualified this argument with the statement that it is no part of the single tax idea to work out benefits for landowners as such.[60] But that some single tax propagandists should hold out the prospect of an increase in land value as a bait to induce landowners to support a partial application of the single tax principle is not strange when we consider the great stress that single taxers have laid upon the rapid growth that Vancouver, Houston, and other cities have enjoyed while partially exempting personal property and improvements.

In the Denver campaign for the first time we meet the bald statement in the propaganda literature of single taxers that the adoption of the single tax amendment would "make land worth more than it is now".[61] The argument proceeds to state: "Wherever the plan has been tried land value has gone up. The power of growing business to boost the value of land is greater than the power of the increased land value tax to depress that value. In hundreds of cities where, in varying degree, single tax has been applied, land is worth more than before, and not one city can be named where it is worth less. The notion that the Denver amendment will reduce land value is silly."

Surely the authors of such arguments have departed far from Henry George's ideas. If they favor the introduction of the full measure of the Henry George single tax, they are trying to tempt owners of land to take the first step toward destroying themselves.

Besides the general appeal to the personal advantage of business men and landowners, a more direct argument *ad*

---

[60] Cf. the comment of the editor of the Single Tax Rev., May-June, 1911, p. 13: "It is no part of the single tax to favor landowners as landowners".

[61] Circular entitled, Lower Taxes on Homes. In this connection cf. the comment of Louis Wallis on the views of the Colorado single taxers, The Public, May 28, 1915, pp. 520-21.

hominem was used with the tax payers. In each of these three Colorado campaigns the single taxers sent out to voters tax schedules which purported to show their comparative burdens under the existing and the proposed systems. According to these tax schedules, the adoption of the amendments would lower the taxes of a considerable majority.

If the single taxers departed somewhat from Henry George in their arguments, their opponents did not fail to hark back to *Progress and Poverty*. More than in any other campaign on the single tax issue, the "anti"s paraded before the people of Colorado Springs and Denver Henry George's views regarding property in land. The secretary of the Colorado Springs single tax organization wrote:

"They were furnished the ground floor of a prominent new building, . . . the windows of which soon appeared thickly covered with cartoons ridiculing the single tax, across the bottom of the window a large banner was placed in the window all the way across, with several such sentences as 'We must make land common property, Henry George', and 'If private property in land be just, then the remedy I have proposed (single tax) is unjust'. This display attracted a great deal of attention from passers-by, and we had no effective way of combatting it".[62]

The opposition repeated such statements as "Single tax is not a system of taxation—not a tax reform—but a means to an end—Land Communism, Land Socialism!" They used in full page newspaper advertisements the cartoon, borrowed from the Seattle anti-single tax campaign, which represented single taxers as rodents literally gnawing at the roots of the life-giving tree which symbolized private property in land.[63] Single tax propagandists must have wished many times that the founder of the movement had

[62] Single Tax Rev., May-June, 1915, p. 169.
[63] The Colorado Springs and Denver anti-single tax campaigns were directed by Charles H. Shields, manager of the Seattle and 1912 Oregon campaigns, to whom the Joseph Fels Fund propaganda has given the opportunity to become a professional anti-single tax worker.

not characterized private property in land as "a bold, bare, enormous wrong, like that of chattel slavery".[64]

Exemption of improvements in the irrigation districts of California[65]

In March, 1909, the California legislature passed a law which required new irrigation districts to pay for the installation and maintenance of their irrigation systems by means of a levy upon land alone. The land-owners of any of the five already existing districts could vote to adopt the same system.[66]

In six irrigation districts the system has been introduced.[67] Two of the five districts in existence when the law was passed have adopted it, Modesto (1911) and Turlock (1915), both of these being located in the San Joaquin Valley. Since 1909 four districts have been organized, Oakdale and South San Joaquin in the San Joaquin Valley, Anderson-Cottonwood in the northern part of the state, and Imperial near the Mexican line. The total area of these is about a million acres. Single taxers have claimed that the system "has brought about wonderful prosperity in these irrigation districts".[68]

Of course the exemption of improvements applies only to the financing of irrigation systems. All of the property in the districts is subject under state constitutional requirements to taxation for county and municipal purposes. The system is thus little more than an application of the principle of special assessments.

[64] Progress and Poverty, bk. 7, ch. 3, p. 356.

[65] The single tax agitation for local option in taxation in California is considered in ch. 13, infra.

[66] Statutes of California and amendments to the codes passed at the 38th session of the legislature, 1909, ch. 303, p. 462.

[67] Cf. letter of E. P. E. Troy in The Public, Aug. 20, 1915, pp. 808-9.

[68] Ibid., p. 809. Cf. also statements relating to this point in Transactions of Commonwealth Club of California, San Francisco, May, 1914, vol. 9, no. 4, pp. 299-303.

CHAPTER XI

THE SINGLE TAX MOVEMENT IN PENNSYL-
VANIA AND NEW YORK

The proposals which the single taxers of Pennsylvania and New York have put forward have been less radical and not so far-reaching as those made by western single taxers. Partly because of this fact and partly because of the dissimilarity of economic conditions the issues under discussion have been somewhat different.

In the western agitations single taxers have directed sentiment against individual or corporate holding of large tracts of unimproved or only slightly improved land. But in the big cities of the East, where the value of land has risen to unprecedented heights, they have made much of the magnitude of the "unearned increment" and of the huge incomes enjoyed by a few by reason of their ownership of valuable sites.

The single tax argument that the exemption of labor products from taxation stimulates production also has had a different emphasis in the eastern campaigns. In the new cities of the West, with their often unhealthy eagerness for quick prosperity, single tax propagandists have promised that a boom such as the city of Vancouver enjoyed would follow the exemption of improvements from taxation. On the other hand they have argued in the eastern cities, where population is dense and rents high, that a lower tax rate upon buildings would stimulate their construction and, by reducing rents, solve the housing problem. Particularly in the New York City agitation has discussion centered about the single taxers' plea that the lighter taxation of buildings would remedy the evils of congestion.

The partial exemption of buildings from taxation in Pittsburgh and Scranton

The staid old commonwealth of Pennsylvania gained the distinction of being the first state of the United States to witness the application, in a manner constitutionally sound, of the plan of land value taxation which, under the name of "single tax", has attracted so much attention of late in western Canada. In May, 1913, the legislature passed a law directing cities of the second class to assess a lower rate of tax upon buildings than upon land. Pennsylvania has divided its cities into three classes in order to get around the constitutional limitations upon municipal autonomy, and the cities of the second class, to which alone this law applies, are two, Pittsburgh and Scranton.[1]

The law provides for an extremely gradual application of the idea of partially exempting improvements from taxation, and one can hardly accuse Pennsylvania of undue haste in moving toward the single tax. For 1914 and 1915 the prescribed rate of tax upon buildings is reduced to ninety per cent of that upon land; for the next three years, to eighty per cent; and so on by reductions of ten per cent every three years, until in 1925 the rate reaches fifty per cent, which obtains thereafter.[2]

Pittsburgh, until 1911, had employed a most peculiar method of taxing real estate.[3] The city's real estate had

[1] Holdsworth, Economic Survey of Pittsburgh, pp. 203-04.
[2] The law is No. 147, in Laws of Pennsylvania, 1913, pp. 209-12.
[3] For discussion of Pittsburgh's land and taxation problems, see Holdsworth, op. cit., ch.'s 10 and 11, and Shelby M. Harrison, The Disproportion of Taxation in Pittsburgh (reprinted from the Pittsburgh District: Civic Frontage, The Pittsburgh Survey, pp. 156-213, 455-68). See also a review of the latter by R. M. Haig in the American Economic Rev., Mar. 1915, pp. 117-19.

been classified as "built up", "rural", and "agricultural", assessed respectively at full rates, two-thirds rates, and half rates. This unjust system—which the legislature of 1911 had abolished—placed a premium, it was alleged, upon the speculative holding of underimproved or vacant land, conveniently classified as "rural" or "agricultural".[4] The 1911 report of the British Board of Trade on "Cost of Living in American Towns" showed that rents in Pittsburgh were materially higher than those in competing cities.[5] Professor J. T. Holdsworth, in his *Economic Survey of Pittsburgh* (1912), pointed out the striking fact that land values per acre were considerably higher in Pittsburgh than in any other American city except New York.[6] He calculated that in Pittsburgh "in the First and Second Wards, comprising the bulk of the wholesale, high-grade retail, and financial sections, the ratio between land values and improvements is about 80 to 20. In the most valuable business area in New York, where land reaches the highest values to be found anywhere, the ratio of land to improvements is 61 to 39".[7] Professor Holdsworth believed that

[4] See the Survey, July 5, 1913, p. 451.
[5] There is a striking presentation of these figures in a pamphlet, An Act to promote Pittsburgh's progress by reducing the tax rate on buildings 40%, p. 3.
[6] Professor Holdsworth gives the following figures (p. 193):

City	Assessed Value of Land per Acre.	Value of Land per Acre on 100% Basis.
New York	$19,887	$19,887
Chicago	8,138	8,138
Cleveland	11,000	12,200
Baltimore	9,500	14,600
Pittsburgh	17,180	19,090
Detroit	5,179	6,470
Buffalo	5,113	7,866
Milwaukee	11,860	11,860
Cincinnati	4,313	4,790
Newark	8,965	12,800

[7] Holdsworth, op. cit., p. 207.

in some districts of Pittsburgh which were best adapted to
manufacturing, exorbitant land prices prevented normal
expansion and deterred prospective newcomers, who could
find in other cities land equally suitable and at the same
time much cheaper.[8] The task of those who held that the
relatively higher taxation of land would secure its most
economic utilization was easier by reason of Pittsburgh's
aggravated land problem.

The passage of the law of May, 1913, was not brought
about by single tax propaganda of the usual sort. But,
though there was no single tax organization to work for
the law, single taxers were actively interested in securing it.
The Survey, July 5th, 1913, states that it was Ben C.
Marsh, Secretary of the New York Congestion Committee,
who first placed before the Pittsburgh people the possibility
of such a rate-change, at the civic exhibit at the Carnegie
Institute in the fall of 1908.[9] Between that time and the
passage of the law, single taxers of Pittsburgh secured a
hearing for several of their best known speakers before
civic and business organizations of the city.[10]

In a special report, December, 1911, the Committee on
Housing of the Pittsburgh Civic Commission strongly recommended that the tax rate for improvements be reduced
gradually to one-half that for land.[11] In the fall of 1911,
this plan received the indorsement of the Keystone Party

[8] Ibid., ch. 11, Uneconomical use of land. Professor Holdsworth,
however, believed that Pittsburgh should "make haste slowly" in the
matter of exempting improvements from taxation, and suggested that
probably "the objects sought to be obtained by this radical change
could be reached much more simply by imposing an extra tax on unoccupied or underimproved land, thus making it unprofitable to hold
land out of use" (p. 212).

[9] The Survey, July 5, 1913, p. 452.

[10] Single Tax Rev., Mar.-Apr., 1912, pp. 46-47, and especially May-
June, 1912, pp. 44-46. See also The Public, May 23, 1913, pp. 489-90.

[11] Civic Bulletin, published by the Pittsburgh Civic Commission,
Jan., 1912, p. 1.

of Pennsylvania, whose platform contained a plank urging
that the assessment of improvements in cities of the second
class be reduced annually ten per cent for five years.[12]
Later the Real Estate Dealers' Association and the Pittsburgh Board of Trade endorsed the measure.[13] Mayor
W. A. Magee favored it, having sent a special investigator
to some of the cities of western Canada to look into their
tax methods.[14]

The bill was introduced at Harrisburg by Representative
A. C. Stein of Pittsburgh. One of the sponsors of the bill,
writing to *The Public,* commented that "those who worked
for the bill during its passage, did not, of course label it a
single tax measure".[15] The Pittsburgh Civic Commission
supported the bill actively, widely circulating among the
legislators and elsewhere an able pamphlet entitled "An
Act to Promote Pittsburgh's Progress".[16] As a result of
the diplomatic methods of the backers of the bill, it became
law with very little opposition. According to W. D.
George, who worked actively for the measure, the city of
Scranton was not heard from while the bill was pending.[17]

The advocates of the measure believe that it is a step in
the direction of a solution of the housing problem. They
believe that lower rents will result because of the encourage-
ment to building and the forcing into full use of under-
utilized land. Also they anticipate the coming of more
factories to take advantage of the liberal exemptions from
taxes.[18]

Regarding the incidence of the changed tax burden it is

[12] Single Tax Review, May-June, 1912, p. 46.
[13] The Survey, July 5, 1913, p. 451.
[14] The Public, May 23, 1913, p. 489.
[15] Idem.
[16] Idem.
[17] Statement to the writer, Jan. 1914.
[18] See the pamphlet, An Act to promote Pittsburgh's progress, p. 6,
et seq. Pittsburgh also exempts machinery from taxation, ibid., p. 10.

argued that, since the land values of Pittsburgh are twice the building values, the measure will tend to reduce the taxes of all property owners whose buildings are worth more than half the value of their land. Particularly have the advocates of the law claimed that it will benefit the owners of homes.

"On the basis of reduced taxation of buildings, out of a total 5,200 buildings [in the 13th ward, which "contains more homes than any ward in Pittsburgh"], 3,982 homes would be reduced 15% to 25% in their taxes, 800 reduced 5% to 10%, and 418 pay the same as under the present system; 2,380 vacant lots would pay an increase of 20%. . . . In a general estimate, there would be over 70,000 home owners benefited".[19]

In the spring of 1915 there was an unsuccessful attempt to do away with reduced taxation of buildings. This attempt aroused considerable public interest in Pittsburgh. The repeal was urged on the ground that the measure was a discrimination against owners of land and a "decided step toward the single tax theory of Henry George".[20] Mayor Armstrong took the leading part in urging the repeal, which was also advocated by the Chamber of Commerce and other interests.[21] The repeal was opposed by a number of organizations, including the Pittsburgh Board of Trade, the Pittsburgh Civic Commission, the Pittsburgh Real Estate Board, by some of the press, and by the single taxers.[22]

The repeal was gotten through both Houses at Harrisburg, but Governor Brumbaugh vetoed it. In vetoing the bill, the Governor said:

"This repealer is opposed by the largest group of protestants that have been heard on any bill. It is advocated by those

[19] Ibid., p. 10.
[20] See the summary of reasons for repeal of the law, cited in The Public, Apr. 30, 1915, p. 427. See also ibid., May 7, 1915, p. 452.
[21] Ibid., May 7, 1915, p. 452.
[22] Ibid., May 28, 1915, p. 522.

now in charge of the fiscal policy of one of the two cities concerned.

"Inasmuch as there is such a conflict of opinion, and inasmuch as the law has scarcely yet been tried it is well to allow it to operate until a commanding judgment decrees its fate. Let the people concerned study freely and fairly the operations of the present law and, if found after two years to be inadequate to the needs of the cities or unfair in its provisions, it can be repealed. To disturb it now when a preponderance of opinion favors it is unwise. For these reasons the bill is not approved".[23]

Single taxers are making an effort to secure the extension to cities of the third class of the plan of taxation now being applied in Pittsburgh and Scranton.[24]

Single tax activity in New York City since 1890

New York City, the adopted home of Henry George when he left California after the publication of *Progress and Poverty,* has thrice been the center of interest of the single tax movement: first in George's two noteworthy campaigns of 1886 and 1887 and the days of the Anti-Poverty Society; again in his last mayoralty campaign of 1897; and now in the movement to halve the tax rate upon buildings, a project actively discussed since 1911. Besides these periods of exceptional single tax interest, New York has been, more than any other city, a center of sustained single tax activity and influence. The "Manhattan Single Tax Club", organized December, 1888, has included in its membership the names of a great many of the leaders of the movement, beginning with Henry George, and has taken a most active part in the furtherance of the single tax cause.[25]

[23] Cited in ibid., June 18, 1915, p. 597.
[24] Ibid., Jan. 29, 1915, p. 108.
[25] See Doblin, Some interesting events in the history of the Manhattan Single Tax Club, Single Tax Rev., Nov.-Dec., 1913, pp. 50-62; Jan.-Feb., 1914, pp. 37-40; Mar.-Apr., 1914, pp. 26-29; May-June, 1914, pp. 17-21.

One reform desired by single taxers and others, and for which the Manhattan Single Tax Club moved as early as 1890,[26] has been enacted into law—the separate assessment of land and improvements. The "New York Tax Reform Association", organized in 1891 by Shearman and other single taxers in order to secure the cooperation of non-single tax reformers in urging fiscal measures desired by single taxers, especially local option in taxation, took an active part in urging this assessment reform.[27] Although the home rule projects have thus far failed of success, the New York State Legislature in May, 1903, passed a law providing for the separate assessment of land and improvements. This law was the result of several years' effort on the part of the New York Tax Reform Association, in which its secretary, Lawson Purdy, took the leading part.[28]

The law provided for an additional column in which the assessors set down "the sum for which, in their judgment, each separately assessed parcel of real estate under ordinary circumstances would sell if it were wholly unimproved".[29] The value of the buildings alone was not to be separately stated, since it was believed that this would have the tendency to cause the under-valuation of land and the over-valuation of buildings. This practice of separate valuation has conduced to great efficiency in the work of assessment in New York City, and in 1911 the New York Legislature provided for extending it to the other cities of the state.[30]

[26] Ibid., Nov.-Dec., 1913, p. 57.

[27] See Post, The New York Tax Reform Ass'n, in The Public, Nov. 22, 1912, pp. 1109-14.

[28] Single Tax Rev., Apr. 15, 1903, p. 24; July 15, 1903, p. 35.

[29] Preliminary Directions to the Deputy Tax Commissioners of the City of New York in relation to the Separate Assessment of Land and Land and Improvements as directed by Chapter 454, Laws of 1903. Under authority of Secs. 887 and 889 of the Charter. New York, July 15, 1903.

[30] Heydecker, Tax legislation in New York, 1911, National Tax Conference, 1911, p. 89.

Another law upon which single taxers look with favor, a law which

*The movement to exempt improvements from taxation in
New York City, 1908-1916*[31]

The proposal to exempt improvements from taxation,
wholly or in part, has been discussed actively in New York
City since 1908. Discussion has centered upon the claim
that reduced taxation of buildings, by stimulating their
construction and hence tending to lower rents, would alle-
viate the evils of congestion. Many who could hardly be
classed as single taxers have been among the advocates of
the proposal.

In March, 1908, an "Exhibit on Congestion of Population" was shown in New York City as the result of the
efforts of a committee of social workers organized in 1906
to study that problem. The exhibit attempted to depict
housing conditions of Manhattan Island, to portray "the
burden of high rents, crowded rooms, high morbidity and
mortality rates, and very high profits of land speculation".[32]
One striking exhibit had two cubes with dimensions of five-
eighths of an inch and four and one-half feet, representing
the value of the land of Manhattan Island respectively in
1624, when it was sold for $24.00, and in 1907, when it had
reached the enormous figure of nearly $3,000,000,000. This
representation bore the legend, "Who created it? Who gets
it?" The exhibit, which was shown in the American Mu-
seum of Natural History in Manhattan and at the Brooklyn
Institute of Arts and Sciences, attracted much attention

the real estate interests opposed, is an amendment of 1913 to the New
York Charter (Ch. 324) providing that buildings in course of construction begun since the 1st of October preceding, and not ready for
occupancy, should not be assessed. See the Single Tax Rev., May-
June, 1913, pp. 29-30.

[31] A good account of the movement, to which the present writer is
indebted, is an article by B. C. Marsh, Land value taxation vs. congestion, Single Tax Rev., Jan.-Feb., 1914, pp. 16-20.

[32] Ibid., p. 17.

and was attended by more than seventy thousand people.[33] In 1909 the Congestion Committee presented an exhibit on City Planning and Municipal Art which directed attention to the "unearned increment" of land values and methods of taxing it in Europe.[34]

As a result of these exhibits and the discussion which they excited, the Board of Aldermen of New York City directed Mayor Gaynor to appoint a City Commission on Congestion of Population to "prepare a comprehensive plan for the present relief and future prevention of congestion of population in the City of New York".[35] The Commission, appointed May 17, 1910, was composed of ten members of the Board of Aldermen and nine private citizens. Its chairman was Jacob A. Cantor and its secretary Benjamin C. Marsh. The latter more than any other man is responsible for the recent discussion of the city land question in relation to congestion and housing. Allan Robinson, president of the Allied Real Estate Interests of New York, who has so actively opposed halving the tax rate on buildings, was also a member. Dr. Frank J. Goodnow, then of Columbia University, who had served as chairman of the Congestion Committee, was chairman of the sub-committee on taxation. This committee held hearings at which a number of well-known tax experts testified, including F. C. Howe, A. C. Pleydell, and E. R. A. Seligman.[36]

The Commission, when it gave its report in February, 1911, followed the recommendation of its sub-committee on taxation, and recommended that the rate of tax upon buildings be half the rate of tax upon land, this reduction to be secured by an equal change in each of five consecutive

[33] Idem.
[34] Ibid., p. 18.
[35] Cf. the Report of the New York City Commission on Congestion of Population, Feb. 28, 1911, p. 3.
[36] Marsh, op. cit., p. 18.

years.[37] As a means to the juster assessment of land, the Commission advised the registry of the prices at which land changed hands for the information of tax officials. The Commission, while not recommending a land value increment tax, urged that public hearings be had on the question in order to ascertain whether New York should adopt it.

In January, 1911, pursuant to a recommendation of the Board of Estimate and Apportionment, Mayor Gaynor appointed an advisory commission "to cooperate with the Budget Committee of the Board of Estimate and Apportionment in ascertaining and reporting on new sources of City revenue".[38] Edgar J. Levey (deceased) was chairman of the commission and Professor Joseph French Johnson was also a member. The report, submitted in January, 1913, recommended as its chief suggestion a land value increment tax of one per cent per year "to be perpetual upon all increments of land values as shown by comparison with the assessed valuation of the year 1912".[39] This proposition differs from the land value increment taxes of Europe in providing for a yearly tax instead of a tax to be paid when the land changes hands, or at long intervals, such as twenty-five years.

In March, 1911, immediately after the Congestion Com-

[37] Recommendations of the New York City Commission on Congestion of Population, recommendation 9 (pp. 32-33), Measures to keep land cheap and promote the provision of good and cheap housing. For the report of the sub-committee on taxation see p. 141 et seq.

[38] Report of the Commission on New Sources of City Revenue, submitted Jan. 11, 1913, p. 1.

[39] Ibid., p. 6. Cf. an article by Joseph French Johnson, The proposed increment tax for New York, Quarterly Jour. of Economics, vol. 27, pp. 539-43, (1913).

For the report of a committee of the Allied Real Estate Interests of New York opposing the proposal, see the Real Estate Mag., Mar. 1913, pp. 22-24.

mittee's report, a bill known as the Sullivan-Short Bill, providing for halving the tax rate on buildings and allowing five years for the change, was introduced into the legislature, but was not allowed to come to a vote. The bill was introduced again in 1912 as the Sullivan-Brooks Bill, only to meet a similar fate. The Progressive Party took up the measure in 1913, and Senator Salant and Assemblyman Schaap introduced a bill providing that the change should take effect if approved at a referendum of the voters of New York City. But this bill fared no better than its predecessors, it, too, being killed in committee.[40]

As the bill to halve the tax rate on buildings was reintroduced after each successive defeat, discussion grew in volume. Interest culminated in the early part of 1914, when the Herrick-Schaap Bill was introduced in the New York legislature.[41] This bill proposed an amendment to the Charter of Greater New York providing that "the Aldermanic Board shall for 1915, in fixing the tax rate for real estate, so apportion such rate that the rate on the difference between the value of the real estate with improvements and its value wholly unimproved shall be ninety per cent of the rate on the value of the wholly unimproved real estate. Every year thereafter the rate on the difference shall be still further reduced ten per cent until the rate shall be fifty per cent of the rate on the value of the unimproved real estate. The act is to take effect immediately, provided that the powers conferred thereunder shall not be exercised . . . until the proposed change is approved by the electors of New York City in November, 1914".[42]

[40] See Marsh's article in the Single Tax Rev., Jan.-Feb., 1914, pp. 18-20.

[41] Cf. Literary Digest, vol. 48, p. 478, (Mar. 7, 1914), Single Tax Talk in New York.

[42] For the text of the bill, see Real Estate Mag., Mar., 1914, p. 41. This issue of the Real Estate Magazine contains the strongest argu-

Public hearings were held in New York and in Albany, at which able spokesmen, for and against the measure, appeared. The New York City press gave much space to letters and editorial discussion of the matter.

The advocates of the proposed change waged a most active campaign of propaganda. The "Business Men's Association to Untax Industry" and the "Society to Lower Rents and Reduce Taxes on Homes", in each of which single taxers were the leaders, were organized to work for the proposal. However, many who were not of the single tax faith supported it. Even Benjamin C. Marsh, the able and active leader of the movement, is not sure that he himself is properly counted a single taxer, though he has been intimately associated with them.[43]

The organizations favoring the measure employed various methods of propaganda. There were street meetings, mass meetings, debates, addresses before various organizations, and a wide distribution of literature. In 1913 and 1914, when it was proposed that the legislature submit the matter for decision to a referendum of the voters of the city, the advocates of halving the tax rate on buildings secured the signatures of 36,000, or nearly six per cent of the total number of voters, who favored such a referendum.[44] Many of these signatures were secured at an "Exhibit on Lower Rents", held in New York beginning in February, 1913, under the auspices of the private Congestion Committee. This exhibit consisted of diagrams, statistics, pictures, and cartoons which presented strongly the case for the proposed measure. In connection with

ment made against the proposal, a brief of the Merchants' Ass'n of New York presented at the legislative hearing on the bill at Albany, Mar. 3, 1914, by Allan Robinson.

For a strong presentation of the arguments in its favor see Marsh, Taxation of Land Values in American Cities, 1911.

[43] Single Tax Rev., Jan.-Feb., 1914, p. 17.
[44] Ibid., p. 19.

222   SINGLE TAX MOVEMENT

the exhibit daily meetings were held. Thousands visited
the exhibit each day, nearly 100,000 in all.[45]

The real estate interests of New York City, ably led by
Allan Robinson, president of the Allied Real Estate Interests, were from the beginning strenuously hostile. They
took the leading part in fighting this proposal to add to
the tax burdens of land-owners. The *Real Estate Magazine*
of New York carried on in its pages an active discussion
both of the single tax and of the proposed measure. Its
managers, besides presenting their own arguments, gave
place to statements of their opponents' views from the pens
of well known single taxers such as Joseph Fels and F. C.
Leubuscher, president of the Society to Lower Rents and
Reduce Taxes on Homes.

Very much of the opposition was based on the ground
that halving the tax rate on buildings was merely an entering wedge for the single tax. The New York *Times* in
an editorial, "Unfit to be voted upon",[46] cited Henry
George's declaration that "there is and can be no just title
to an exclusive possession of the soil, and that private
property in land is a bold, bare, enormous wrong, like that
of chattel slavery". This, said the *Times,* indicated the
end aimed at by the Society for the Reduction of Taxes on
Homes.

Regarding the referendum, the *Times* voiced the feelings
of many opponents of the measure when it stated in the
editorial cited that, since "nobody loves a landlord, . . .
tenants would be unanimous for lower rents, or for making
any experiment with lower rents as an objective". It was
also argued that the matter, involving as it did complicated

[45] For descriptions of the Exhibit, see The Public, Feb. 28, 1913,
pp. 198-200; Mar. 7, 1913, pp. 221-22; Single Tax Rev., Jan.-Feb.,
1914, p. 19.
[46] Feb. 12, 1914.

questions as to the incidence and effects of taxation, was much too intricate to become the subject for a popular vote.[47] On the other hand, the advocates of the referendum charged that their opponents, in fighting it, feared that the vote would be in favor of halving the tax rate on buildings. They charged that they were unwilling to trust the voters' decision in the matter.

On the 20th of February, 1914, the mayor and Board of Estimate and Apportionment held a hearing on the measure. F. C. Leubuscher appeared in behalf of it, and Professor E. R. A. Seligman spoke in opposition. After the hearing, the following resolution was adopted:

"Resolved, That the Board of Estimate and Apportionment of the City of New York earnestly deprecates the passage of the Herrick-Schaap bill, or any similar legislation, until the question involved in this proposed measure has been given the careful investigation which its importance demands, and the Mayor, through the Department of Taxes and Assessments and such other means as the city authorities may see fit to employ, has made a thorough and impartial study of the subject of taxation upon lands and buildings."[48]

On the 3d of March, 1914, there was a hearing on the Herrick-Schaap Bill at Albany.[49] This hearing was attended by more than two hundred real estate men. Allan Robinson and several single tax speakers took part in the discussion. The fate of the bill was the same as that of its predecessors; it was not allowed to come to a vote.

Again, in the spring of 1915, State Senator W. J. Heffernan of New York City introduced a measure[50] which proposed for 1916 a rate of tax upon buildings ninety per

[47] Cf. Literary Digest, op. cit.
[48] Single Tax Rev., Mar.-Apr., 1914, p. 23.
[49] Single Tax Rev., Mar.-Apr., 1914, p. 24.
[50] The writer is indebted to Benjamin C. Marsh for a copy of the bill. The essential part of it is printed in Haig's report, Some Probable Effects of the Exemption of Improvements from Taxation in the City of New York, p. 11.

cent of that upon land, this reduction to be followed by eight further reductions of ten per cent and a final reduction of nine per cent, so that at the end of ten years the rate of tax upon buildings would be one per cent of that upon land. The bill provided that the plan should not take effect unless adopted by a referendum of the voters of New York City at the general election of November, 1915. But this measure was not permitted to emerge from committee.

In April, 1914, Mayor Mitchel, pursuant to the resolution of the Board of Estimate and Apportionment, appointed a committee of twenty-five, known as the Committee on Taxation of the City of New York. Mr. Alfred E. Marling was chairman, Professor Seligman chairman of the Executive Committee, Mr. Frederic C. Howe secretary, and Mr. Laurence Arnold Tanzer executive secretary.[51] The mayor instructed the Committee to make an investigation considerably broader than that contemplated in the above resolution, i.e. "taxation upon lands and buildings", since he requested them "to make a comprehensive and exhaustive study of the several methods of taxation in use here and in other cities of this country and abroad, and of such methods and devices as have been, or may be, during the continuance of your investigation, suggested as calculated to effect an improvement in the ways and means of creating revenue for payment of the cost of the city government."[52]

Shortly after organization the Committee entrusted Dr. Robert Murray Haig of Columbia University with the task

[51] The other members of the Committee were R. S. Binkerd, George Cromwell (resigned), F. H. Field, J. N. Francolini, J. J. Halleran, Hamilton Holt, J. W. Jenks, A. L. Kline, F. C. Leubuscher, Walter Lindner, C. C. Miller, G. V. Mullan, L. H. Pink, Lawson Purdy, David Rumsey, O. R. Seitz, F. B. Shipley, R. E. Simon, F. S. Tomlin, C. T. White, D. F. Wilcox, and C. H. Woodward.

[52] Final Report of the Committee on Taxation of the City of New York, 1916, p. 11.

of making a field investigation of the so-called single tax experiments in western Canada and in Houston, Pueblo, Pittsburgh and Scranton. Advocates of the exemption of improvements had urged that the policy had brought highly desirable results where it was being applied. Dr. Haig made his investigation in the summer of 1914 and presented his results in a report on *The Exemption of Improvements from Taxation in Canada and the United States*. This report, which the Committee published in the fall of 1915, presented a full statement of the facts in the case together with cautious generalizations and conclusions.[53]

After completing this work Dr. Haig prepared for the Committee a second report entitled, *Some Probable Effects of the Exemption of Improvements from Taxation in the City of New York*. He undertook to determine, from an analysis of the New York City assessment rolls for 1914, "which sections of the city, which types of property and which economic classes would pay greater taxes and which smaller,"[54] were land to be taxed at a higher rate than buildings. Two proposals for exemption were considered: the taxing of buildings (1) at a rate half that upon land, and (2) at a rate one per cent of that upon land. Whether a tax-payer's bill would increase or decrease in the case of a given piece of property was dependent upon the relation of land value to building value, this ratio being 65.94 : 34.06 for Manhattan and 61.47 : 38.53 for the entire city. In 1914 the levies upon land and improvements, respectively, were 84 and 52.8 millions; had the first plan been in effect

[53] In the New York controversy each side claimed to be supported in its position by Haig's findings. For a summary of his conclusions by the present writer cf. a review in the American Economic Rev., Mar., 1916, pp. 158-61, also the Annals of the American Acad. of Polit. and Social Science, Mar., 1916, pp. 239.

[54] Haig, Some Probable Results of the Exemption of Improvements from Taxation in the City of New York, p. 11.

they would have been 104.1 and 32.8 millions, and under
the second plan they would have been 135.9 and .8 millions.[55] Under the first plan in Manhattan the tax burden
would have been increased from 92.4 to 94.7 millions; the
tax rate upon land from 1.78 to 2.20; and the tax burden
upon land from 57 to 70.5 millions. Under the second plan
the tax burden would have totaled 98.3 millions, 91.9 millions of this from land, and the rate upon land would have
been 2.86.[56] Under either plan Brooklyn would gain a
large reduction, and only the presence of much vacant land
would prevent substantial decreases in the relative burdens
of the other boroughs. All the calculations were subject
to the assumption that land values would remain constant,
neither diminished by heavier taxes nor increased by the
growth of the city or forces which the change itself would
set in motion. The total tax bills of the following types of
property would be reduced: sky-scrapers, up-town tenements and apartment houses in Manhattan, and homes and
apartments generally in the out-lying sections. The following types would receive increases: down-town tenements
and most single-family houses in Manhattan, and, of course,
vacant and poorly improved land in all sections. In Manhattan every assessment section south of 96th street would
receive a substantial increase. Dr. Haig concluded, first,
that "the change promises ultimate benefits of considerable
importance to all tenants and to many of the home-owners
in the out-lying boroughs," which benefits, however, "may
be very slow of realization"; and, second, that "the owners
of land would be charged with the cost of these benefits,"
which cost would be "considerable."[57]

In November, 1915, the Committee held a series of public

[55] Ibid., p. 24.
[56] Ibid., pp. 22, 26, 27.
[57] Ibid., p. 135.

hearings on the proposal at which about forty advocates and opponents of the plan appeared.[58]   The Committee also drew up five elaborate series of questions relating to various aspects of the problem, submitting these for answer to individuals and organizations interested in the problem of "untaxing buildings."[59]   A number of briefs, pro and con, were submitted to the Committee, the ablest of these being the brief in favor of untaxing buildings submitted by Benjamin C. Marsh on behalf of the Society to Lower Rents and Reduce Taxes on Homes.[60]

The Committee presented its final report in January, 1916.[61]   It recommended "against the adoption of the principle of untaxing buildings, gradually or otherwise," and "against a supertax on land values as a means of raising the additional revenue required in the immediate future."[62] The Committee, however, favored an increment tax on land values similar to that proposed by the Commission on New Sources of City Revenue in 1913, namely a flat annual one per cent rate upon all increments calculated from the year of the enactment of the law as a base.[63]   The Committee, besides recommending a number of administrative changes, favored "a state income tax as a partial means of

[58] The testimony taken at these hearings is printed in the Final Report of the Committee, pp. 237-370.

[59] For these series of questions together with the answers submitted, cf. ibid., pp. 127-73.

[60] For these briefs cf. ibid., pp. 174-235.

[61] This report, with the majority and minority reports, the answers to the series of questions, the briefs submitted, and the testimony taken at the public hearings, is a valuable collection of data relating to the untaxing of buildings.

[62] Ibid., p. 15.

[63] The Committee suggested, however, that the base "should be not the year 1916, but any year between 1910 and 1914 which marks the highest assessed valuation, provided the property has not been sold in the meantime" (p. 101).   The Committee drafted an increment tax bill (pp. 392-93).

securing the additional revenue required in the immediate future", or "in the event of the adoption of a state income tax not proving feasible, an abilities tax, composed of a habitation tax, an occupation tax and a salaries tax."[64] There was considerable diversity of opinion among the members of the Committee regarding most of these recommendations. A substantial minority dissented from nearly every one, and those favoring one were in several cases not those favoring another.

The majority in recommending against untaxing buildings urged that the change would interfere with complex property rights, that "the tendency of the scheme would be to a more intensive use of land" and would require "laws to regulate the height of buildings and to provide for a proper zoning system," and that "in the Borough of Manhattan, at least, the burden would be relatively heavier upon the owners of the less expensive parcels of real estate." Conceding the possibility of "a temporary decrease of rents," the report took the position that the extent of the benefits of the proposal was "questionable" and that it would be "neither fair nor wise to cause the owners of real estate, and especially the owners of the more modest parcels of real estate, to suffer diminution in the amount of their invested capital because of vague and uncertain benefits to other classes that might ultimately be expected."[65]

The minority report and dissenting memorandums advocating the untaxing of buildings were signed by seven members, and two of the majority while opposing the plan under existing conditions believed that "the theory of untaxing buildings is logical and right."[66]   The minority

[64] Ibid., p. 15.
[65] Ibid., pp. 32-35.
[66] These two were Messrs. Pink and Holt (ibid., p. 35). The minority report was signed by Messrs. Leubuscher, Wilcox, Purdy, Howe, and Shipley. Those filing dissenting memorandums were Messrs. Binkerd and Tomlin (ibid., pp. 59-60).

argued that the policy would tend to discourage land speculation and that it "would tend mildly to stimulate building
operations, and particularly to cause the replacement of
obsolete and inadequate buildings with more modern and
better ones." It would tend toward lower rents and improved housing, more home owning in the suburbs, greater
prosperity, less unemployment, and higher wages, and
"would institute a fundamental change for the better in
our taxing system, which in the long run would bring
benefits, small in detail, but immense in the aggregate, to
many millions of human beings."[67]   The minority met the
confiscation of property in land argument with the statement that the policy of untaxing buildings "would not
affect vested interests in land so seriously as to differentiate
it from other fiscal measures and governmental policies that
are never questioned on moral grounds."[68]

Following the presentation of the final report of the
Committee came something of a lull in public interest. But
the propaganda work continues. The advocates of untaxing buildings expect to re-introduce their measures at successive sessions of the New York legislature.

[67] Ibid., pp. 58-59.
[68] Ibid., p. 52. The argument went on to state: "For example, right
under our very eyes the city, by its deliberately adopted rapid transit
policy, is spending vast sums of money for improvements which, it
is known in advance, will destroy values in certain sections, and create
them in others. The city is making some men poor while it makes
others rich, and, what is more, is making those who are injured by
them help pay for the improvements that are destroying their property" (p. 52).

CHAPTER XII

THE TACTICS OF THE SINGLE TAX MOVEMENT

Single taxers and local option in taxation

The present movement for local option in taxation, or "home rule", as it has been attractively named, originated in New York City about 1890. It was the outgrowth of a suggestion of Thomas G. Shearman, who believed that the granting of local option in taxation would increase the possibility of securing somewhere the adoption of the single tax. Shearman believed that single taxers would stand a better chance to secure local option legislation if they could have the coöperation of some who were not of their number, and, with this in view, he became the chief mover in the organization of the New York Tax Reform Association, formed in 1891 to enlist the opponents of personal property taxation in a movement to secure local option legislation which would permit the abolition of this form of taxation in New York City.[1]

The first League for Home Rule in Taxation was formed under the leadership of single taxers in New York City in 1891.[2] *The Standard* commented upon this organization as follows:

"This organization offers the best plan for practical single tax work yet devised. It does not agitate for the single tax, but for a law that will allow every county to decide for itself whether to tax land values alone, or improvements alone, or

[1] See L. F. Post, The New York Tax Reform Association, The Public, Nov. 22, 1912, pp. 1109-14.
[2] The Standard, Nov. 4, 1891, p. 5. See also Single Tax Rev., Nov.-Dec., 1913, pp. 60-62.

personal property alone, or any two, or all three. No fair man can object to such a law. It will revive democracy in its best form."[3]

As a result of the activity of the League for Home Rule in Taxation and the New York Tax Reform Association, the legislature of New York has had before it at nearly every session since 1891 measures providing for local option and the separate assessment of land and improvements. In many other states also, home rule measures of one sort or another have been frequently before the legislators or voters. The voters of the state of Washington in 1898 voted down a local option amendment which was opposed as a single tax measure.[4] The *National Single Taxer,* October, 1899, mentioned eleven states in which such measures "have been up recently".[5] In 1902 Colorado rejected a constitutional amendment for local option which authorized specifically the exemption of personal property and improvements but forbade the exemption of land.[6] For a number of years past single taxers have tried to secure local option in Rhode Island.[7]

Of late the home rule proposition has been most prominent in the West. At the 1910 election Oregon voted by a slim majority for a home rule amendment[8] which combined with it, as Professor Bullock has said, "a provision, delightfully inconsistent with the principle of 'home rule', by which it was declared that no poll tax should be levied in Oregon".[9] But before the single taxers could take any

[3] The Standard, Dec. 9, 1891, pp. 2-3.
[4] Supra, p. 184.
[5] These states were California, Colorado, New York, Ohio, Washington, Minnesota, Illinois, Massachusetts, New Mexico, Rhode Island, and Michigan. See National Single Taxer, Oct., 1899, p. 4.
[6] Supra, p. 157 et seq.
[7] Single Tax Rev., Jan.-Feb., 1910, pp. 29-31; Jan.-Feb., 1912, pp. 44-46.
[8] Supra, p. 170 et seq.
[9] Proceedings of National Tax Conference, 1911, p. 287.

action under this law it was repealed, 64,000 to 47,000, in the anti-single tax land-slide of 1912.[10]

In California at the elections of 1912 and 1914 home rule amendments were before the people. The Joseph Fels Fund Commission contributed liberally to the financing of these campaigns through the California League for Home Rule in Taxation, a single tax organization. The advocates of the measures, in their speeches and literature, have, as in other Pacific Coast single tax campaigns, made much of the progress of Vancouver and Victoria, British Columbia, under the policy of exempting improvements from taxation, a policy made possible through their enjoyment of the privilege of local option. The voters of California rejected the measure each time; in 1912—243,959 to 169,321; and in 1914—375,634 to 267,618.[11]

In 1912 Colorado, by a vote of 49,596 to 44,778,[12] adopted an amendment to Section 6 of Article XX under which cities and towns of over 2,000 population receive extensive home rule powers, and "may, without regard to the general laws of the state, enact such laws and ordinances on the subject of municipal taxation as they may desire".[13] This law, however, was not proposed by single taxers. It

[10] Supra, p. 180.
[11] Single taxers have sometimes relied upon the belief that the vote of cities would support them in their movements for local option in taxation. The evidence from these California elections regarding this point is not decisive. In 1912 local option won in San Francisco but was beaten decisively in Los Angeles. In 1914 it carried in the latter city but was badly beaten in the former. See the California Blue Book, 1913-15, pp. 310, 409.
[12] The figures for the vote are from The American Year Book, 1912, p. 182.
[13] Cited from the summary of legislation in the Special Report on Taxation of the Bureau of Corporations "covering the tax movement throughout the United States during 1912", Washington, 1914, p. 413. See also a citation of a part of the amendment in the Proceedings of the National Tax Conference, 1914, p. 454.

was not even known to many of them, until, in 1913, acting
under it, the Pueblo single taxers began a campaign which
led to the exemption in that city of fifty per cent of the
value of improvements in 1914, and ninety-nine per cent
in 1915.[14]

The Wisconsin legislature in 1914 passed a resolution to
amend Section 1 of Article VIII of the constitution so as
to permit the legislature to authorize cities, towns, villages,
and counties to vote "to exempt from taxation, in whole or
in part, designated classes of property".[15] The value of the
property exempted, however, was to be included in state
taxes, or state and county taxes, as the case might be. This
measure, to become effective, needed to pass the next session
of the legislature and be ratified by the people, but it failed
to pass at the session of 1915.[16] Single taxers favored its
adoption, as did many who were not single taxers, believing
that it would add flexibility to Wisconsin's tax system.[17]
The State Tax Commission in its report of 1914 did not
commit itself, pointing out both advantages and objections
to the proposal.

Ohio single taxers are initiating at the present writing
(1916) a measure granting to municipalities, townships, or
school districts the option to choose between the existing
general property tax system and a system of exclusive land
taxation for local purposes. Some single taxers have criticized the proposal as not granting "real home rule in
taxation".[18]

A survey of the movement for local option in taxation

[14] This law, however, was repealed in Nov., 1915, before the ninety-
nine per cent exemption could become operative. See ch. 10, supra.
[15] For the text of the amendment and a discussion of its merits, see
the Report of the Wisconsin Tax Commission, 1914, pp. 128-31.
[16] Letter from Wisconsin Tax Commission, dated Nov. 4, 1915.
[17] Report of the Wisconsin Tax Commission, 1914, p. 130.
[18] Cf. discussions of this proposal in The Public, July 30, 1915, p.
736, and Aug. 13, 1915, p. 784.

shows that it originated with single taxers and that nearly every agitation for home rule has been initiated and backed by them. In most instances the single tax issue has been injected to a greater or less extent. In the two California campaigns for local option, the arguments for the measures in the voters' text books referred to the experience of western Canada in exempting improvements from taxation, and are recognizable as single tax arguments.[19] As to the Oregon campaign of 1910 Charles V. Galloway of the Oregon State Tax Commission said:

"Interest in local (county) option or home rule in taxation was made to order. It is indeed doubtful that there is or ever has been in Oregon any real demand for local option in taxation except to promote the single tax program. We have now come to look on 'local option in taxation' and 'single tax' as terms practically synonymous".[20]

[19] Cf. the following passage from the affirmative argument in the official pamphlet, Amendments to Constitution and Proposed Statutes with Arguments Respecting the Same, to be Submitted to the Electors of the State of California at the General Election on Tuesday, Nov. 5, 1912 (p. 31): "A suggestion, hardly amounting to an objection, has been made that possibly some community might seek to stimulate business and industry by exempting certain classes of property from taxation, and that this might operate to compel other communities to follow the example thus set or lose commercial prestige. It is said that this might produce internecine warfare. But this is not warfare, it is business. If one community can stimulate business and industry by this means, it would furnish a good example for others, and soon we would see the whole state adopting the same means of 'stimulating business and industry'. This is really the chief virtue of the amendment. *It makes it possible to stimulate business and industry*". Cf. also the corresponding voters' pamphlet for the election of Nov. 3, 1914, pp. 11-12.

Indeed, it is claimed that the 267,618 who voted for the 1914 California local option measure are "single tax voters". (Joseph Fels Fund Bulletin, June, 1915, pp. 2-3.) This claim is manifestly unjustified. Although the single tax issue was involved, the issue was not so joined on the measure that one could properly class these voters as in any way committed to the single tax proper.

[20] Proceedings of National Tax Conference, 1911, p. 249.

In general it may be said that, aside from those who have worked for home rule in order to secure for cities the right to abolish the personal property tax, home rule has had few advocates who do not lean towards the single tax. In practice, then, the question of the desirability of local option in taxation is not very much broader than the question of the desirability of permitting localities to vote independently on the question of exempting personal property and improvements.[21] As Professor Bullock has said: "Local option in taxation turns out to mean, in most cases, local option in exemption".[22] While some of the proposed local option amendments, e.g., that of California in 1912, have been drawn to admit the broadest local liberty in constructing a revenue system, those more typical of the wishes of single taxers either have provided specifically, as in Colorado in 1902, that the power of local exemption should not extend to the exemption of land, or, as in California in 1914, have not included land in the list of property which localities may be privileged to exempt. The Ohio proposal goes the farthest, since the only possible option in departing from the existing tax system would be the adoption of the land tax system for local purposes.

[21] The most important general discussions of the merits of local option in taxation are the following: Tuttle, Local Option in Taxation, Municipal Affairs, vol. 2, pp. 395-410, (1898); Wolff, Home Rule in Taxation, Proceedings of First National Tax Conference, 1907, pp. 107-20; Bullock, Local Option in Taxation, Proceedings of National Tax Conference, 1911, pp. 271-87, and discussion of local option, ibid., 288-97; Report of the Oregon Board of State Tax Commissioners, 1911, pp. 22-27; Discussion of Home Rule and Reform in Taxation, Convention of League of California Municipalities, Santa Barbara, 1911; Transactions of the Commonwealth Club of California, San Francisco, vol. 7, pp. 375-460 (Oct., 1912), and ibid., vol. 9, pp. 259-88 (May, 1914); Secrist, Home Rule in Taxation, Quarterly Jour. of Economics, vol. 28, pp. 490-505 (1914); and Report of the Wisconsin Tax Commission, 1914, pp. 128-31.

[22] Bullock, op. cit., p. 277. Bullock concludes that "except for the single taxer, the plan has few advantages and many dangers" (p. 281).

Considering the sort of local option measures which have been proposed and the manner in which they have been advocated, there is much to bear out the view of Professor Bullock that with the single taxers local option is "a mere question of tactics rather than . . . a question of principle", and that "if political control of any state ever passes into the hands of the single taxers, it is probable that the principle of home rule in taxation will lose much of its present popularity".[23] One of the sponsors of the proposed Ohio amendment said in reply to single taxers who had objected to its narrowness:

"Our decision to support the former type of measure was dictated by frankness. Wherever home rule in taxation has been promoted by single taxers, they are immediately accused of trying to bring about the single tax by stealth. We do not propose to risk any doubts or suspicions as to the nature of our purposes nor the personnel of our backing.

"Home rule in taxation, as an abstract proposal, has never greatly enthused any voting population."[24]

It should be remembered, however, that single taxers, with their extreme individualism and Jeffersonian view of decentralization,[25] do have a real leaning, apart from tactical considerations, toward the granting of extensive home rule powers to localities.

With single taxers, then, home rule in taxation is generally favored as the best method for making possible the securing of the single tax. The hope of the single taxers is that, local option gained, the single tax will be applied somewhere as the result of concentrated attack upon the most favorable opening, a city or county. Thereupon,

[23] Ibid., p. 274. Cf. in this connection the statement of a writer in the Single Tax Rev., Jan.-Feb., 1915 (p. 4), that "they consider it [local option] only as the 'shortest road to single tax'". (Arnold, The Present Program and Status of the Single Tax Reform.)

[24] The Public, Aug. 13, 1915, p. 784.

[25] Cf. The Life of Henry George, p. 604.

subtle economic forces will be set in motion which, single taxers believe, will compel its general adoption. They believe that either (1) the object lesson of its advantages where it is being applied will be of such a positive nature that other cities and counties will be led by self-interest to institute the system; or that (2) if for any reason they should be reluctant, an economic pressure which cannot long be resisted will force them to it, since investors and manufacturers will be attracted to the non-improvement-taxing localities, the penalty of delay being the risk of being left behind in the race for prosperity.[26]   Thus one locality after another would be induced or forced to adopt the single tax, and the working of this economic pressure, single taxers believe, would in practice make impossible the choice under home rule of any tax system other than theirs.   To quote Professor Bullock again, "it is believed that, while the law might extend local option to all localities, economic forces would effectually deny it to any community that did not desire to exempt all personal property or adopt the single tax".[27]

Opponents of the principle of home rule believe that the operation of any *system* of taxation is best controlled by

[26] Formerly single taxers emphasized the persuasive influence of the object lesson of advantages rather than the club of economic pressure as the force relied upon to bring about the spread of the system.   The former consideration was stressed the more in the Delaware campaign. (Supra, ch. 8.)

[27] Bullock, op. cit., p. 281.   Cf. also the following comment from a report adverse to local option in taxation, Transactions of the Commonwealth Club of California, San Francisco, May, 1914, vol. 9, p. 270: "A system of exemptions by a single community might prove profitable to that community as a whole, but any such temporary advantage would soon be nullified by the actions of other communities and the net result of the competitive bidding would simply be that all of our exemptions would be exhausted and we would be on a single tax basis."

central authority, and oppose decentralization.[28] They fear the possible consequences of granting to localities the right to exempt, pointing out that in many cases where states have granted a limited local option in the matter of temporary exemption of new manufacturing plants, an undesirable competition of localities has ensued, the law serving "as a cudgel rather than a bait" in the hands of certain business interests.[29] The views of the late A. B. Nye, Controller of California, are worthy of citation in this connection:

"Home rule in taxation is a phrase which sounds well, and it is especially attractive when the plausible advocate holds forth the inducement that under it each community can establish that plan of taxation which best suits its needs or attracts its fancy. But this is not consistent with the other argument, which is also emphasized, that home rule gives every community a means of aggression or of defense, by enabling it to bid against other communities with tax exemptions, and thus capture or retain business. For a city or county which can thus be put on the defensive, and compelled to relieve property of taxation in order to avoid the loss of business which some other town or county is seeking to acquire, can hardly be said to have a perfectly free will in matters of taxation. Indeed, one of the first, and probably most far-reaching, effects of the system would be to set up a keen competition between rival communities, in which the prize of victory would be business advantage and the weapons would be tax exemptions. As in most battles, all of the combatants would be damaged more or less, and the principal gainers would be certain business interests which can well afford to pay taxes, but which would in this way be offered a fine chance for escaping them.

"It is in this inevitable competitive contest that the single taxers see their advantage in home rule. Their motto is, 'Never tax anything which can run away', and as land is the

[28] For development of this argument, see T. S. Adams, Separation of the Sources of State and Local Revenue as a Program of Tax Reform, Proceedings of National Tax Conference, 1907, pp. 515-27.

[29] New Hampshire Tax Commission, 1908 (p. 154), quoted by Bullock, op. cit., p. 278.

most immovable of all things, they argue that the almost certain result of a few years of home rule competition will be the exemption of other forms of property and the raising of all revenues by land taxation. In this forecast I entirely agree with them.

"It is not worth while to make an argument against single tax. Assume, if you please, that it is the correct theory of taxation; but if it is to be established in our household we want it to come in through the front door, in broad daylight, and not after dark, through a rear window which has been inadvertently left open."[30]

Opponents of the single tax and of the heavier taxation of land naturally fight home rule in taxation, since it opens up the possibility of their being obliged to wage guerilla warfare against these proposals.

Single taxers and direct legislation

Most single taxers advocate the initiative and referendum as "the highest known method of democratic government—the referendum as a people's veto, the initiative as a people's command".[31] This advocacy dates back at least to 1893, when the National Single Tax Conference at Chicago unanimously adopted a resolution favoring the initiative and referendum and also proportional representation.[32] Many of the leading advocates of these measures, e.g., W. S. U'Ren of Oregon, have been single taxers. The Fels Fund Commission has taken an active part in the direct legislation movement, lending aid to it in New Mexico, Arizona, Colorado, Arkansas, Minnesota, and Ohio.[33]

[30] Transactions of the Commonwealth Club of California, San Francisco, Oct., 1912, vol. 7, no. 4, pp. 402-03. This number contains a valuable discussion of home rule in taxation.

The single tax reply to the argument presented in this citation is that such a state of affairs has not come about in western Canada. Ibid., pp. 392-93; 412-13.

[31] The Public, Nov. 22, 1912, p. 1107.

[32] Justice, Jan. 12, 1895, p. 7.

[33] Supra, ch. 9.

Single taxers favor the initiative in particular because the getting up of a petition effectually opens the way for their campaigns in spite of hostile legislatures, and because it affords a means of popular education regarding the single tax. Jackson H. Ralston, a member of the Joseph Fels Fund Commission, said at the 1910 Fels Fund Conference: "As for direct legislation, it bears to single tax as close a relation as a lock does to the door".[34]

Some single taxers have criticized the Commission for devoting too much attention to work in behalf of direct legislation, believing that the system now obtains in enough states to give a field for single tax experiment with initiative measures. One critic urged that "labors for further extension of the system may well be left to other hands, while single taxers devote themselves to the more important work of teaching men their economic rights".[35]

Single taxers and the separate assessment of land and improvements

The practice of separately assessing land and improvements, which most students of taxation hold conduces to greater accuracy and fairness than the practice of making a single lump-sum valuation, has claimed the active support of single taxers.

We have already discussed the origin of this practice in California, where separate assessments were made as early as 1852.[36] California probably became the first state to adopt the system when the Code of 1872 prescribed it for the entire state. The city of Buffalo, New York, adopted it in 1876.[37] The New York State Board of Assessors, in

[34] Report of the Single Tax Conference held in New York City November 19-20, 1910, under the auspices of the Joseph Fels Fund Commission, Cincinnati, 1911, p. 17.
[35] Single Tax Rev., Sept.-Oct., 1910, p. 35.
[36] Supra, p. 62 et seq.
[37] Lawson Purdy, in Single Tax Rev., Apr. 15, 1903, p. 26.

their report of 1878, recommended "that all assessors, in order to arrive at the full and true value of the real estate, be required to assess the value of the land and buildings thereon separately".[38] In 1892 the system was applied to cities of the first and second classes in New Jersey.[39] Its adoption for New York City in 1903 and for the cities of that state in 1911, largely as the result of the efforts of single taxers, we have already mentioned.[40] The practice of separate assessment of land and improvements, besides being prescribed for California and the cities of New York state, is provided for by the following states: Arkansas, Idaho, Maine, Minnesota, Nebraska, New Hampshire, New Jersey, Rhode Island, South Dakota, Utah, Wisconsin, and Wyoming.[41]

Single taxers favor the New York system—of placing in separate columns the value of land and the value of land plus improvements—since they believe that to state separately the value of improvements introduces a tendency to overvalue them.

The making of separate assessments has rendered possible comparison of the values of land and improvements. By revealing the tremendous amount of unearned increments of land values, particularly in cities, it has furnished single taxers with figures which have become powerful arguments in their hands.[42] The propaganda literature

[38] Cited by Lawson Purdy, ibid., p. 26.
[39] Ibid., p. 25.
[40] Supra, p. 216.
[41] This statement is based upon an examination of a Census Bulletin of 1914, Taxation and revenue systems of state and local governments (a digest of constitutional and statutory provisions relating to taxation in the different states in 1912), Washington, 1914, pp. 24, 65, 101, 121, 140, 149, 153, 204, 215, 234, 263, and 271. This list is probably not a complete representation of the localities where separate assessment of land and improvements is practised.
[42] See Albert Firmin, The Land Rent of Manhattan, 1813-1912, a

used in the later single tax campaigns has made extensive
use of such statistics.

The relations of single taxers to political parties

When in 1887 the defeat of the United Labor Party had
destroyed its power, single taxers faced the problem of a
method of advance. Henry George believed that the best
work could be done at that time through the Democratic
Party, which President Cleveland's noteworthy tariff message of 1887 had practically committed to tariff reform.
There were some, indeed, who wished to keep the movement "pure" by steering clear of alliances with political parties not committed to the single tax. But Henry George
believed that independent political action would be futile
and confusing, and to this belief he won over the more substantial single taxers.[43] From that time until the present
most single taxers have affiliated themselves with this party,
being particularly attracted by its advocacy of tariff reform and states' rights. Few have been Republicans, because single taxers generally oppose the stand of that party
on the tariff question and imperialism, and regard it as a
defender of "Wall Street" and "privilege".

A great many single taxers were in the Populist movement because of their approval of free silver, government
ownership, popular election of senators, abolition of national
banks, and other measures which that party demanded.
The Populist platform of 1892 contained a radical declaration against land monopoly.

On the silver issue single taxers generally went with
Bryan, both because of his money views and because of
a declaration on the land question which was much quoted

Century of Tribute, Single Tax Rev., Nov.-Dec., 1913, pp. 63-75; and
the Tenants' Monthly (New York), Sept. and Oct., 1915.
    [48] Supra, ch. 7.

in single tax literature of the time.[44]   Also they believed
that he represented the popular ideal in government as opposed to the Mark Hanna doctrine.[45]   Some of the more
influential single taxers of the East, however, opposed the
silver movement, and, led by Shearman, Garrison, Shriver,
Murphy, and Fillebrown, issued a circular which stated:
"We do not maintain that the single tax is, or ought to be,
identified with the [sic] gold standard any more than with
the silver standard; but we do hold that our cause cannot
afford to be associated with a proposal that must have dishonest results, with whatever honesty of purpose it may be
advocated".[46]   But the rank and file of the movement regarded the action of this group of leaders somewhat in the
light of treason.[47]   In fact, there has hardly been a novelty
of money reform that has not found adherents among
single taxers.

The Progressive Party included a number of single taxers,
e.g., Raymond Robins of Illinois; E. B. Osborne, Everett
Colby, and George L. Record of New Jersey; and Amos
Pinchot of Pennsylvania.   Single taxers acclaimed Roosevelt when, writing in the *Century Magazine,* October, 1913,
he declared for municipal self-government in taxation and
the heavier taxation of the unearned increase in the value
of land.[48]

The question of independent single tax political action
did not down when Henry George declared against it in
1887-1888.   In 1899 single taxers ran candidates for city

[44] Supra, p. 150.

[45] For George's reasons for supporting the Bryan movement, see The
Life of Henry George, pp. 580-83.

[46] Cited in Justice, Nov. 7, 1896, p. 3.

[47] When the Executive Committee of the Massachusetts Single Tax
League failed to endorse Bryan, a meeting of five hundred single
taxers on Boston Common adopted resolutions protesting against the
gold standard.   See Justice, Aug. 8, 1896, p. 4, and Oct. 17, 1896, p. 2.

[48] Century Magazine, vol. 86, pp. 834-35 (1913).

offices in Philadelphia; in 1901 in Cincinnati; and in 1902 in Chicago.[49]   As an outgrowth of the recent activity of single taxers in New York City, the Land Value Tax Party was organized.[50]   This party ran candidates at the city election of 1913.

Single taxers as candidates and public officials

Henry George, in his three New York campaigns, set an example to his followers in seeking public office as a means to further the progress of his theories.   Besides Henry George there have been a considerable number of single taxers in connection with whose candidacy the single tax issue has been raised.

A number of single taxers, mainly Democrats, have been members of Congress and several have been governors of states.   Tom L. Johnson did good service for the cause as a congressman and later as mayor of Cleveland.[51] Henry George's son, Henry George, Jr., was a member of the Sixty-third Congress representing New York.   Many single taxers have held offices of lesser prominence, as members of state legislatures and in city governments, especially in connection with the tax departments.

Political activity and educational propaganda

The revival of single tax political activity which has been brought about under the direction of the Joseph Fels Fund Commission has led to considerable discussion as to whether political activity is the best means of advancing the cause. Some single taxers have questioned the wisdom of these political campaigns, believing that educational propaganda has been neglected.   Chief among the critics of single tax

[49] National Single Taxer, Feb., 1899, p. 19; Feb.-Mar., 1901, p. 13; Single Tax Rev., Jan. 15, 1903, p. 48.
[50] Single Tax Rev., Sept.-Oct., 1913, pp. 42-51.
[51] See Johnson's autobiography, My Story, New York, 1911.

tactics is Charles B. Fillebrown, who believes that "if any one thing is prominently in evidence, it is that the formal combination of the single tax with political action and methods has been uniformly disastrous to the single tax".[52] Fillebrown believes that George's three New York campaigns and the attempt to capture Delaware (which Fillebrown at the time supported[53]) were productive of more harm than good to the cause. Regarding the more recent political activities, he wrote:

"In the last two years political methods have once more been invoked in connection with the expenditure of a couple of hundred thousand dollars of most generous money and much vigorous and unselfish effort by speakers and organizers to carry elections in Missouri, Washington, Oregon and other parts of the country. With what result?—that to-day in those regions the press is closed and the farmers' minds are closed, and that both will be so much the harder to open in future.

" . . . It cannot be gainsaid that the political method as a means of putting the single tax on the statute books has been abundantly tried and found wanting, and the reasons for its failure are not far to seek. Voters cannot be persuaded to decree an important legislative innovation which they do not fully understand and concerning which it is easy for the opposition in the heat of a campaign, to deceive or confuse the mind."[54]

Fillebrown believes that "persistent education of the masses and the classes—by word of mouth and still more effectively by the printing press—upon the pure issue of the single tax as the normal and just basis for obtaining public revenue", is the true means and method of advancing the cause.[55]

Most single taxers do not agree with these views, believing that political campaigns offer the best possible op-

[52] Fillebrown, Thirty Years of Henry George, Boston, 1913, p. 8.
[53] See Justice, Feb. 29, 1896, p. 1; May 23, 1896, pp. 1, 4.
[54] Fillebrown, op. cit., pp. 11-12.
[55] Ibid., p. 12.

portunity for carrying on a campaign of education. At the
Joseph Fels Fund Conference held in Washington in 1914,
the issue was raised in connection with the reading of a
letter in which Fillebrown presented his views. On vote as
to whether political action or educational propaganda should
be the main work of the organized single tax movement,
the members of the convention, enthusiastic over single
tax successes in Pueblo, Pittsburgh, and Scranton, voted for
the former with only a murmur of negative votes.

It is an important practical question for single taxers as
to whether any given political campaign is timely. Whatever advance the single taxers can make when their program is understood, they can manifestly expect little when
it is not understood.

Single tax organizations and their activities[56]

The several single tax political campaigns have evoked a
variety of methods of propaganda, in the way of literature
distribution, newspapers, speaking campaigns, personal
work, and campaign organizations. We have already
treated them as they have developed in connection with
particular campaigns. Also ardent individual propagandists have employed various methods, such as vacant lot
signs, single tax "stickers," single tax letter-heads and
blotters, the circulation of literature with their letters, and
the production of "Single Tax Cigars." It remains to
consider some of the more permanent agencies of the
movement.

Since the organizing movement of 1888-90 there has
been an ebb and flow in the number and influence of the
single tax organizations of the country. We have seen that
in 1889 there were one hundred and thirty-one organiza-

[56] A description of the Joseph Fels Fund of America is given in ch. 9,
supra.

tions.[57] The *Single Tax Review* (September-October, 1915) listed forty-six organizations in the United States,[58] which number, however, is not directly comparable to the number listed in 1889, because some of the organizations in the later list have a wider field, with branch organizations.

The local organizations have been centers from which single tax influence has radiated. Their activities include the holding of stated meetings, the maintenance of reading rooms and the circulation of literature, the organization of "Single Tax Reading Circles", the offering of classes or lectures on "political economy", and the placing of speakers before various organizations. These single tax organizations have often participated actively in the agitation of the tax question, generally with a view to securing the proposal of a single tax or home rule in taxation measure before a state legislature or for the vote of the electorate.

An organization which has done good propaganda work for the single tax cause is the "Henry George Lecture Association", established in 1899 with headquarters at Chicago.[59] F. H. Monroe is its president. Its work consists in placing single tax speakers before organizations of various sorts in all parts of the United States, and in this way it has exerted a wide influence. The Henry George Lecture Association has published a directory of those who have subscribed one or more times to its work since 1903; this directory is the best index of single taxers which has been published, and contains twenty-five hundred to three thousand names.[60]

[57] Supra, p. 138.
[58] Single Tax Rev., Sept.-Oct., 1915, pp. 314-15.
[59] The headquarters of the Association are at 538 S. Dearborn St., Chicago.
[60] Edition of Nov. 8, 1912. This directory "is issued for the convenience of subscribers only and to facilitate acquaintance and organization".

Another sort of propaganda organization is the "Single Tax Information Bureau", best developed by E. B. Swinney of Brooklyn. The report of this Bureau shows that from 1903 to 1910 there were more than 12,000 requests for literature, and that more than 350,000 pieces of literature were sent out.[61]

There has never been an active, continuing national single tax organization in the United States. The "Single Tax League of the United States", formed at the National Conference of 1890,[62] proved to be an organization mainly on paper. At a national conference held in New York in 1907, the "American Single Tax League" was formed,[63] but it likewise has not played a very prominent part in the subsequent history of the movement. The "Women's National Single Tax League", organized in 1898, has held annual conventions.[64] The Joseph Fels Fund Commission has effected an informal national organization, cemented by means of its annual conferences.[65]

Single tax periodicals.

Almost continuously since Henry George established his weekly, *The Standard*,[66] in New York in 1887 there have been authoritative organs of the single tax movement, some of which have exerted wide influence. When in August,

[61] Single Tax Rev., Jan.-Feb., 1911, pp. 52-53.
[62] Supra, p. 139.
[63] The Single Tax Rev., Jan.-Feb., 1908, pp. 12, 18. For its first annual report, see ibid., Mar.-Apr., 1909, pp. 50-52.
[64] Ibid., July-Aug., 1912, pp. 55-59. Women have played an important part in single tax work, and there is scarcely a single taxer who is not an ardent advocate of woman suffrage.
[65] Supra, ch. 9.
[66] Supra, p. 109. Complete files of The Standard are in the New York City Public Library, the Library of Columbia University, and the John Crerar Library, Chicago.

1892, *The Standard* suspended publication, the St. Louis *Courier*,[67] and *Justice*,[68] a weekly published in Philadelphia and later in Wilmington, Delaware, became the main single tax organs.

In 1896 the *Courier* became the *National Single Taxer*,[69] published first at Minneapolis and, after 1898, at New York, part of the time a weekly and part of the time a monthly. In 1901 the *National Single Taxer* evolved into the *Single Tax Review*,[70] published at New York City, which since that time, has been the chief organ of the movement. Joseph Dana Miller has been its editor from the start. The *Single Tax Review* appeared quarterly until 1908; since that time it has appeared bi-monthly.

The *Joseph Fels Fund Bulletin*, a four page monthly published at Cincinnati, is the official organ of the Joseph Fels Fund Commission. It was established in January, 1913.

Besides the specialized single tax periodicals there are several periodicals which, edited by single taxers, have actively advocated the single tax.

The *Public*,[71] founded by Louis F. Post in 1898, is a weekly published at Chicago. Samuel Danziger has edited *The Public* since 1913, when Post resigned to become Assistant Secretary of Labor. The Joseph Fels Fund Commission has contributed to the support of *The Public*.[72]

[67] So far as the writer knows there is extant no file of the St. Louis Courier.
[68] The files of Justice, 1895-98, are in the Library of Princeton University.
[69] A nearly complete file of the National Single Taxer is in the New York City Public Library.
[70] Complete files of The Single Tax Review are in the New York City Public Library and the Library of Princeton University.
[71] The New York City Public Library has a nearly complete file of The Public.
[72] Supra, p. 167.

The San Francisco *Star,* published by J. H. Barry since 1884, and the St. Louis *Mirror,* edited by W. M. Reedy, have advocated the single tax as a main part of their editorial policy.

There also have been many local periodicals devoted to the interests of the single tax cause in various parts of the country. The names of those that are now defunct are too numerous to mention. The more important of the local single tax periodicals published at the present writing (1916) are: the Fairhope, Alabama, *Courier;* the *Tenants' Monthly,* New York City; the *Single Taxer,* Denver; *Tax Talk* and *Everyman,* Los Angeles; and *The Ground Hog,* Cleveland.[73] Besides, there are newspapers and periodicals throughout the United States which favor the single tax.

In the nineties the papers of the Middle West using "patent insides" were supplied with single tax copy through various newspaper syndicates, a work which must have had considerable influence. The "American Economic League", which is the press bureau department of the Fels Fund Commission organization, supplies single tax matter regularly to several hundred newspapers.

The single tax colony at Fairhope, Alabama.[74]

"The Fairhope Industrial Association"—whose name was changed in 1904 to the "The Fairhope Single Tax Corporation"—was organized in February, 1894, at Des

[73] Cf. a list of periodicals in the Single Tax Rev., Sept.-Oct., 1915, p. 315, and in other issues.

[74] The writer is indebted to E. B. Gaston, Secretary of the Fairhope Corporation during almost the entire period of its history, for material upon which to base this account, and to F. F. Anderson for a copy of the latter's pamphlet criticizing the Fairhope experiment.

For general accounts of the Fairhope experiment, see Gaston, Fairhope, the Home of the Single Tax and the Referendum, New York Independent, vol. 55, p. 1670 (1903); G. L. Tucker, A Single Tax

Moines, Iowa.[75] Its founders wished to establish a colony
which should apply single tax principles so far as was
possible under the existing laws of American common-
wealths. The search for a location was assigned to a committee of two, who made an investigation of a number of
possible situations in the Southern states.[76] As a result of
their search, the colonists selected a location on a high bluff
on the eastern shore of Mobile Bay, sixteen miles from the
city of Mobile.

On the 14th of January, 1895, ground was broken at
Fairhope. The founders consisted of five families, who
subscribed two hundred dollars each for membership. With
this a tract of three hundred and fifty acres was purchased
at prices of from $1.25 to $6.00 per acre.[77] This land was
deeded to the corporation, which became the landlord of the
settlement. Since the colonists were not experienced agri-
culturists, they had a rather hard time at the start. Real
pioneer work confronted them and the first year's work
consisted largely of clearing the ground and raising a
small crop, a part of which was sold.[78]

The Fairhope plan is based upon an arrangement by

Community, New York Nation, Apr. 2, 1896, p. 269; P. Trenchard,
The Only Single Tax Colony in the World, The World Today, vol.
11, pp. 1211-13 (1906) ; Helen C. Bennett, A Single Tax Colony Which
Has Made Good, Colliers, vol. 49, pp. 24, 44-46 (Sept. 14, 1912) ; and
W. A. Hinds, American Communities and Coöperative Colonies, Chi-
cago, 1908, pp. 505-12.

Arden, Del., is another single tax colony whose plan, however, is
nothing like as completely worked out as that of Fairhope. For a
description of Arden, see Single Tax Rev., Oct. 15, 1907, pp. 41-42;
New York Independent, vol. 71, pp. 299-304 (1911).

[75] Constitution of Fairhope Single Tax Corporation, 1911, p. 1.
[76] Tucker, op. cit., p. 269.
[77] Gaston, op. cit., p. 1671; Gaston, Fairhope Single Tax Colony,
in a prospectus, Fairhope, Ala., The All-Year Resort of the South, n. d.
[78] Tucker, op. cit., p. 269.

which the corporation holds all land "as trustee for its entire membership." Persons over the age of eighteen years whose applications are approved by the Executive Committee may become members of the corporation upon payment of one hundred dollars; but upon petition of ten per cent of the membership the application is submitted to a vote of the membership. The husband or wife of a member may become a member by signing the constitution.[79] The constitution provides that the lands "shall be equitably divided and leased to members at an annually appraised rental which shall equalize the varying advantages of location and natural qualities of different tracts".[80] Rentals are determined once a year by the Executive Council, subject to a referendum of the members. Leases convey full right to the use and control of the land and the ownership and disposition of improvements on it so long as the lessee pays the annually appraised rentals.[81] These leases are assignable to members of the corporation. Transfers of leases, accompanied by sales of improvements, are said to be quite common. Indeed, it is claimed that transfers are more readily made, since purchasers need consider improvements alone—investing none of their capital directly in land.[82] The secretary of the corporation stated that in years but one tenant has been dispossessed for non-payment of rent.[83]

The rentals provide a fund from which are paid "all taxes levied by the state, county or township, on the property of the corporation or any of its members held within

[79] Constitution of Fairhope Single Tax Corporation, 1911, Art. II.
[80] Ibid., Art. VIII, Sec. 2.
[81] Ibid., Art. VIII, Sec. 3.
[82] Gaston, op. cit., p. 1676.
[83] Fairhope Courier, May 22, 1914, p. 4.

its jurisdiction, moneys and credits excepted".[84]   The corporation also pays the road and poll taxes ($4.00 and $1.50 respectively) of its lessees.[85]

Fairhope has never been a colony made up of single taxers alone.   Indeed, not all the founders were orthodox in that faith, their number including communists and other radicals.[86]   One of the single tax founders stated that "all through our later history we have had with us probably a majority who strongly espoused the socialistic faith".[87]   The numerical growth of Fairhope has come, not so much from single taxers, as from radicals of various stripes and from those who were attracted by Fairhope's desirability as a resort.   In 1908 the town of Fairhope was incorporated under the laws of Alabama.

The history of Fairhope has not been a record of complete harmony.   There have been critics without and discontent within.[88]

The discontent culminated in a suit for dissolution of the Fairhope Single Tax Corporation, brought in April, 1914, by Alexander J. Melville.[89]   The text of this complaint summarizes the chief items of discontent, which were: that the rentals fixed were out of all proportion to the value of the use of the land, and that they were "made openly for the purpose of raising the amount necessary to pay the company's obligation and without regard to actual

[84] Constitution of Fairhope Single Tax Corporation, 1911, Art. XIV.
[85] Gaston, Fairhope Single Tax Colony, op. cit.
[86] The Public, May 7, 1915, p. 447.
[87] Bellangee, Fairhope, Its Problems and Its Future, Single Tax Rev., May-June, 1913, p. 20.
[88] See Memorial of Protesting Fairhope Tenants, Single Tax Rev., Apr. 15, 1905, pp. 43-44; The Fairhope Monitor, vol. 1, no. 1, June, 1913; Bellangee, op. cit., pp. 17-27; and F. F. Anderson, Fairhope, A Study in Primitive Altruism, 1913.
[89] The text of the complaint is in the Fairhope Courier, May 22, 1914.

rental value"; that the tenants were burdened to pay taxes
on the unleased and unproductive land of the corporation;
that overhead expenses were too high, since the town and
the Fairhope corporation maintained duplicate administrative organizations; that the management was inefficient and
that Fairhope's show of prosperity had been kept up only
by the gifts of Fels and other outside single taxers; and that
the administration was "obstinately undemocratic" in that
the constitution denied to non-members a voice in deciding
upon policies.[90]

In June, 1915, the Supreme Court of Alabama overruled
the decision of the Mobile Chancery Court, which had decided against Fairhope, and dismissed the suit.[91] The Fairhope corporation met the charges brought against it to the
satisfaction of the Court. As to the charge that rentals
were excessive E. B. Gaston, secretary of the Fairhope corporation, stated that "the rents are now, as they have all
along been, such as to make it very much more to the
interest of the land user to locate on the corporation's land
than to purchase of other land owners".[92] He said that the
proceeds from timber on unleased lands were more than
sufficient to meet the taxes on them. Regarding the criticisms of management and administration, it was replied that
Fairhope was not a government but a voluntary association

[90] Anderson, op. cit., pp. 6-7. The most persistent criticism of Fairhope has been that its management is a self-perpetuating oligarchy.
Critics have pointed out that the constitution is practically unamend-
able. It requires a three-fourths vote of the total membership of the
corporation to amend (Art. VII, Sec. 7), and a considerable number
of the members reside away from Fairhope.

[91] See The Public, July 23, 1915, pp. 716-17, for a citation of the
opinion of the Court.

[92] Fairhope Courier, May 22, 1914, p. 2. This issue of the Courier
contains Gaston's answer in behalf of Fairhope to the charges made
in the complaint.

with definite aims, and that control must be kept within
the membership of the corporation to insure the carrying
out of these aims.[93] The defenders of Fairhope charged
that the suit was really intended as an attempt to discredit
the single tax.

Fairhope's promoters point to its prosperous condition as
evidence of the success of their idea. They claim that
Fairhope, with a population of about 700, "has notoriously
outgrown every other settlement on the eastern shore".[94]
Four-fifths of the population of the town of Fairhope and
practically all of its business institutions are on corporation land.[95] The total land holdings (1914) of the Fairhope Single Tax Corporation are about four thousand
acres.[96] There are more than 250 lessees,[97] the rents
ranging from twenty-five cents to about $2.00 per acre for
farm land and from $4.00 to $45.00 for residence lots.[98]
The value of the corporation's land holdings is estimated
at more than $100,000.[99] For 1915 the gross rental was
$5,792.14, and the surplus over taxes and fixed charges was
$1,438.39.[100] This surplus goes to running expenses and
public improvements. These include the support of public
utilities, which must be provided by the corporation since
the constitution forbids the granting of franchises.[101] The
utilities include a phone system, a water works, and a wharf,
the latter being the most successful venture.

[93] See Single Tax Review, July-Aug., 1913, pp. 49-50.
[94] Fairhope Courier, May 22, 1914, p. 2.
[95] Idem.
[96] A generous benefactor, presumably Joseph Fels, gave 2,200 acres
of this. Anderson, op. cit., pp. 2, 6-7.
[97] Fairhope Courier, May 22, 1914, p. 1.
[98] Gaston, Fairhope Single Tax Colony, op. cit.
[99] The Public, May 7, 1915, p. 448.
[100] Idem.
[101] Art. X.

Single taxers are not unanimous in their attitude toward Fairhope. Some believe that it is "one of the most practical and valuable efforts being made today [1909] for the cause".[102] Others agree with Henry George's opinion of "a single tax city", expressed in *The Standard* in 1889, that "the single tax cannot be fairly tried on a small scale in a community not subject to the single tax",[103] and that the success or failure of such an experiment proves nothing at all regarding the larger aspects of the program.

[102] Statement of Joseph Fels, Daniel Kiefer, H. F. Ring, and J. J. Pastoriza, in Fairhope Courier, Jan. 8, 1909, pp. 3, 7.

[103] The Standard, Nov. 2, 1889, pp. 2-3.

CHAPTER XIII

THE SINGLE TAX AND THE TAXATION OF
LAND VALUES

What is the single tax?[1]

In the case of the term *single tax* the general meaning
has given place to a special meaning. In the general sense
the term refers to a plan of raising public revenue under
which there would be but a single tax. There have been
several such proposals other than Henry George's single
land tax, notably the *impôt unique* of the French Physiocrats and the single income taxes which some of the socialists have urged.[2] But to-day the term single tax—or, as
some of its advocates are preferring to write it, *singletax*[3]—
distinctively suggests George's proposal or some variation
of it.

Henry George's own words in *Progress and Poverty* offer
perhaps the most workable definition of the single tax—the

[1] The aim of this section is to consider the connotation of the term
single tax rather than to present the single tax argument. For that
cf. the works of Henry George, Thomas G. Shearman, C. B. Fillebrown,
and Louis F. Post, also the propagandist writings of other single
taxers. There is a considerable literature of pamphlets giving good
presentations of the single tax argument. One of the best brief ex-
positions, which the Fels Fund Commission has given a wide circulation, is The Taxation of Land Values, by Frederic C. Howe.
[2] For a discussion of the anticipations of Henry George's single tax
cf. ch. 1, supra.
[3] Cf. Post, The Taxation of Land Values, preface to fifth edition,
Indianapolis, 1915.

proposal "to abolish all taxation save that upon land values".[4]   There are good reasons for restricting to this meaning the employment of the term. Since 1887, when Henry George and Thomas G. Shearman devised the term single tax,[5] it has been used in this sense both widely and discriminatingly. Furthermore the pretty well defined group of followers of Henry George who call themselves single taxers accept it with this meaning. Nevertheless there is no uniformity of usage. The term single tax has suffered so from careless use that it has become almost as difficult to define as socialism.

Popularly a miscellaneous lot of schemes, varying all the way from Henry George's plan for state appropriation of land incomes to proposals for taxation of the future "unearned increment" of land values, have been dubbed single tax. We often hear it stated that western Canada, or New Zealand, or England under the Lloyd-George budget of 1909, or Houston, Texas, or some other place enjoys the single tax. Had there been an adjective, "single-taxic", it might have been possible to have obviated in part such unprecise usage. It is difficult to justify applying the title single taxer to one not sharing George's view of the general exploitative nature of private receipt of income from land. Clearly the term single tax is strained until it is meaningless when applied to plans of taxation which contemplate merely special taxation of land, without doing away with commodity, income, inheritance, or business taxes.

It should first of all be kept in mind that the single tax, as Henry George proposed it in *Progress and Poverty* (1879), was primarily a project for social rather than fiscal reform. The fiscal aspect, however, has received dispro-

---

[4] Progress and Poverty, bk. 8, ch. 2, p. 404.
[5] Supra, p. 109 et seq.

portionate emphasis because of the opportunism of single
taxers, their working for laws to increase taxes upon land as
a step in the direction of the full measure of the single tax.
"The wide-spreading social evils which everywhere oppress
men amid an advancing civilization", wrote George, "spring
from a great primary wrong—the appropriation, as the
exclusive property of some men, of the land on which and
from which all must live".[6] It was to remedy this wrong, to
prevent the continued appropriation by land-owners, a favored class, of what nature had designed for all, that Henry
George proposed the single tax, which was to absorb annually as nearly as possible the entire use or rental value of
all lands. The single tax thus was not in itself the end of
Henry George's scheme; it was his ingeniously devised
method for abolishing private property in land and applying
land values to the common use.

   Henry George believed that there were two fundamental
economic wrongs in the existing economic organization of
society: (1) private ownership of land, or, as some single
taxers would prefer to state it, private receipt of income
from land; and (2) the levying of taxes upon anything
other than land. Private ownership of land, the value of
which increases with progress, was the chief cause of poverty and misery, while the burdens of taxation, which bore
most heavily upon the poor and industrious, aggravated
these evils.

   Henry George's remedy is closely related to these premises. Rejecting the formal abolition of private land titles
with or without state purchase of land, he proposed "to
appropriate rent by taxation."[7] To cite a much quoted
paragraph:

[6] Progress and Poverty, bk. 7, ch. 1. p. 338.
[7] Ibid., bk. 8, ch. 2, p. 404.

"I do not propose either to purchase or to confiscate private property in land. The first would be unjust; the second, needless. Let the individuals who now hold it still retain, if they want to, possession of what they are pleased to call *their* land. Let them continue to call it *their* land. Let them buy and sell, and bequeath and devise it. We may safely leave them the shell, if we take the kernel. *It is not necessary to confiscate land; it is only necessary to confiscate rent.*"[8]

Henry George's single tax was thus to be made high enough to absorb the entire use or rental value of all lands,[9] thereby taking all of the value of land for the common use. Since the selling value of a piece of land is but the present value of the expected future incomes which the owner hopes to gain by reason of his ownership, the selling value of land would fall to zero were the tax to take annually the entire use value. Henry George intended that land ownership should be utterly profitless under the single tax.

Since in his opinion a land tax of such dimensions would provide an ample revenue for the state,[10] all other taxes could readily be abolished. The effect of this, Henry George believed, would be "to lift the whole enormous weight of taxation from productive industry."[11]

George confidently believed that the carrying out of the single tax program would usher in the economic millenium. It would "solve the labor problem, do away with involuntary poverty, raise wages in all occupations to the full earnings of labor, make overproduction impossible until all human wants are satisfied, render labor-saving inventions a blessing to all, and cause such an enormous production and such an equitable distribution of wealth as would give to

[8] Ibid., p. 403.
[9] Infra. pp. 262-63.
[10] Some critics of the single tax have disputed this proposition.
[11] Progress and Poverty, bk. 9, ch. 1, pp. 432-33.

all comfort, leisure, and participation in the advantages of an advancing civilization".[12]

Henry George's single tax thus is more than a mere tax. It is a far-reaching proposal which has back of it a complete system of economic doctrine with extensions into the fields of politics and social theory. Single taxers have often urged that the term single tax is descriptive not so much of their philosophy as of the method by which they would seek to realize their ideals. In 1889, shortly after the name single tax had become attached to the movement, Henry George wrote:

"The term single tax does not really express all that a perfect name would convey. It only suggests the fiscal side of our aims. And in reality the single tax is not a tax at all. But it is a tax in form, and the term is useful as suggesting method. . . .

"What we want to do is not merely to impose a certain kind of a tax, but to get rid of other taxes. Our proper name, if it would not seem too high flown, would be 'freedom men', or 'liberty men', or 'natural order men', for it is on establishing liberty, on removing restrictions, on giving natural order full play, and not on any mere fiscal change that we base our hopes of social reconstruction. . . .

"We want as few taxes as possible, as little restraint as is conformable to that perfect law of liberty which will allow each individual to do what he pleases without infringement of equal rights of others."[13]

In the course of the development of the American single tax movement but one modification of what we may term "the Henry George single tax" has gained any standing within the movement, the so-called "single tax limited". This we shall now discuss.

[12] Single Tax Platform, adopted by the National Conference of the Single Tax League of the United States, New York, Sept. 3, 1890. This platform was drafted by Henry George. It was reaffirmed by the 1912 Fels Fund Conference (The Public, Dec. 6, 1912, p. 1163). This platform is given infra as Appendix A.

[13] The Standard, Mar. 2, 1889. Cf. supra, pp. 110-11.

The "single tax limited"

The central thought of the single tax limited is that, if the revenue derived from land taxation should prove more than enough for the ordinary needs of the state, the surplus should remain in the hands of land-owners instead of being used for an extension of governmental expenditure. The basis for a distinction between the single tax limited and the Henry George single tax is of course the assumption that something less than the whole of income from land would adequately supply government needs on the present scale. On this point opponents of the single tax have adduced contradictory arguments. Some have urged that George's plan would provide revenues so enormous as to lead to wholesale waste and corruption; others have figured that it would be inadequate to meet the needs of the state. The term single tax limited was coined by Henry George himself in 1888 when, in the course of an address, he took occasion to contrast the position of "single tax men limited" with that of "single tax men unlimited", which latter position he endorsed.[14]

George believed that the state should take by taxation the whole of the "economic rent" of land, "as near as might be".[15] How nearly this might be done in practice he was not sure. Discussing in *The Standard* (1889) the question,

[14] These terms were first used by Henry George in an address which is printed in The Standard, Dec. 29, 1888, p. 3: "There are some who see the injustice of present taxation. There are some who would go so far as to substitute for our present modes of raising revenue this equal, simple, cheap method that does not hamper production, and then stop. Them we may call single tax men, limited. We who want to go the whole way—we are single tax men unlimited. But there is no reason why we should not, and every reason why we should, go together until we get to the point where our limited friends want to stop. They can then stop, if they choose, while we keep on."

[15] The Standard, Aug. 17, 1889, p. 2.

"How nearly may all 'economic rent' be taken?", he said: "This is a point as to which I am not and never have been clear. . . . About the best . . . anyone . . . could do in this regard would be to formulate some plan that should take *about* the whole of economic rent".[16]   The plan which George believed best was to let land-owners retain a margin as a sort of commission for collecting and paying in rent. If such a margin were left there would remain a selling value for land, thereby making it easier to assess.   The chief objection to such a plan, George believed, was that "in this way we could not collect the full amount of economic rent".

Henry George believed that, were the state to appropriate land incomes entirely, the resulting revenue would be greater than the present revenue of governments, and that the disposal of this increased revenue would involve an extension of the sphere of government activity.   To cite George's words:

"This revenue arising from the common property could be applied to the common benefit, as were the revenues of Sparta. We might not establish public tables—they would be unnecessary; but we could establish public baths, museums, libraries, gardens, lecture rooms, music and dancing halls, theatres, universities, technical schools, shooting galleries, playgrounds, gymnasiums, etc.   Heat, light, and motive power, as well as water, might be conducted through our streets at public expense; our roads be lined with fruit trees; discoverers and inventors rewarded, scientific investigations supported; and in a thousand ways the public revenues made to foster efforts for the public benefit.   We should reach the ideal of the socialist, but not through governmental repression.   Government would change its character, and would become the administration of a great co-operative society.   It would become merely the agency by which the common property was administered for the common benefit."[17]

Thomas G. Shearman of New York City was the first prominently to advocate the single tax limited.   Shearman

[16] Idem.
[17] Progress and Poverty, bk. 9, ch. 4, p. 454.

had been an earnest advocate of free trade and of the abolition of the personal property tax before reading *Progress and Poverty*. His conversion, in the early eighties, to the belief that land alone should be taxed came after an approach from the side of taxation rather than from the side of "natural rights". Hence he was disposed to view the single tax as a fiscal rather than a social reform proposition. Shearman first presented his views in the columns of *The Standard* in 1888 and 1889. Later he amplified them in his *Natural Taxation, an Inquiry into the Practicability, Justice and Effects of a Scientific and Natural Method of Taxation* (1895), a work which has gone through several editions and exerted wide influence.

Shearman believed that the amount of the tax which the state should require of land-owners should be "whatever amount the state really needs, for the effective but economical administration of government".[18] He calculated that taking half of the net income from land would suffice.[19] He opposed an artificial increase of public expenditures merely to absorb the surplus of land rents, believing that graft and corruption would enter were a surplus to be collected. However, Shearman modified the difference between his position and George's by giving the opinion that the gradual extension of the sphere of governmental activity and the corresponding increase in public expenditures would make an increasing demand upon owners of land.[20]

The terms single tax limited and single tax unlimited have not been very widely employed. This is partly on account of

---

[18] Shearman, Natural Taxation, ch. 9, sec. 17, 1911 ed., p. 133.

[19] Ibid., ch. 10, sec. 12, p. 157. "All attainable statistics thus point to the conclusion that the entire cost of the most expensive and even extravagant governments in civilized countries could be placed upon ground rents, without taking in taxation even half of the present net income of land-owners from that source alone."

[20] Ibid., ch. 9, sec. 17, pp. 133-34.

their obvious awkwardness but mainly because the distinction between the two has not been prominent in the history
of the movement. The center of discussion has nearly
always been the Henry George single tax. There is no
numerical evidence as to the relative strength of the advocates of the single tax limited. But such evidence as there
is indicates that nearly all of those supporting the exclusive
land tax believe that economic justice will not be obtained
short of diverting the whole of land income, as nearly as
possible, from the individual land-owners into the coffers
of the state.[21] Few would be willing to stop with the single
tax limited. To quote a statement of the single tax creed
by the editor of the *Single Tax Review*:

"The single tax is an instrument for effecting the resumption
of social wealth for social needs—not merely for the needs of
government as now administered, but going beyond it, if
necessary, in order to take all the land value. It therefore has
nothing in common with 'the single tax limited,' save as
political steps to the ultimate goal."[22]

Such prominence as the single tax limited has had has
resulted from the prominence of its two chief advocates,
Thomas G. Shearman and C. B. Fillebrown, who have been
since George perhaps the ablest and most successful propagandist writers. It is their activity which has given the impression that a substantial branch of the movement advocates the single tax limited.[23]

[21] Reference to the single tax limited is rare in single tax literature,
and the writer, in talking and corresponding with single taxers in all
sections of the United States, has, with one or two exceptions, neither
met nor heard of any of its present-day advocates other than Mr.
Fillebrown.

[22] Single Tax Review, Mar.-Apr., 1914, p. 44. Cf. also Joseph Fels,
The Single Tax Coming, in Real Estate Mag., New York, Feb., 1914, p.
10.

[23] The relative moderation of both Shearman and Fillebrown resulted
in the withdrawal of each from the ranks of the regular single taxers.

Some single taxers have designated as advocates of the single tax limited those who support single tax measures at the polls but who are not full-fledged single taxers. The number of these, however, is considerably larger than the number of the advocates of exclusive land taxation, since the measures proposed in the United States have nearly always involved but a very partial application of single tax principles.[24] Many who have had but little comprehension of Henry George's program have voted for such proposals, and there is small justification for calling them single taxers at all.

Attitude of present-day single taxers to the doctrines of Henry George

It sometimes is said that single taxers to-day have become unorthodox, that they are considerably less radical in their doctrines than was Henry George. We shall now consider whether this proposition is correct.

Some have assumed that the relative moderation of the immediate steps which single taxers urge involves the giving up of the Henry George idea that private property in land should be abolished by taxing its annual use value into the public treasury. But there is no reason to think that this opportunism represents more than a precept of political wisdom. A further consideration which has conduced to the idea that single taxers no longer hold as radical views as

Shortly before his death (1900) Shearman wrote to a friend: "In all times it has been the misfortune of reforms that some of their advocates have made it impossible for others to do any effective work for them for considerable periods. . . . There is no one left, except Mr. Fillebrown, with whom I can co-operate" (Cf. Fillebrown's pamphlet, Thomas G. Shearman and his Natural Taxation, Boston, 1915, p. 9, note). About a dozen years later Mr. Fillebrown was constrained to withdraw from the Massachusetts Single Tax League. Infra. p. 271.

[24] Cf. supra, ch.'s 9-12, also infra, pp. 288-90.

did George is an unduly broad construction of the terms single tax and single taxer. We are not warranted in classing as single taxers those who merely favor special taxation of land without contemplating essential changes in existing tax systems. Evidently neither single tax opportunism nor the growing movement toward special taxation of land indicates a relaxation in the devotion of single taxers to the faith "once delivered to the saints".

Modifications of the single tax (defined as the exclusive land tax) are possible in two directions: (1) by providing that land-owners should receive compensation, in whole or in part, were the value of their land to be taxed out of existence; (2) by departing from the singleness of the single tax and admitting to a limited extent taxes other than the land tax.

The first of these possible modifications has not been suggested by single taxers, although one of the most persistent objections to the single tax has been that those happening to have their capital invested in land should not be required to bear the entire cost of the change, should the introduction of the single tax be determined upon. There is in the United States no movement for "land nationalization" with compensation to present owners which is comparable to the British movement with this objective.[25]

Modifications in the second direction, of departing from the singleness of the single tax program, require more consideration. As a matter of principle single taxers have pretty consistently opposed all taxes other than land taxes, but as a practical matter they have sometimes been less consistent. They have been persistent and active enemies of consumption taxes, particularly when these embody the principle of protection. They likewise have opposed the

[25] Cf. Hyder, The Case for Land Nationalization, London, 1914.

"general" features of the general property tax and have urged the exemption of personal property and improvements. To inheritance taxes they have given little consideration, though opposed in theory to them as to all taxes other than those upon land.[26]

The position of single taxers regarding taxes levied for the purpose of restriction, such as liquor taxes, has not been uniform. Henry George, in his *Our Land and Land Policy* (1871), had favored restrictive taxes,[27] but he later came to disbelieve in them, partly because of his *laissez faire* political theories and partly because he felt that liquor taxes and licenses were mainly responsible for the participation of the liquor interests in politics.[28] Most single taxers have opposed these taxes and licenses for similar reasons, although it is worthy of note that several recently proposed single tax measures have provided that taxes and licenses pursuant to the police power should not be disturbed.[29]

Single taxers have been actively hostile to the principle of the income tax, since it exemplifies the ability to pay basis as contrasted with the benefit principle.[30] As Louis F. Post wrote:

"The value of the service which the public gives to each individual is fairly measured by land value taxation. We should then no more think of taxing citizens in proportion to their ability to pay regardless of the benefits they receive from the public, than an honest merchant would think of charging his customers in proportion to their ability to pay regardless of the value of the goods they buy of him."[31]

They oppose it because it taxes "earned" incomes alike with "unearned" incomes (i.e., those gained from land owner-

[26] Cf. Fillebrown, The A-B-C of Taxation, ch. 11, Inheritance and Income Taxes.
[27] George, Our Land and Land Policy, pp. 111-12.
[28] George's address, How to Destroy the Rum Power (pamphlet).
[29] Cf. supra, pp. 187, 189, 192, 203, 204.
[30] Cf. supra, p. 144.
[31] Post, The Taxation of Land Values, p. 9.

ship). However as a practical matter some single taxers have advocated the income tax, believing it to be a revenue method greatly preferable to tariff and other indirect taxes. In the latter part of 1915 single taxers were active in organizing the "Association for an Equitable Federal Income Tax", formed to urge the federal government to "secure at least three hundred million dollars by a rapidly progressive individual income tax".[32] But some single taxers questioned the wisdom of this movement, feeling that such an income tax would be so much preferable to existing revenue methods that it would be yet more difficult to dislodge. Single taxers favoring the income tax would doubtless reconcile their advocacy with single tax principles by claiming not to regard it as a finality.[33] Nevertheless the fact of their advocacy is significant of a relaxation of the strictness of the word *single* in the perhaps unhappy title single tax.

It appears, then, that single taxers have modified Henry George's doctrines but little. About the only deviation from the single tax as proposed in *Progress and Poverty* is the single tax limited, whose two chief advocates, Thomas G. Shearman and Charles B. Fillebrown, have gained little following for their ideas among single taxers. *Progress and Poverty* is much more truly the Bible of single tax than is Marx's *Capital* of socialism. The disciples of *Progress and Poverty* have relatively greater faith in its infallibility as a repository of economic truth. "Revisionism" and "re-inter-

[32] Cf. a brief of this Association, Why the federal government should secure at least three hundred million dollars by a rapidly progressive individual income tax, New York, 1916.

[33] Louis F. Post, advocated the income tax in an address cited in The Public, Dec. 24, 1915, p. 1248. But he stated to the writer that this advocacy was only because he regarded the income tax as preferable to indirect taxes, and did not involve a relaxation of single tax principles.

pretations" on the part of socialists have qualified the Marxian doctrines, but George's work has suffered comparatively little from onslaughts of "higher criticism" within the ranks of the faithful. For single taxers *Progress and Poverty* remains in the strictest sense the law and the gospel.

Indeed, the social, economic, and political philosophy of Henry George has tended to become a sort of creed which his followers accept with but few qualifications. This has resulted primarily from the fact that single taxers look to a single book of a single leader. Single taxers have an apt phrase, "Do you see the cat?", which means, "Do you see things from the single tax viewpoint?" The expression was contributed to single tax phraseology by Judge Maguire, Henry George's San Francisco friend.[34] Judge Maguire told the story of a landscape picture which bore the sign, "Do you see the cat?" A first glance at the picture failed to reveal the hidden feline, but after closer study the figure of the whole animal burst suddenly into view. Thereafter one might see in the picture nothing but cat.

It remains, however, in considering the attitude of present-day single taxers to the doctrines of Henry George to consider the re-interpretation which Mr. Fillebrown has given. Although Mr. Fillebrown has not a large following among single taxers proper, he ranks as the most influential of present propagandists.[35]

Fillebrown's re-interpretation of Henry George

Mr. Fillebrown's differences from his fellow single taxers are both tactical and doctrinal. The former, which center about the relative merits of educative propaganda (which Mr. Fillebrown champions) and political action, we have

[34] Cf. Post, The Taxation of Land Values, pp. 177-78.
[35] Cf. Supra, pp. 159-62.

already discussed.[36]   Although his divergent opinions led
him to withdraw from the Massachusetts Single Tax
League,[37] other single taxers have not stressed points of
difference which grow out of Mr. Fillebrown's relative moderation and his desire to attract to the single tax those whom
the radicalism of most single taxers would repel.

Mr. Fillebrown has striven to interpret Henry George in
the most conservative spirit possible.   But in so doing he has
undertaken what must be regarded as a crusade to convince
his readers that George's views are actually less radical than
they appear to be.   He says:

"I have frequently found myself standing between him and
many false and harmful impressions that have operated to his
prejudice and to that of his cherished reform.   Among these,
the insistence upon a full one hundred per cent rate, and the
abolition of private property in land as Henry George's standard measures for sound doctrine, have been painfully wasteful
and enervating. . . .

"If those devout followers of Henry George who still insist
that he should go down to posterity as advocating the destruc-
tion of private property in land would exercise his care to
avoid misinterpretation, they would thereby better serve him
and the reform he so wonderfully expounded."[38]

Mr. Fillebrown, a single taxer limited, holds that George
did not advocate taking in taxation the entire ground rent
of land.   To quote Q. 17 from *A 1915 Single Tax Catechism*:

"Q. Did not Henry George hold that the full ground rent of
land should be taken in taxation?

[36] Cf. supra, pp. 105-07, 159-62, and 244-46.
[37] Cf. Single Tax Rev., Jan.-Feb., 1914, p. 55.   Mr. Fillebrown's difference from his fellow single taxers was not over his advocacy of
the single tax limited, but was on the question of the tactical advisa-
bility of political action for the single tax, and the question as to
whether it might be said that "private property in land" would persist
under the single tax.
[38] Cf. Fillebrown's pamphlet, Land: the Rent Concept, the Property
Concept, Boston, 1915, p. 15.

"A. No! Not only did he concede a margin of rent to the landlord, but as a matter of fact, as Thomas G. Shearman said, 'not all the power of all governments' could collect in taxation all of ground rent."

This is perhaps literally correct since George was not sure that it would be administratively possible to collect every penny of ground rent for the state.[39] But the emphatic "No!" errs plainly in emphasis, since George unquestionably desired to render land ownership utterly profitless and urged that all the "economic rent" of land be taken, "as near as might be".[40] This fact, and not the possibility that the single tax might leave to land-owners a bare fraction of land value, is the significant fact regarding George's view of property in land.

Mr. Fillebrown believes that George is misinterpreted when it is said that he proposed to abolish private property in land. To quote Q. 12 from *A 1915 Single Tax Catechism:*

"Q. Did not Henry George believe in the abolition of private property in land?
"A. Assuredly not. If he did, why was it that he suggested no modification whatever of present land tenure or 'estate in land'? If he did, how could he have said that the sole 'sovereign' and sufficient remedy for the wrongs of private property in land was 'to appropriate rent by taxation'?"

In all of his writings Mr. Fillebrown has urged that Henry George did not propose to do away with private property in land. This idea he regards as particularly "false and harmful" to the progress of the single tax cause.

"If you say that private property in land is unjust, or that private ownership of land is unjust, the tendency is to close many minds to further consideration of a statement which to them savours too strongly of confiscation. One may attack with vigour the private appropriation of ground rent (what

[39] Supra, pp. 262-63.
[40] Idem.

land is worth for use), and be easily understood, while an attack upon private ownership in land is very apt to be misunderstood."[41]

Mr. Fillebrown believes that George's meaning is more clearly expressed by interpolating into his writings as follows:[42]

"If private property in [*the economic rent of*] land be just, then is the remedy I propose a false one; if, on the contrary, private property in [*the economic rent of*] land be unjust, then is this remedy the true one."

And also:

"Whatever may be said for the institution of private property in land [*as it exists to-day*], it is therefore plain that it cannot be defended on the score of justice."

And again:

"It may be confidently asserted that when Henry George said, 'Private property in land is unjust', he meant—as the whole principle and spirit of his teaching require us to believe, and as the context of controverted passages shows—that private property in land *values* is wrong."[43]

It is difficult to follow Mr. Fillebrown in seeing an essential economic difference between private property in land and private property in the rent or the value of land. Private property in the rent of land means simply private property in the use-value of land, and it is upon the value of the uses of land that the value of the land itself depends. Property in land or in anything else is worth while in proportion to its value. When Henry George proposed to tax the rent of land or land values into the public treasury he proposed to deprive land-owners of property in the rent of land or in land values, hence of their private property in land, to the extent of the capitalized value of the tax. Mr. Fille-

---

[41] Fillebrown, The A-B-C of Taxation, New York, 1916, p. 96.
[42] Fillebrown, Land: the Rent Concept, the Property Concept, p. 11.
[43] Fillebrown, The A-B-C of Taxation, p. 99.

brown apparently maintains that private property in land
would persist even under a land tax taking one hundred per
cent of the annual use-value of land.   But it is plain that
this is a sort of private property that no one would care to
own.

Hardly anyone but Mr. Fillebrown, either single taxer
or critic, has ever questioned that the author of the statement that "private property in land is a bold, bare, enormous wrong, like that of chattel slavery"[44] did intend to
abolish private property in land.   This surely is the plain
meaning, both in letter and in spirit, of George's writings
and speeches.   But as Professor Haney has well said: "It
is idle to discuss the question whether the single tax would
confiscate land or not.   Who wants the orange after the
juice is squeezed out?"[45]

In characterizing Mr. Fillebrown's position as a single
taxer it is difficult to avoid erring by way of emphasis,
since it is necessary to dwell upon what are merely his
doctrinal pecularities.   Important as he regards these ideas
—and he includes them in each of his writings—we cannot
but regard them as incidental and not essential.   The important point about Mr. Fillebrown's work is that his *The
A-B-C of Taxation* (first published in 1909) is a restate-
ment of the single tax argument which is probably the strongest and most influential single tax book since the appearance
of *Progress and Poverty.*

The central thesis of *The A-B-C of Taxation* is that the
single tax is justified because "land value is a social product,
i.e., it is created principally by the community through its
activities, industries, and expenditures".[46]   "The people

[44] Progress and Poverty, bk. 7, ch. 3, p. 356.

[45] Haney, The Single Tax, in Studies in the Land Problem in Texas,
Bulletin of the University of Texas, 1915, no. 39, p. 167.

[46] Fillebrown, The A-B-C of Taxation, p. 155.   This idea is found in
Progress and Poverty.   "There is a value created and maintained by

turn the crank of a great tax mill; the taxes that go into the hopper come out ground rent, no tax quality lost, no rent ingredient added."[47] Since taxes upon land cannot be shifted, "the selling value of land is an untaxed value and land owners who invest to-day are entirely exempt from taxation".[48] The chief difference from the argument of *Progress and Poverty* is indicated by the title *The A-B-C of Taxation;* the emphasis is on the fiscal more than the social reform side. Mr. Fillebrown proposes the single tax limited, with particular reference to the raising of local revenue. And in urging his proposal he does not undertake to require the acceptance with it either of every detail in Henry George's theory of distribution or of certain doctrines regarded by many single taxers as inseparable accompaniments of the single tax, such as the "natural rights" dogma, municipal ownership, direct legislation, and fiat money.

The difficulty of estimating Mr. Fillebrown's position as a single taxer is increased by the appearance in 1914 of his little book, *Taxation,* in a series of popular books on social science.[49] Several passages in this do not harmonize well with essential single tax doctrines,[50] and it is difficult to reconcile them with the principles of *The A-B-C of Taxa-*

the community, which is justly called upon to meet community expenses. Now, of what values is this true? Only of the value of land." (Bk. 8, ch. 3, p. 418.)

[47] Ibid., p. 6.

[48] Ibid., p. 159.

[49] Fillebrown, Taxation, Chicago, 1914.

[50] Cf. the following passages: "Accordingly in distributing the tax burden, the financier must endeavor to have it fall as evenly as possible upon all classes of society" (p. 26); "In the construction of a tax system the first essential is financial productiveness" (p. 37); and "The wealth represented by this personalty is bound both legally and morally to contribute to the support of the government, as much as is the realty, but obviously it will not do so unless its owner is honest to an exceptional degree" (p. 45).

tion as they appear, with no important changes, in a 1916 edition.

The single tax and proposals for special taxation of land:
(1) unearned increment taxes

The present movement for the special taxation of land has a dual root: (1) in John Stuart Mill's propaganda for taxing unearned increment, and (2) in Henry George's propaganda for the single tax. Corresponding with this dual root are two types of tax proposals.[51]

The first of these types of special land taxes proposes a levy against future increases in land values. Probably the first to suggest such a tax was the Scotchman, William Ogilvie, who published in 1782 *An Essay on the Right of Property in Land with respect to its Foundation in the Law of Nature*. Ogilvie believed that "a tax on all augmentation of rents, even to the extent of one half the increase, would be at once the most equitable, the most productive, the most easily collected, and the least liable to evasion of all possible taxes".[52] James Mill advocated such a tax in his *Political Economy* (1821),[53] as did his son, John Stuart Mill, in his *Political Economy* (1848).[54] The latter was active in forming in 1870 the "Land Tenure Reform Association", whose program called for "the interception by taxation of the future unearned increase of the rent of land."[55]

[51] A third type of special land tax—a tax on vacant lands—has been suggested but not very actively discussed. The main purpose of those who have suggested such taxes for the United States has been generally to meet the single tax argument regarding speculation in vacant land. Such taxes have been levied in Canada (cf. Haig, The Exemption of Improvements from Taxation in Canada and the United States, p. 261).

[52] Cf. supra, pp. 5-6.

[53] Cf. supra, pp. 21-23.

[54] Cf. supra, pp. 22-23.

[55] Cf. supra, p. 22.

This form of tax was first actually placed in operation by the Germans in the port of Kiauchau in 1898.[56] Those responsible for the experiment had apparently heard of neither John Stuart Mill nor Henry George. The plan at once attracted attention in Germany,[57] being adopted first by Frankfurt-on-Main in 1904. By 1910 it was in force in 457 cities and towns in Germany.[58] In 1911 an Imperial unearned increment tax was adopted which replaced in the main the local taxes.[59] The noteworthy Lloyd-George budget of 1909 introduced into England an unearned increment tax which takes for the state a fifth of all increases in land values greater than ten per cent.[60] In 1913 the province of Alberta, Canada, adopted what is probably the first tax of this kind to be put in force on the American continent.[61]

No unearned increment taxes have been adopted in the United States, although they have been actively discussed. Such taxes have been proposed for a number of cities, notably New York. The report of the New York Commission on New Sources of City Revenue, submitted January, 1913, urged as one of its chief recommendations "an increment tax of one per cent per annum to be perpetual upon all increments of land values as shown by comparison with the assessed valuations of the year 1912",[62] a proposal which differs from the European taxes in providing for a yearly tax rather than a tax collected when the property is trans-

[56] Cf. Seligman, Essays in Taxation, 1913, pp. 505-06.

[57] Ibid., p. 507 et seq.

[58] Report of the Commission on New Sources of City Revenue, New York, 1913, p. 49.

[59] Seligman, op. cit., p. 510 et seq.

[60] Ibid., p. 491 et seq.

[61] Haig, op., cit., pp. 73-75.

[62] Report of New York Commission on New Sources of City Revenue, Jan. 1913, p. 6. Cf. supra, p. 219.

ferred, or periodically when there is no transfer. The Commission estimated that in ten years the annual yield of this tax would approximate $15,000,000.[63] The Committee on Taxation of the City of New York, which reported in January, 1916, recommended a similar tax.[64]

The principle of the unearned increment tax is different from that of the single tax, since to tax future increases in land values is not the same as to levy more heavily upon present land values. The principles of a tax upon future increments in land values admits definitely the validity of the vested rights of present owners of land, whereas the single tax as definitely denies the validity of these rights. Two considerations should be borne in mind regarding the theory of taxing future unearned increment in land values. The first is that the unearned increment includes only that increase in the capital value of land in excess of the price at which it was bought. "So far as increases in land value can be foreseen they are included in the present worth of the land, and the new purchaser does not thereafter, viewed as an investor, get any 'unearned' increment except from *unforeseen* or miscalculated changes."[65] The second consideration is that whatever increase in land value may be due to the labor or investment in the property on the part of the owner is not unearned increment. The problem of distinguishing these elements, particularly in the case of agricultural land, offers both theoretical and administrative difficulties.

Some have described the single tax as a measure to collect unearned increment for the state. In defense of this usage about all that can be said is that one may maintain that historically the present value of lands represents an unearned

[63] Ibid., p. 7. Cf. also pp. 39-60.
[64] Cf. Final Report of the Committee on Taxation of the City of New York, 1916, pp. 101, 392-393, also supra, p. 227, and note 63, p. 227.
[65] Fetter, Economic Principles, New York, 1915, p. 363.

increment to certain individuals.   But present owners obviously have not gained unearned increment if, since acquiring their land, it either has remained stationary or has fallen
in value.   Therefore it would seem desirable to apply the
term unearned increment tax only to a levy against *future*
increases in the capital value of land.[66]   To characterize the
single tax as a tax upon unearned increment is confusing.

Different though the two sorts of taxes are, discussion of
the single tax has furthered discussion of the unearned increment tax.   Both are proposals to add to the tax burdens
of land-owners.   Both likewise are supported by "social product" and "unearned income" arguments which are similar.

Some single taxers have opposed the unearned increment
tax as a temporizing measure.   However, probably the majority would not oppose it.   Louis F. Post has said:

"It does take a *part* of the land value of properties on which
it falls, which is certainly better than taking none; and, what
is probably more important with this and all other kinds of
land value taxation than the mere fact of the tax, is the nature
of the agitation.   Everywhere opposed as confiscation of private interests in land, it is everywhere defended as the taking
for the community of what belongs to the community.   Such
agitations are especially promotive of the full single tax idea.
. . . Their chief value . . . is their tendency to develop an
appreciation in public opinion of the fundamental fact that land
values are community values and belong to the community."[67]

There are very many who accept hardly any of the essential single tax doctrine who are active advocates of the un-

[66] Dr. Haig has pointed out that "yield increments" and "capital
increments" have   sometimes been confused (Quarterly Jour. of Economics, Aug. 1915, p. 833).   Capital increments, of course, can only
arise from actual or prospective yield increments.   Such increment
taxes as have been adopted or discussed levy against capital increments.   There is little reason for applying the term unearned increment to yield increments without a qualifying adjective.

[67] Taxation of Land Values, pp. 87-88.

earned increment tax. The ground for urging such a tax is
the remarkably rapid rate at which land values have increased in American cities. In New York City during the
nine years 1906-15 land values increased from $3,367,233,-
746 to $4,643,414,776, an increase of more than a billion and
a quarter dollars, or 38 per cent.[68] In more rapidly growing
western cities increases have been more remarkable in their
rapidity. During the eight years 1906-14 the land values of
Los Angeles increased from 203 to 481 millions.[69] Mr.
Fillebrown has called attention to the fact that the land
values of Boston increased during the period 1887-1907
from 322 to 653 millions, remarking that "those who agree
with John Stuart Mill that it would be sound public policy
and no injustice to land-owners to take for public purposes
the future increase in ground rent will be interested to
note what an opportunity for putting such a plan in operation in Boston" is shown to have been lost in 1887.[70]

(2) The exemption of improvements from taxation

The second sort of proposals for special land taxation
involves a heavier direct levy upon present land values, together with the partial or total exemption from taxation of
improvements and personal property. Unearned increment
taxes have been the more widely discussed of special land
taxes in England and more especially in Germany, but in the
United States and Canada interest has centered upon proposals of this second sort.

In the three western provinces of Canada—Saskatchewan,
Alberta, and British Columbia—partial or total exemption is

[68] Report of Department of Taxes and Assessments, New York City,
1915, p. 20. Cf. also Scott Nearing, Land Value Increase in American
Cities, in The Public, Nov. 26, 1915, p. 1151.

[69] Nearing, op. cit., p. 1152.

[70] Fillebrown, The A-B-C of Taxation, pp. 23-24.

generally practised.[71]   Hardly a municipality in those provinces does not tax improvements at a lower rate than land,
and many, including the cities of Vancouver, Victoria, and
Edmonton, exempt them entirely.   Single taxers have advertised extensively the claim that the remarkable development
of this section during the period from 1908 to 1912-13 was
due to the fact that long strides toward the single tax had
been taken.   This argument or assertion has been prominent
in recent single tax agitations in the United States.

The movement for exemption of improvements in the
United States has achieved but little so far as legislation
goes.   Exemption is now legally being applied only in Pittsburgh and Scranton, in which cities the rate of tax upon
buildings is being reduced by ten per cent steps triennially
until it will be half that upon land by 1925.[72]   But since
1908 the movement has become more and more prominent.
Exemption of improvements has been a political issue of
importance in several parts of the country.   The chief factor
which has made for the increased prominence of this issue,
besides the attention given to claims regarding the prosperity of western Canada under so-called single tax,[73] has
been the propaganda activity made possible by the Joseph
Fels Fund endowment, established in 1909 "to put the single

[71] For a complete account of the Canadian movement cf. Haig, The
Exemption of Improvements from Taxation in Canada and the United
States, a report prepared for the Committee on Taxation of the City
of New York, 1916.

[72] Supra, pp. 210-15.

[73] Because the claims of ardent propagandists have been so commonly of the *post hoc ergo propter hoc* sort, opponents of exemption
of improvements had their innings when the tide of prosperity receded
and a somewhat severe depression set in.   They urged that the system,
by over-stimulating building activity, had paved the way for a particularly serious period of economic stagnancy.

tax into effect somewhere in the United States within five years".[74]

The present status of the movement to exempt improvements from taxation in the United States appears from the accounts in previous chapters of the several single tax campaigns. In the following chapter it is further considered in its relation to the present status of the single tax movement.

[74] Supra, pp. 163-68.

CHAPTER XIV

CONCLUDING SURVEY

In *Progress and Poverty* George confidently predicted that his book would find readers and his teachings apostles. Both predictions have been remarkably fulfilled. His writings have enjoyed a circulation wider perhaps than those of any other writer upon economic subjects. In the introduction to the twenty-fifth anniversary edition (1905) Mr. Henry George, Jr., stated that, "embracing all forms and languages, more than two million copies of *Progress and Poverty* have been printed to date; and that including with these the other books that have followed from Henry George's pen, and which might be called 'The Progress and Poverty Literature', perhaps five million copies have been given to the world". Equally striking has been the realization of George's faith that his teachings would make converts. They have gained an unusual following. President Benjamin Ide Wheeler has said:

"From the teachings of Henry George there flows a stream of idealism that seldom has been equalled. Whenever you find single taxers you will find men and women who are interested in what is going on in the world for reasons other than personal reward. They are earnestly seeking the good for its own sake, and for what they believe to be the good of the country."[1]

The interest which *Progress and Poverty* kindled may be said to have reached its culmination following George's campaign for the mayoralty of New York City in 1886. Following his notable showing of strength in that campaign

[1] Single Tax Rev., Mar.-Apr., 1911, p. 37.

some enthusiasts predicted the triumph of the full single tax within a comparatively short period, believing that it would be carried to success by a great national workingmen's party.[2] But the development of the movement since 1886 has not been what was then anticipated. The early rate of growth has not been matched, and it is doubtful whether the number of believers in the full single tax has increased much since Henry George's death in 1897. Land-owners today may in some localities be worried over the prospect of heavier land taxes, but they manifest little uneasiness over the firmness with which private property in land is established. Judging by the extent to which essential single tax principles have been enacted into law, or by the extent to which full-fledged converts have been won, single tax progress has not been great.

Results have not come, indeed, as many single taxers have expected them to come. But it does not follow that the movement has been uninfluential. Shortly before his death Henry George remarked in the course of an address that he had given his lifetime to the dissemination of his single tax doctrines. A voice from the audience inquired, "And what have you accomplished?" George replied facetiously, "I have taxed New York's halls to their utmost capacity." Opponents of the single tax would not now deny that the appearance of *Progress and Poverty* was an important event in the history of thought on economic and social problems, or that the single tax movement has been a force of very great importance in stimulating public interest in economic problems and in molding opinion regarding questions of fiscal and social reform.

The aim of this final chapter is to present a concluding survey of the present status of the movement, its place in the history of thought on economic and social questions, and

[2] Supra, p. 104.

its influence and significance. In describing the present status of the movement the two most obvious considerations are (1) legislative accomplishments, and (2) number of adherents.

Legislative accomplishments

The legislative achievements of the single tax movement have been few in the United States. The only direct application of the single tax principle to be found at the present writing (1916) is in the cities of Pittsburgh and Scranton, which are on the way to reach a 50 per cent exemption of buildings in 1925.[3] It is a noteworthy fact that this exemption was prescribed by a law of 1913 passed by the Pennsylvania legislature, and not by popular vote. The exemption of improvements in the irrigation districts of California, which has been advertised as a step toward the single tax, is really hardly more than an application of the principle of special assessments.[4]

If we exclude cases of irregular and extra-legal exemption of improvements, as in Houston, Texas,[5] the history of the movement shows just three cases where single tax principles have been adopted. In Hyattsville, Maryland, in 1892 exemption of improvements and personal property was prescribed by the town authorities under a special provision of the town charter, but was frowned upon by the courts in the following year.[6] In Everett, Washington, the measure adopted by popular vote in 1912 was ruled against by the State Tax Commission and was of such doubtful constitutionality as not to be contested in the courts.[7] In

[3] Supra, p. 210 et seq.
[4] Supra, p. 208.
[5] Supra, p. 197 et seq.
[6] Supra, p. 145 et seq.
[7] Supra, p. 185 et seq.

Pueblo, Colorado, an initiative measure adopted in 1913 was repealed in 1915 before taking full effect.[8]

Single taxers believe that in a time not much more than a generation the movement has made striking progress in several important countries. But the United States, the birthplace of the single tax movement, does not stand first in achievements. A single taxer recounting the accomplishments of the movement would point to western Canada, where nearly all the municipalities tax improvements at a lower rate than land and where there are also special provincial land taxes; to Australasia, with its forty years of experimentation along similar lines; to England, where the Lloyd-George budget of 1909 levied four new taxes upon the theretofore favored landholders; to Germany, with its pioneer adoption of unearned increment taxes; and to movements of varying strength in the Scandinavian countries, Spain, and parts of South America.[9] It should be remembered, however, that not all these movements for heavier taxation of land are based upon single tax principles. The movement for taxing future unearned increments of land values is rooted in the work of John Stuart Mill and the experience of the German colony of Kiauchau rather than in the single tax propaganda.[10]

Why has land taxation made less headway, comparatively, in the United States? Professor Carver thus compares the progress of land taxes and inheritance taxes.

"The inheritance tax has made more headway than the land tax. The arguments for one seem to be about as strong as for

[8] Supra, p. 202 et seq.

[9] For a brief account of these achievements cf. Fillebrown, Thirty Years of Henry George, with a Record of Achievements, 3rd edition, Boston, 1915; Garrison, The Case for the Single Tax, Atlantic Mo., Dec., 1913, pp. 745-46; Post, Taxation of Land Values, Indianapolis, 1915, pp. 174-76; also supra, p. 15, note.

[10] Supra, pp. 276-80.

the other. The inheritance tax, however, has stood on its merit and has not been championed as an engine of social reform. It has had no body of ardent apostles to set up a fiery cross and preach a crusade against a fortunate class. The land tax has been thus handicapped, which may account for its slow progress. In the ardency of reform, arguments are used which ignite certain inflammable spirits but repel all thinking men."[11]

Mr. Fillebrown is convinced that stress upon political campaigns rather than upon pure propaganda of education has comparatively retarded the American movement.[12] But perhaps the main reason is that in the United States land is already heavily taxed under the general property tax and is also subject to special assessments on account of local improvements. Mr. Fillebrown has stated that "it is probably true that a larger percentage of ground rent is reclaimed by the community through taxation in the states of Massachusetts and New York than in any other territory in the world".[13] Likewise land has been legally taxable on its selling value—though "some American towns are indeed in the habit of assessing vacant lots with considerable tenderness"[14]—whereas some foreign systems have only taxed realized income and have omitted to tax vacant land. Some of the European land tax reforms have been designed to remedy abuses which were relics of mediaeval times.

The number of single taxers

The evidence as to the number of single taxers in the United States is not very satisfactory. There has been no national dues-paying single tax organization comparable to the Socialist Party, doubtless because the strong individualistic tendencies in single tax theory have militated against

[11] Carver, Essays in Social Justice, Cambridge, 1915, p. 304.
[12] Supra, pp. 105 et seq., 244 et seq.
[13] Fillebrown, op. cit., p. 15.
[14] Seligman, Essays in Taxation, 1913, pp. 488-89.

such centralization. The single tax societies, of which the *Single Tax Review,* January-February, 1916, listed fifty, are mainly local organizations, and vary much in strength. There are no figures as to their total membership.[15]

The size of the popular vote cast for the measures which single taxers have urged is often cited as indicating. the strength of the movement. The following table summarizes the votes for the measures proposed during the years 1912-15.[16]

Place	Date	Vote for	Vote against
Missouri	1912	87,000	508,000
Everett, Washington	1912	4,858	2,637
Seattle	1913	10,578	21,260
Oregon	1914	65,495	136,193
California	1914	267,618	375,634
Colorado Springs, Colo.	1915	944	7,241
Denver	1915	7,988	27,125
Pueblo	1915	3,042	3,255
Houston, Texas	1915	5,659	1,963
Total		453,182	1,083,308

NOTE.—The Oregon figures give the vote on the measure getting the larger vote of the two submitted. The California vote is on local option in taxation, the measure being opposed to a certain extent as a step toward the single tax. The Pueblo vote is on the repeal of the single tax measure adopted in 1913, 2,711 to 2,171. The Houston figures are for the re-election of Tax-Commissioner Pastoriza over his opponent, the issue being exemption of improvements.

The figures represent the vote the last time single tax measures were up, when they have been up more than once in any of these places.

The vote in favor of the above measures proposed by single taxers is 29.5 per cent of the total vote on them. If

[15] The best published index of single taxers is a directory of the Henry George Lecture Association. Cf. supra, p. 247.

[16] Full accounts of the campaigns in which these measures were involved are given supra, ch.'s 9, 10, 11, and 12. A tabular summary of the measures, with brief descriptions of them together with the votes and percentages, is given in Appendix B.

we leave out of the total the big and unfavorable vote of Missouri, where bitter prejudice was aroused among the farmers, and also California's big vote on the question of local option in taxation,[17] the percentage of votes for the single tax measures is 33.0 instead of 29.5. This is a substantial minority, but yet far from a majority.

Proposals for exemption of improvements have a two-fold backing. Initiating them and most active among their supporters are the single taxers, who urge such measures as an opening wedge for the full single tax program. But since these measures are in the main moderate as compared with the full single tax they have gained the support of a great many who believe in single tax principles only to the extent of partially or wholly relieving improvements and personal property from taxation under the general property tax, and who do not accept George's views of the exploitative nature of land income generally.

It is evidently impossible to estimate very exactly what share of the 450,000 supporters of these measures were actually single taxers—advocates of the exclusive land tax for all public revenues. Some would go so far as to count the entire number as single taxers.[18] Bnt this is manifestly unwarranted since, for example, more than three-fifths of the 450,000 was made up of those voting for home rule in taxation in California in 1914, this vote not even being a test of the strength of sentiment for exemption of improvements, much less of the strength of the single tax.[19] There is no reason to think that single taxers are more than a fraction of the number who have voted for these relatively limited measures. Mr. Benjamin C. Marsh stated that in New York City "relatively few of those endorsing the halv-

[17] Supra, p. 191 et seq. and pp. 232 and 234 n.
[18] Joseph Fels Fund Bulletin, June, 1915, pp. 2-3.
[19] Supra, pp. 232, 234, and 234 n.

ing of the tax rate on buildings are single taxers, probably not over five per cent."[20]

The supporters of exemption of improvements include several elements besides the single taxers. Some have voted for them, not because they regarded them as wholly desirable, but because they considered them to be preferable to the general property tax as administered. In almost every election labor organizations have supported the single taxers. The socialists generally have voted gladly for measures where the issue has been joined on a question of vested property rights. In some cases, as in Everett and to a certain extent in California, the co-operation of socialists has been close. Finally, there is a considerable number who, without accepting the whole single tax doctrine, have become convinced of the desirability of partial or total exemption of improvements from taxation together with an extension of land taxes.

Single taxers have been somewhat chary about committing themselves to numerical estimates of strength. Examination of the literature of the movement reveals hardly any such estimates, if we except the calculations of voting strength based upon the votes in favor of the comparatively moderate measures which single taxers have urged since 1908. In 1909, when the Joseph Fels Fund Commission was beginning its work, Mr. Daniel Kiefer, chairman of the Commission, wrote in the *Single Tax Review* that "with no definite statistics at hand, the belief is that there are at least fifteen to twenty thousand avowed single taxers in the United States".[21] In March, 1916, the Fels Fund Commission had 35,000 names on its list, including both single taxers and those favorable to the single tax.[22]

[20] Single Tax Rev., Jan.-Feb., 1914, p. 20.
[21] Ibid., Sept.-Oct., 1909, p. 53.
[22] Letter to the present writer, March 24, 1916. But it was stated that this list is not regarded as a complete list of single taxers, since new

Mr. Joseph Dana Miller, editor of the *Single Tax Review*, in a letter of March 24th, 1916, wrote as follows in answer to the present writer's request for an estimate of numbers:

"It is a difficult question to answer. But I should say that there are in the United States between 25,000 and 50,000 convinced single taxers who are in the possession of the full vision; there are probably many more who have been favorably influenced, and whose numbers are still more difficult of estimate.

"There can surely be no fewer than the number stated after an agitation of thirty years during which time nearly a million copies of *Progress and Poverty* have been circulated, and vaster quantities of miscellaneous literature.

"An intellectual conviction such as ours will not manifest itself in *organized* numbers, nor in public confession of faith. The element of error which with a basis of truth sometimes carries along superficial reforms swiftly, is lacking; were it based on error with a mixture of superstition it would increase its adherents prodigiously, like protectionism or the tulip mania; as it is, the actual number of believers must remain more or less a matter of doubtful conjecture."

Doubtless some single taxers would dissent from these estimates, which necessarily cannot be much more than shrewd guesses. But it is plain that merely to set down the number of single taxers comes short of doing justice to the strength of the movement. Professor Alvin S. Johnson has said:

"The single taxers . . . are as a rule members of our dominant middle class. Moreover, their strength is especially great in that wing of the middle class which is active in molding public opinion, the 'intellectuals', to borrow an excellent descriptive term from Russian politics. Among the single taxers are to be found writers and educators, members of the legal and medical professions, social workers and ministers of the gospel. It is this fact of an exceptionally influential personnel that chiefly lends political importance to the movement."[23]

names continually are being added of those who long have been single taxers.

[23] Atlantic Mo., Jan., 1914, p. 27.

The single taxers and their adversaries

Scarcely any book published on an economic subject has given rise to more controversy than *Progress and Poverty*. Discussion of the single tax question has called forth a great volume of controversial literature, which has ranged in form from books to newspaper letters and editorials, and in spirit from sympathetic criticism to violent vituperation.

There has been no lack of efforts to "refute" *Progress and Poverty*. Following its publication in 1879 came numerous reviews, each contributing an argument or a judgment, and, as it became more and more prominent with successive editions, as Henry George came to occupy a larger place before the public eye by virtue of his further writings, his lectures, and his political activity, more elaborate refutations began to appear. We meet in succession General Walker and Professor Sumner, with their harsh and rather arrogant attacks;[24] the Duke of Argyll, denouncing "the prophet of San Francisco";[25] W. H. Mallock, W. T. Harris, G. B. Stebbins, Edward Atkinson, and John Rae, with their statistics, their general criticism, and their defense of the existing social order;[26] T. H. Huxley, with his assault upon the resurrected doctrine of "natural rights";[27] Professor Seligman, with his criticism of the single tax as a fiscal measure;[28] and a host of others.

[24] Supra, p. 82 et seq.
[25] Nineteenth Century, vol. 15 (1884), pp. 537-59.
[26] Mallock, Property and Progress, New York, 1884; Harris, Right of Property and the Ownership of Land, American Jour. of Social Science, No. 22, 1887, pp. 116-55; Stebbins, Progress From Poverty, Chicago, 1887; Atkinson, remarks in the single tax debate, Saratoga, 1890, American Jour. of Social Science vol. 27, 1890, pp. 55-72, 122-24; Rae, Contemporary Socialism, 1891.
[27] Huxley, Collected Essays, On the Natural Inequality of Men; Natural Rights and Political Rights; and Capital—the Mother of Labour. These essays first appeared in the Nineteenth Century, vol. 27 (1890).
[28] Seligman, Essays in Taxation, 1913, ch. on the Single Tax

Something of a lull in the controversy followed in the dozen years after Henry George's death in 1897. But the political activity consequent to the establishment of the Joseph Fels Fund in 1909 has occasioned a renewal of more active discussion. Many arguments against the single tax have been made primarily for local consumption, while others have interested a larger audience.[29]

Yet among all this literature there hardly exists a comprehensive exposition of the case against *Progress and Poverty*. The reason is that this remarkable book raised so many issues that it would take a volume of large scope than has yet been written on the subject to give a full consideration of them all. Such a work would needs survey nearly the whole field of economic, social, and political theory, with excursions into the realm of ethics. The ideas of *Progress and Poverty* have been pretty thoroughly threshed out in the course of the discussion. George's many critics have attacked him at what they have considered the most vulnerable spots. But the seeker for a comprehensive statement of the objections to the single tax can find it only in piecing together scattering criticisms in books, chapters, and miscellaneous literature.

In the preface to the fourth edition of *Progress and Poverty*, a year after publication, Henry George declared that he had met no objection that was not fully answered in the book itself. He asserted in his last volume, *The Science of Political Economy*, that "its reasoning has never been successfully assailed".[30] Single taxers always have maintained that the arguments of *Progress and Poverty* have never been answered.

[29] Among recent criticisms of the single tax that which perhaps has attracted most attention is Professor Alvin S. Johnson's The Case Against the Single Tax, Atlantic Mo., Jan., 1914, pp. 27-37.
[30] P. 203.

Most single taxers have been somewhat impatient of opposition. Convinced that they had the simple and practical
means to open the door of equal opportunity to all, they
have generally regarded opposition either as *prima facie*
evidence of stupidity, or as springing from a desire to maintain existing social injustice. Single taxers employ the term
"privilege" to signify the entrenched hostile forces which
have a strong personal interest in opposing their propaganda.[31] These forces, single taxers urge, can make an
unfairly strong resistance because of their insidious control
of politics, the press, and even the universities.

Henry George had believed that, "should *Progress and
Poverty* succeed in commanding anything like wide attention there would be at least some of the professed teachers
of political economy who, recognizing the ignored truths
which I had endeavored to make clear, would fit them in
with what of truth was already understood and taught".[32]
But he was disappointed in his expectation. Economists
generally have rejected the essential ideas for which he so
earnestly contended.

How his disappointment in this respect embittered him
appears from the tone of his *The Science of Political
Economy*, published posthumously in 1898.[33]

"What were their training and laborious study worth if it
could be thus ignored, and if one who had never seen the in-
side of a college, except when he had attempted to teach

[31] Since George's time single taxers have made increasing use of the
term privilege. Cf. Henry George, Jr., The Menance of Privilege, New
York, 1905, and F. C. Howe, Privilege and Democracy in America,
New York, 1910. The idea of privilege means more than mere land
ownership. It includes ownership of such natural resources as mines,
oil and gas wells, timber and water-power; ownership of franchises,
whose value is socially created; and gain due to favoring laws, e.g.,
the tariff. Cf. Howe, op. cit., p. 68.
[32] George, The Science of Political Economy, preface.
[33] The citations here given are from pp. 204-08.

professors the fundamentals of their science, whose education
was of the mere common school branches, whose *alma mater*
had been the forecastle and the printing-office, should be admitted to prove the inconsistency of what they had been teaching as a science? It was not to be thought of. . . .

"It would not have been merely to accept a new man without
the training of the schools, but to admit that the true science
was open to anyone to pursue, and could be successfully continued only on the basis of equal rights and privileges. It
. . . would have converted them and their science into opponents of the tremendous pecuniary interests that were vitally
concerned in supporting the justification of the unjust arrangements which gave them power. . . . Thus the professors of
political economy, having the sanction and support of the
schools, preferred, and naturally preferred, to unite their differences, by giving up what had before been insisted on as
essential, and to teach what was an incomprehensible jargon
to the ordinary man, under the assumption of teaching an oc-
cult science, which required a great study of what had been
written by numerous learned professors all over the world, and
a knowledge of foreign languages. So the scholastic political
economy, as it had been taught, utterly broke down.

"The new science speaks of the 'science of economics' and
not of 'political economy'; teaches that there are no eternally
valid natural laws; and, asked if free trade or protection be
beneficial or if the trusts be good or bad, declines to give a
categorical answer, but replies that this can be decided only
as to the particular time and place, and by a historical investigation of all that has been written about it. As such inquiry
must, of course, be left to professors and learned men, it leaves
the professors of 'economics', who have almost universally
taken the places founded for professors of 'political economy',
to dictate as they please, without any semblance of embarrass-
ing axioms or rules. . . .

"So general is this scholastic utterance that it may now be
said that the science of political economy, as founded by Adam
Smith and taught authoritatively in 1880, has now been utterly
abandoned, its teachings being referred to as teachings of 'the
classical school' of political economy, now obsolete.

"What has succeeded is usually denominated the Austrian
school, for no other reason that I can discover than that 'far
kine have long horns'. If it has any principles, I have been
utterly unable to find them. The inquirer is usually referred
to the incomprehensible works of Professor Alfred Marshall;

. . . to the ponderous works of Eugen V. Böhm-Bawerk;
. . . or to a lot of German works written by men he never
heard of and whose names he cannot even pronounce."

Most single taxers accept substantially George's estimate
of professional economists and current economic thought.
They suggest two possible reasons why economists do not
accept the single tax. The first is that they are ignorant of
"the true science of political economy", as taught by Henry
George.[34] The second is that they are hypocrites who, in
accepting positions in plutocratic institutions, are either explicitly venal or implicitly accept the collar of the millionaire.[35] Single taxers have cited cases of alleged infringement upon freedom of teaching as examples of how economists of leading institutions are muzzled. They have been
fond of quoting Macauley's sarcastic comment that the law
of gravitation might not be generally accepted to this day
were important financial interests concerned in disputing its
truth. They declare that economists, in order to evade consideration of fundamental matters of right and wrong in
social adjustments, indulge in evasions and hair-splitting
like mediaeval schoolmen. They charge that economists
take pride in "stilted involution" by means of "statistics,
percentages, algebraic demonstrations" and other "mental
paraphernalia", to which "our camp is illy adapted".[36]

[34] Referring to such statements Mr. Fillebrown criticizes his fellow
single taxers for "a supercilious, patronizing style of writing that
violates good taste." (Fillebrown's pamphlet, Henry George and the
Economists, Boston, 1914, pp. 6-7.)

[35] Henry George, Jr., wrote in his The Menace of Privilege: "Of
course a university must teach political economy. . . . But with Princes
of Privilege among its regents or trustees and its heaviest contributors,
how can the real science of political economy which condemns privilege
as robbery be taught? If it were so taught, the nobles of government
favor would not for a moment lend their countenances and open their
purses to the institution" (p. 288).

[36] Demuth, Professional Economists vs. Single Taxers, Single Tax
Rev., Jan.-Feb., 1914, p. 33. Cf. also Love's assaults upon the profes-

This is hardly the place to undertake a justification of the economic profession. But we may note some considerations pertinent to the single tax arraignment.

A review of the literature of the controversy over the single tax idea gives evidence that many opponents of the single tax, economists among them, have not always been fair or reasonable. Some economists could be mentioned who apparently have assumed that condemnation from authority was in itself nearly adequate to dispose of the single tax, as when Professor Sumner declared that George's opinions were worthless because he had not fortified himself "by any correct study of sociology", or when General Walker wrote that the publication of *Progress and Poverty* was "certainly a curious phenomenon of the time, and a very disagreeable phenomenon".[37]   Men with a burning zeal for what they believe to be "the noblest cause the world has ever known" cannot be blamed for resenting such a spirit of opposition. To attack an economic faith like that of the single taxer is almost as delicate a matter as to attack the tenets of a religious belief, and many critics have needlessly been harsh. On the other hand it would be easy to gather a goodly list of single taxers who have been exceedingly impolite controversialists.

Furthermore single taxers may justly claim that students of the history of economic thought have been neglectful of the significance and influence of *Progress and Poverty*, which perhaps has been the most widely read of modern books on social problems. For example Henry George com-

sion, ibid., July and Oct., 1901; Jan., 1902; Apr., and July, 1903; Oct., 1904; and Jan., 1905. Cf, also a series of letters between President Jordon of Stanford University and J. H. Stallard, a single taxer, published in 1899 under the title, The True Basis of Economics; and the Single Tax Rev., Mar.-Apr., 1916, pp. 95, 96 and 101,
    [37] Supra, pp. 82, 84.

plained that in Ingram's *History of Political Economy* "writers of France, Spain, Germany, Italy and northern nations are referred to in the utmost profusion, but there is no reference whatever to the man or the book that was then exerting more influence upon thought and finding more purchasers than all the rest of them combined".[38]

But single taxers would find difficulty in showing that the teachers of political economy in most leading institutions are subject to pressure which has the effect of preventing a perfectly frank discussion of economic problems. Economists in these institutions subscribe to no creed and give no pledge other than to seek and to teach the truth. None recognize more clearly than professional economists that in dealing with problems of social justice it is easy to touch "the sensitive pocket-book nerve"; none appreciate more fully the menace to progress which is involved in suppression of freedom of teaching. When occasional attempts are made to quell inconvenient criticism, none are keener to make public the facts than professional economists. Fortunately public opinion is being educated to the point where any efforts to withdraw from students of social problems the privilege of disagreeing with the upholders of the total beneficence of existing social arrangements find small support.

In condemning professional economists *en masse* single taxers should not overlook the fact that economists probably suffer much more criticism for espousing than for rejecting so-called radical ideas. To the minds of many conservatives the universities today are hotbeds of "socialism". It is possible to mention many ideas formerly or still spoken of as radical which have gained much of their strongest sup-

[38] George, The Science of Political Economy, p. 206. Ingram's History of Political Economy first appeared in the 1885 edition of the Encyclopedia Brittanica.

port from economists, e.g., social insurance, public control of private monopolies, municipal ownership, collective bargaining on the part of workingmen, free trade, progressive taxation of incomes and inheritances, and taxation of the unearned increment of land values.

Finally, a good deal of the single taxers' criticism of opponents involves a naïve sort of egotism. The man who insists that all who may disagree with him are fools, frauds, or hypocrites may believe it thoroughly. But to the "man from Mars" or some equally neutral observer it would seem that the possibility of other honest and intelligent opinions is not thereby precluded. We all know of the juror who complained of his eleven stubborn colleagues. Nothing is more complex than the group of difficult problems termed "the social problem". It is unreasonable for a man seriously to assert that there is room for intelligent belief in but a single ideal of social justice or a single means of attaining it. The reason why earnest students reject the single tax doctrine is that they have not become convinced of its justice or expediency.

In the course of the long and—as opponents of the single tax now will admit—fruitful controversy to which *Progress and Poverty* has given rise, many objections have been entered. Some of these have been irrelevant, and others have been of minor significance. Some points are still in dispute, as, for example, certain of the social effects of land taxes. But there are several objections to the single tax idea which nearly all the critics have urged persistently. These recur with a striking sameness in most discussions of the question. It is these objections, presumably, which have had the most weight in preventing a wider acceptance of the single tax. These objections we shall take up in the following section.

Some persistent objections to the single tax[39]

Henry George painted a most attractive picture of the beneficent results to be expected from the application of the single tax. But his essential doctrines have commended themselves only to a comparatively small minority of those who give thought to social problems. The persistent objections which have stood in the way of a broader acceptance of single tax principles appear to single taxers, of course, to be utterly inadequate. They have replied to them time after time.[40] But the way in which these objections persist in reappearing indicates that critics of the single tax are unconvinced by the single tax rebuttal.

The main proposition in the single tax argument is that property in land differs so from property in other goods that society and not private owners should receive the fruits of its ownership. Hence it is proposed that the single tax should collect ground rents in lieu of taxes. Single taxers have employed two lines of argument in undertaking to prove this proposition. The first of these lines of argument

[39] This section deals with some of the objections that have stood in the way of a more general acceptance of the full single tax argument. The question as to how far the state should depend upon land taxes is a further question and is too much controverted to be considered here. Single taxers have converted many to a belief in heavy taxation of land, but the arguments for this view are not on the same basis as the arguments for the Henry George single tax. There are many favoring heavier land taxes or exemption of improvements who do not believe that there is something peculiarly exploitative about private ownership of land. For excellent statements of the arguments for and against heavier land taxation, presented from the points of view both of advocates and opponents, cf. Final Report of the Committee on Taxation of the City of New York, 1916.

[40] Cf. for example the following from a Fels Fund leaflet entitled, An Economist Who Needs Economic Instruction: "Professor Haney's unfamiliarity with Henry George's works is evident on his presentation of objections which Henry George had answered long ago."

is based upon Henry George's theory of property rights; the second upon his economic theories.

In *Progress and Poverty* Henry George declared that property rights to products of labor spring from "the natural right of the individual to the use of his own faculties".

"What constitutes the rightful basis of property? . . . Is it not, primarily, the right of a man to himself, to the use of his own powers, to the enjoyment of the fruits of his own exertions? . . . As a man belongs to himself, so his labor when put in concrete form belongs to him.

"And for this reason, that which a man makes or produces is his own, as against all the world."[41]

From this reasoning Henry George deduced the proposition that taxation of products of labor was nothing other than robbery.[42] But private property in land, he declared, infringed the "natural rights" of men.

"Let the parchments be ever so many, or possession ever so long, natural justice can recognize no right in one man to the possession and enjoyment of land that is not equally the right of all his fellows. . . . Though the sovereign people of the State of New York consent to the landed possessions of the Astors, the puniest infant that comes wailing into the world in the squalidest room of the most miserable tenement house, becomes at that moment seized of an equal right with the millionaires. And it is robbed if the right is denied."[43]

[41] Progress and Poverty, bk. 7, ch. 1, p. 332.

[42] "The truth is that customs taxes and improvement taxes, and income taxes, and taxes on business and occupations and on legacies and successions, are morally and economically no better than highway robbery or burglary, all the more disastrous and demoralizing because practiced by the state. There is no necessity for them. The seeming necessity arises only from the failure of the state to take its own natural and adequate source of revenue—a failure which entails a long train of evils of another kind by stimulating a forestalling and monopolisation of land which creates an artificial scarcity of the primary element of life and labor." (George, A Perplexed Philosopher, 1892, pp. 282-83.)

[43] Progress and Poverty, bk. 7, ch. 1, pp. 337-38.

Nearly all the critics of the single tax have felt that this natural rights line of argument is entirely without weight. What are natural rights? it is asked. They are merely rights which Henry George or some other thinker believes would be established in society as it *ought* to be. To quote Professor Ritchie:

"When traditional custom or constituted authority comes to be unsatisfactory to certain more reflective minds, there arises a discrepancy between it and what seem to be the natural instincts or feelings of the individual, a discrepancy between law and conscience; and so, as we have seen, reformers try to go back to an authority more venerable than parliaments and kings; more venerable even than immemorial usage: they 'appeal from tyranny to God', from the mere custom of the multitude to the feelings that Nature has emplanted in the breast of each of us."[44]

But Professor Ritchie goes on to say, "The unfortunate thing is that these instinctive feelings differ so much in different persons". Many men have contended earnestly for the recognition of certain natural rights. But the difficulty is that they have not all contended for the same natural rights. Conceptions of what constitute natural rights do not agree.[45] An indefinite number of different ideas of natural rights is evidently possible. In the absence of a special revelation from heaven on the subject, who shall decide?

Political scientists urge that to appeal to the sanction of

[44] Ritchie, Natural Rights, London, 1894, p. 85.

[45] It has often been argued that the right of property in general is a natural right, and it has even been held that property in slaves is a natural right. The Kentucky Constitution of 1850, art. 13, Bill of Rights, sec. 3, declared: "The right of property is before and higher than any constitutional sanctions; and the right of the owner of a slave to such slave, and its increase, is the same, and as inviolable as the right of the owner of any property whatever." Cited in Ely, Property and Contract in their Relation to the Distribution of Wealth, New York, 1914, p. 532.

alleged natural rights is in reality nothing more than naïvely
to beg the question. Professor Ely states that "generally
the term natural rights simply carries with it what Jeremy
Bentham calls dogmatism in disguise. . . . It presents no
argument for the position taken but sets up the position
taken as its own reason. You say, this appeals to you on
the ground of natural rights; I say it does not appeal to me;
you have simply your position over against my position."[46]
Critics hold that to appeal to natural rights is a purely
gratuitous attempt to strengthen the argument; it is what
T. H. Huxley once called "superfluous rhetorical confec-
tionery".

The test which most students of social problems today
would apply to institutions and laws is not an *a priori* idea
of natural rights but the test of social utility. The single
tax may or may not be a good thing, but single taxers can
make their case only by showing that it is just and will
promote the general welfare. Realizing this, many single
taxers have abandoned "the proud claim of securing an immediate intuitive verdict from the supreme tribunal of
natural equity".[47] The theory of property is not an absolute theory, but one of social utility. The idea of *natural*
rights is incompatible with social existence. "Rights are
acquired in and through society."[48] What social adjust-

---

[46] Ely, op. cit., p. 504.

[47] Daniels, Public Finance, New York, 1899, p. 82. But the single
tax leaflet cited in note 40 supra declares: "The most astounding assertion—to be made by an 'economist'—is that it is 'an antiquated
metaphysical theory', which 'bases ownership on effort expended and
would allow title only in those who have made things'. Well, if labor
is not the proper basis of ownership, then there are but two other
possible foundations—theft and gift. . . . Does the peculiar brand of
political economy taught by Professor Haney, give theft the preference
over labor?"

[48] Ely, op. cit., p. 504.

ments shall be, what limitations shall apply either to property or to individual actions, what property shall be public and what private, are matters to be decided, not on abstract grounds or by *a priori* ideas, but on grounds of social welfare.

The single tax proposal, besides calling for the taxing of ground rents into the public treasury, involves the abolition of all other taxes.[49]   But single taxers have not succeeded in gaining a very wide acceptance for the idea of doing away with all taxes save upon land.   They have not had much difficulty in finding objections to present methods of raising revenue, and they have done an important service in urging these objections.   But against two sorts of taxes the single tax argument has carried little weight, namely, income and inheritance taxes.   Single taxers have tacitly recognized this fact, since their arguments have but rarely been directed against these taxes.

It will be recalled that Henry George advocated the taxation of inheritances in his earliest writings,[50] although he abandoned this idea in *Progress and Poverty*.   Of late a number of single taxers have publicly advocated the income tax.[51]   In 1915 some of them were active in the Association for an Equitable Federal Income Tax, organized in New York City.   Early in 1916 the Joseph Fels Fund, which stands for single tax orthodoxy, circulated widely an address by Herbert S. Bigelow entitled, What Shall We Do With Our Millionaires?, the letter accompanying this pamphlet declaring that it was "the best brief piece of single tax propaganda literature yet produced".   But this pamphlet advocated both income and inheritance taxes.   Now that the

[49] Professor Ely has pointed out that George really denies the right of taxation.   (Op. cit., pp. 255-56, 260-61.)

[50] Supra, pp. 48-49.

[51] Supra, p. 269.

issue has been raised among single taxers some have taken a firm stand against these taxes,[52] and the Fels Fund has come in for some criticism for circulating this pamphlet. The present writer does not believe that many single taxers would now advocate income or inheritance taxes as permanent parts of a tax system. Of those favoring the income tax some have made the reservation that it is merely preferable to existing tax methods but not to land taxation. But the fact that they have advocated these taxes at all goes to show that the coming of a single land tax cannot be discerned with the naked eye. It signifies a tendency to relax the strictness of the phrase single tax, and may presage a weakening of the view that condemns all taxes but land taxes upon *a priori* grounds.

The commonest of all objections to the single tax, and the one which doubtless has carried most weight, is that it would be unjust to owners of land. A typical statement of this objection is the following:

"Our American nation, acting through both federal and state government, has extended a general invitation to the people to acquire full property in land; and the invitation has been accepted by Americans, while people have come from the ends of the world to acquire property in land, in accordance with our own conditions. . . . Now it is seriously proposed, because of an abstract doctrine of natural rights, to deprive the land owners of their land values. It is not believed . . . that the American conscience will ever accept this proposition. If a mistake has been made, it is the mistake of the nation, and not of one particular class in it."[53]

Single taxers have replied to this objection many times, commonly stating that it is conclusively answered in chapter XI of George's *A Perplexed Philosopher,* a chapter which has been circulated widely as a tract. They have been stick-

[52] Cf. especially a letter from F. W. Garrison in The Public, Mar. 31, 1916, pp. 296-97, and a reply by B. C. Marsh, ibid., Apr. 14, 1916, p. 344.
[53] Ely, op. cit., p. 779.

lers for not compensating present landholders, urging that
to do so would be to recompense robbers for the abolition
of their privilege of plunder. It is said that if any compensation should take place the land owners should compensate
the landless who for generations have been robbed of their
natural inheritance.

Very frequently single taxers have drawn an analogy
between abolition of private property in land and abolition
of private property in slaves, placing ownership of human
beings and ownership of land alike under the same moral
condemnation. Henry George wrote:

"Our boasted freedom necessarily involves slavery, so long
as we recognize private property in land. Until that is abolished, Declarations of Independence and Acts of Emancipation
are in vain. So long as one man can claim the exclusive
ownership of the land from which other men must live, slavery
will exist, and as material progress goes on, must grow and
deepen! . . .

"The truth is, and from this truth there can be no escape,
that there is and can be no just title to an exclusive possession
of the soil, and that private property in land is a bold, bare,
enormous wrong, like that of chattel slavery."[54]

Accepting such a view of the moral basis of the institution
of private property in land, single taxers have held that
compensation to present owners in the event of its abolition
would be iniquitous.[55] But opponents have protested that it
is a gratuitous affront to intelligence to compare ownership
of human beings, whose welfare should be the end of economic activity, with ownership of land, an inert thing.

Single taxers have not been able to convince many that
private ownership of land is ethically on a different basis

[54] Progress and Poverty, bk. 7, ch.'s 2 and 3, pp. 355-56. Cf. also
Post, The Taxation of Land Values, 1915, pp. 126-28.
[55] Single taxers have been impatient with the view that slave owners
should have been compensated under any circumstances. They have
said that if there was to be any compensation, slaves were entitled to it.

from other property, or that to expropriate owners of existing land values is more just than to expropriate owners
of other property values. Opponents urge that the single
tax argument at this point rests upon the not very substantial basis of the *a priori* view of property rights held by a
small minority of the community—the single taxers. Men
have trafficked in land for generations and it has been an
object of investment just as other forms of wealth. It is
argued that universally to take land values from their present owners would be not to repair an old injustice but to
make a new one.

Single tax and socialism as rival reform programs

In considering the single tax and socialism as rival radical
programs of social reform we may compare (1) the theories,
and (2) the movements.

The most fundamental difference in the two theories is
found in the respective views of single taxers and socialists
as to wherein "exploitation" consists. The former believe
that it arises from private ownership of natural resources
and "socially created values", and their program is directed
toward recovering these for the community by taking their
income in taxation. But the socialists believe that by virtue
of private ownership of the instruments of production in
general—machinery, buildings, etc., as well as land—non-
producers are able to exploit the wealth-producing classes.
Hence the socialists would have society secure control of the
means of production and exchange.

Derived from these fundamental ideas are the single tax
and socialist theories of the distribution of wealth. Single
taxers hold that there are three classes of income: that from
land, rent; that from capital, interest; and that from labor,
wages. The first of these classes of income they regard as

unearned, the others, earned. Socialists on the other hand recognize but two sorts of income, "of which one is given to labor in the form of wages, and the other to capitalists, landlords, employers and other 'gentlemen at large' under the form of interest, rent, and profits".[56] Socialists urge that George's theory, by failing to distinguish between property in the produce of a man's own toil and property in the produce of other men's toil, classes many unearned incomes as labor incomes.[57]

Single taxers and socialists have frequently criticized one another's position.[58] They have met in debates and have engaged in literary combats. The followers of George declare that, "instead of competition being the demon which has its hand upon the throat of labor, as the socialists would have us believe, it is rent, which follows in the wake of advancing production and swallows up all the increase in wealth which springs from the increased skill and efficiency of labor, and the invention of labor saving machinery".[59] There is indeed "merciless competition among the disinherited [of land], but it has no basis in nature". With land values socialized and freed from the grasp of the monopolist, and with wealth production freed of tax burdens, single taxers believe that competition would be equal and stimulating in its results and wages would rise.

[56] Gronlund, Socialism vs. Tax Reform; an Answer to Henry George, New York, 1887, pp. 23-24.
[57] Cf. Edmond Kelly, Twentieth Century Socialism, New York, 1910, p. 124.
[58] The earliest controversy took place in 1887. Supra, p. 118 et seq. Gronlund presented the socialist case in a pamphlet, The Insufficiency of Henry George's Theory, July, 1887. George replied in the columns of The Standard, July 30 and Aug. 6. Gronlund then made a rejoinder in August under the title Socialism vs. Tax Reform; an Answer to Henry George. George also publicly debated the issues with S. E. Schevitch in October in New York City.
[59] J. B. Sharpe, in The Standard, Dec. 24, 1890, p. 7.

The socialists regard George's remedy as wholly inadequate. Private control of the tools of production in a highly organized industrial régime they regard as of greater economic significance than private ownership of land. If the land were socialized, they ask, how would the worker manage to get a home built? And would it be fair to relieve from taxation the owners of big factories?[60]

The single tax and socialist movements first came into real contact with each other in 1886-87. At that time the advocates of either reform were struggling to control the United Labor Party, which in 1886 came so near to making Henry George mayor of New York City. It will be recalled that George's friends secured control of the United Labor Party's New York State convention in 1887 and expelled the socialists, who thereupon organized the Progressive Labor Party which later merged into the Socialist Labor Party.[61]

At this time Henry George invited the socialists to work with him in undertaking to socialize the value of land. "Let the socialists come with us, and they will go faster and further . . . than they could go alone; and when we stop they can, if they choose, try to keep on."[62] The socialists, in turn, claimed to be with George in his main proposal. "We want to abolish the wage system. In order to do that, it is necessary to abolish private property in capital. According to our ideas land is a most important bastion in the fortress Capital. . . . With his land theories and his tax system, . . . [George] deals mighty blows at this bastion."[63]

[60] Cf. Gronlund, op. cit.; Hillquit, Socialism in Theory and Practice, p. 294; A. M. Simons, Single Tax vs. Socialism, Chicago, 1899.

[61] Supra, pp. 121, 123.

[62] The Standard, Aug. 6, 1887, p. 4.

[63] Gronlund, Socialism vs. Tax Reform, p. 25.

Single taxers and socialists, however, have not co-operated very much. Both have been too busy making propaganda for their respective doctrines. Also the advocates of each have been very insistent upon the wrongness of the theories of the other. Single taxers have found fault with the socialists for a wrong diagnosis of the cause of social ills, while socialists have criticised the single tax on the ground that it is an inadequate remedy. The chief case where single taxers and socialists have worked together was in Everett, Washington, one of the few places where single taxers have been successful with their proposals. In Everett the socialist vote was an important factor contributing to the adoption of the single tax measure. There has been some co-operation also in California.

The two movements have developed quite differently in the United States. At the beginning socialism was exotic, a German movement beginning to make its way in this country, while the single tax movement was American. In 1886-87 they did not differ so greatly as regards the class to which each appealed, although the single tax movement had a much greater number of "intellectuals". But since 1887 the single tax movement has developed a much greater part of its strength, comparatively, among the middle class, while socialism is more typically a class movement with its greater strength among the workers.

The present socialist movement in the United States centers around the organized Socialist Party with its 115,000 members.[64] The voting strength of the movement in the

[64] For an excellent discussion of the present form and program of the socialist movement, cf. Mr. Hillquit's testimony before the Federal Commission on Industrial Relations, 1915. Socialists have circulated this testimony in pamphlet form under the title, The Double Edge of Labor's Sword; Discussion and Testimony on Socialism and Trade-Unionism before the Commission on Industrial Relations, by Morris Hillquit, Samuel Gompers, and Max J. Hayes, New York, 1914.

presidential election of 1912 was about 900,000. Single taxers on the other hand have no national party of enrolled members. They work through disparite organizations in all parts of the country, exhibiting little national co-operation except in so far as it may be accomplished through the Joseph Fels Fund Commission.[65]

It sometimes has been asked why the socialist movement has come into greater prominence and enjoyed a greater numerical growth than has the single tax. A chief reason is that the former lends itself better to agitation. The socialist protest is more simple, being directed against the great inequalities in the distribution of wealth. But the single tax is a step more complex since it undertakes to introduce a theoretical distinction between kinds of wealth, a distinction not readily grasped by the man in the street, to whom socialism makes a stronger appeal. A protest against the mere magnitude and economic power of individual wealth is simpler, and to the average mind appears more logical, than a protest directed against ownership of one form of wealth, land, and that not necessarily in the hands of the economically strong. The average man notices rather the amount of swollen fortunes than the kind of goods in which they happen at the moment to be invested.

Both the single tax and socialism have had their chief influence in the United States, not in securing any very considerable part of the legislation they desire, but as forces helping to mold opinion regarding social problems. The further programs of either movement are so far removed from present possibility that both have tended toward opportunism—working for specific proposals each urged on its own basis. The ideal of either program is more or less a matter of academic discussion. Professor Simkhovitch has

---

[65] Supra, p. 242 et seq.

stated that "socialists today have the alternative of becoming plain social reformers or of being out-and-out utopians", and that "whether they call themselves revisionists, reformists, laborites or plain socialists, whether they go on respecting the old melodramatic phrases or not, the overwhelming majority of the socialists of today are tending to be reformers".[66] Much the same might be said of single taxers. They continue assiduously to discuss the abolition of all taxes save those upon land, but to the observer the realization of Henry George's dream does not seem near at hand. Single taxers like socialists have the option of being either utopians or plain social reformers, working to justify their proposals as steps toward the ideal shared alike by single taxers, socialists, and the great mass of others desirous of the attainment of social justice.

Influence of the single tax movement

It has appeared from the foregoing discussions that the American single tax movement has not had large accomplishments either in the way of legislation secured or number of adherents gained for its essential principles. Nevertheless the movement has exerted a most important influence upon opinion. How widely this influence has been diffused is evident from the tremendous circulation of Henry George's writings and from the extent of the single tax propaganda. We may consider the influence of the movement under three heads: influence upon tax reform, upon economic thought, and upon the attitude taken by Americans toward social questions.

Henry George urged the single tax as a measure of social reform and not primarily of fiscal reform. But the

[66] Simkhovitch, Marxism vs. Socialism, New York, 1913, pp. xi and 292. For a socialist view cf. Spargo and Arner, Elements of Socialism, New York, 1913, ch. 23, on Socialism and Social Reform.

line of least resistance for single taxers has been to work to change existing tax systems in the direction of the single tax, and its advocates have taken active part in discussions of tax problems.

Single taxers have found a ready object of criticism in existing tax methods, and they have not come short of their opportunity to point out faults. In this they have performed a most valuable public service. They have occupied a prominent place in the ranks of tax reformers. So far as destructive criticism goes they have frequently been in close agreement with those having other tax ideals. They have persistently laid bare the theoretical and administrative defects of the general property tax; they have shown the injustice of poll taxes; they have set forth the burdensomeness of federal indirect taxation; they have labored assiduously to relax the rigid tax clauses of state constitutions; and they have worked ardently for the juster and more efficient administration of taxes.

The single taxer who has been identified most prominently with the tax reform movement was Thomas G. Shearman. He had been an active worker for this cause before his conversion to the single tax, but his conversion increased his zeal. In 1891 he was instrumental in organizing the New York Tax Reform Association.[67] Until his death in 1900 he devoted a considerable part of his time to speaking and writing on tax reform and the single tax. His *Natural Taxation* (1895) contains one of the strongest indictments of the evil features of the general property tax which has ever been written. Shearman was one of the few single taxers who have been disposed to view the single tax as mainly a fiscal proposition. *Natural Taxation* caused very much discussion of tax problems and tax reforms.[68]

[67] Supra, p. 216.
[68] Cf. the Shearman Number of the National Single Taxer, Jan., 1901.

The list of single taxers who have taken an active personal interest in tax abuses of their respective localities would be a long one. Hardly an issue in the file of any single tax paper fails to recount the efforts of some of the faithful in different parts of the United States in directing attention to specific evils. This activity has consisted in showing up corruption or inefficiency in the work of assessment, such as the undervaluation or omission from the rolls of vacant land or the relative underassessment of large holdings or valuable plots of land as compared with homes. In this connection single taxers have published lists of "favored tax-payers". They have compiled statistics to show how the general property tax tends to bear heavily upon the farmer. They have pointed out many times how taxation of personal property sets a premium upon dishonesty, and how attempts to enforce it defeat their end. The total effect of such specific interest in tax matters has been of much importance.

Single taxers also have urged the extension of the principles of excess condemnation and special assessments— these on the ground of their benefit theory of taxation. They hold that these principles afford "an object lesson which can be used with great effect in pushing the single tax".[69] Recently they have advocated defraying the cost of subways in New York and Chicago by means of special assessments upon the property benefited.

As a result of the single tax propaganda many students of taxation have become converts to the belief that an extension of land taxes is desirable for both fiscal and social reasons.[70] Not counting those who favor unearned in-

[69] Hathaway, Special Assessments and the Single Tax, in The Standard, Jan. 27, 1892, p. 3.

[70] Mr. Fillebrown's A-B-C of Taxation in particular has exerted wide influence in behalf of this idea. Canada's experience with special land taxes has also furthered its acceptance.

crement taxes—the justification for which is not based upon strictly single tax reasoning—there are many who favor partial or total exemption of improvements from taxation. Single taxers have won considerable acceptance for the view that most taxes other than those upon land are repressive in their tendency, although, in the view of many, they have greatly exaggerated the magnitude of the repressive effects. Professor Carver reaches the following conclusion regarding the adjustment of taxes in his *Essays in Social Justice:*

"Inasmuch as permanent taxes as permanent sources of public revenue should be levied in such a way as to repress productive enterprise as little as possible, and inasmuch as,—which means the same thing,—permanent taxes should be collected in such a way as to avoid as much as possible the shifting of the burdens, it follows that they should be levied mainly upon the land, incomes, and inheritances."[71]

Finally, single taxers have directed attention to the social effects of taxation. The principle of using the taxing power as a means of social reform has unquestionably gained a wider acceptance as the result of the single tax agitation.

In 1890 Francis A. Walker, delivering the presidential address before the American Economic Association on the subject, The Tide of Economic Thought,[72] declared that political economy, especially in the United States, had "suffered inexpressibly from public indifference", and that "the few who have professionally cultivated it have had things all their own way simply because no one cared enough about it to contest or even to criticize the conclusions they might reach". For this state of affairs Walker declared the economists themselves had largely been to blame, for, with their smug and uncompromising individualism, they had

[71] Carver, Essays in Social Justice, p. 429. Cf. in this connection Carver's ch. on The Single Tax.
[72] Publications of American Economic Association, vol. 6 (1891).

been "as distinctly separated from the mass of the people as have been the astronomers".[73]

But by 1890, Walker declared, indifference to the importance of economic problems no longer obtained. Men were beginning to see and feel the vital importance of industrial relations, and economic questions were taking precedence over all others in the public thought. The change in opinion was having its effect, too, upon the professional economists.

"We may have to put off some of the airs which we have thought rather becoming to us; we may have to get out of our chairs, and teach as we walk among our fellow men, like the philosophers of the old Academy; we may have to translate our lectures into more popular form and modern phrase. But . . . we ought to rejoice, with all our hearts, that the people, the whole people, are coming, for the first time, to take a deep, earnest, passionate interest in the subjects to which we have devoted our lives."[74]

One of the chief factors responsible for the increasing interest to which Walker referred, an interest which since 1890 has greatly enlarged and quickened, has been the single tax movement.[75] It has been said that *Progress and Poverty* "exploded the fiction that economic works must necessarily be dry reading".[76] The circulation of George's writings has been truly remarkable. They have had their influence directly, being read by all elements of the people,

[73] Ibid., p. 19.

[74] Ibid., p. 20.

[75] Professor Ely wrote in The Labor Movement in America, New York, 1886 (p. 126): "Now, one may object to Henry George's teachings—as I do most decidedly—and yet rejoice at the good which his works are doing in stimulating the thoughts and promoting the generous aspirations of the people. It would, indeed, not be an easy matter to over-estimate the educational value of that one work *Progress and Poverty*. A not inconsiderable part of the wholesome growth of interest in economics is due to its publication."

[76] Scanlon, The Quarter-Centennial of the Single Tax Movement, Westminster Rev., vol. 164 (1905), p. 644.

both well-educated classes and workingmen.[77]   The wide circulation of this literature, aided by the speaking campaigns of George and others and the political agitations, made many converts.   But the propaganda has had further important results which have appeared in less direct ways. For every convert there have been several who, perhaps for the first time, found a real interest in economic problems.   Professor Brooks tells of a thoughtful farmer in the West who said:

"If I had not read two books, Henry George, in the early eighties, and later Bellamy, I should have grubbed along and never thought anything was wrong.   Those books set me thinking how the things we grow and make are divided up.   I have read ever since, and gone to a good many lectures."[78]

The Henry George movement has been to American economic thought in large part what socialism has been to economic thought in Europe.   It has been a stimulating challenge, making necessary a rigorous re-examination of currently accepted ideas.   Such a challenge was much needed by the rather self-satisfied American economists of the eighties.   It was a force operating to shake them out of their rut, to broaden the field of interest, and to make clearer to all the vital importance of economic problems. The result of the challenge of *Progress and Poverty* has not been the general acceptance of Henry George's system of economic thought.   But the fact that economic thought has been broader and deeper in the years since 1880 than in the century preceding is due in no small degree to the publication of *Progress and Poverty*.[79]

[77] Cf. supra, ch.'s 4, 5 and 6, especially pp. 87-88, 90 et seq.

[78] J. G. Brooks, The Soc. l Unrest, New York, 1903, pp. 136-37.

[79] Professor W. T. Harris declared in 1887 that George's book "has had nearly as wide an influence as the books of Malthus and Ricardo— and that influence is still rapidly spreading." (Harris, The Right of Property and the Ownership of Land, Jour. of American Social Science Association, vol. 22, 1887, p. 120.)

Professor Ely wrote in The Labor Movement in America, pp. 283-84:

The single tax movement has had a most important effect in molding opinion on social problems. In 1890 Professor Ely wrote:

"Perhaps the greatest service of all which Mr. George has rendered is to be found in the discussions of right and wrong in economic affairs and institutions which he has provoked. There have always been plenty to advocate the economic rights of the individual, and it is very fortunate that now, at least, a few leaders of thought are urging us to look at rights from the standpoint of the public as well as the individual. . . . The question is frequently asked: 'Are property rights safe?' I have no fear about the property rights of the individual, but I have much fear that the property of the public will be stolen in the future as it has too frequently in the past. Henry George and others like him are helping to protect the property of the public, and for this the millions whose rights are too often overlooked ought to be grateful."[80]

One outstanding illustration of this is in the changed public attitude today toward the granting of franchise privileges. Too often in the past municipal government has been regarded as "an eleemosynary foundation for the gift of franchises".[81] These privileges, sometimes of almost priceless worth, have been given in the past for the asking or bartered for a private consideration. The arousing of public opinion so that municipalities shall place the rights of the community above the greed of monopolists and require an equivalent for the grant of these franchises has been due in no small measure to the single tax agitation and to the work of single tax reformers. Single taxers have insistently urged that private individuals shall not use the machinery of the law for personal gain, whether it be in

"*Progress and Poverty* has not been published ten years, yet it is now possible to affirm without hesitation that the appearance of that one book formed a noteworthy epoch in the history of economic thought both in England and America."

[80] Christian Advocate, New York, Dec. 25, 1890, p. 856.
[81] Zueblin, American Municipal Progress, New York, 1916, p. 359.

purchasing franchises, or lobbying for favoring tariffs, or corrupting courts.

Another most important way in which the single tax movement has exerted influence has been in directing attention to the vital importance of the conservation of national resources. In 1871 Henry George in his first book, *Our Land and Land Policy,* pointed out eloquently and vigorously how the policy pursued by the federal government and by most of the states was squandering the country's land, forest, and mineral wealth for the benefit of the fortunate or favored few. Single taxers have been among the most persistent and influential advocates of conservation. They have actively opposed the efforts which from time to time have been made to induce Congress to grant away the remainder of the nation's natural resources to those who covet them without requiring a due return. Throughout the single taxers have taken the long time social point of view, and in so doing they have rendered a most valuable service both to the present and to future generations.

Finally, the American single tax movement has been a powerful force insistently directing attention to the vexed problem of poverty. Men have pondered this problem more seriously ever since *Progress and Poverty* was written. Through the propaganda of Henry George and his followers hundreds of thousands have been led to consider how the condition of mankind may be ameliorated. Never before has the pressing importance of social reform been felt as in the last generation. The most vital message of Henry George's life and work was the urgency of social reform. Whatever be the fate of the remedy for which he so earnestly contended, one thing is sure. Henry George made it plain that no true civilization can avoid the duty of finding a means to "extirpate poverty" and "to lighten the burdens of those compelled to toil".[82]

[82] Progress and Poverty, Introductory, p. 8.

APPENDIX A

Adopted by the National Conference of the Single Tax League of the United States, at Cooper Union, New York, Sept. 3, 1890*

We assert as our fundamental principle the self-evident truth enunciated in the Declaration of American Independence, that all men are created equal, and are endowed by their Creator with certain unalienable rights.

We hold that all men are equally entitled to the use and enjoyment of what God has created and of what is gained by the general growth and improvement of the community of which they are a part. Therefore, no one should be permitted to hold natural opportunities without a fair return to all for any special privilege thus accorded to him, and that value which the growth and improvement of the community attach to land should be taken for the use of the community.

We hold that each man is entitled to all that his labor produces. Therefore no tax should be levied on the products of labor.

To carry out these principles we are in favor of raising all public revenues for national, state, county and municipal pur-

*The second Single Tax Conference, held at the Columbian Exposition, in Chicago, affirmed August 30, 1893, this platform, except the last paragraph, "With respect to monopolies," etc. For this paragraph the Chicago Conference substituted the following: "In securing to each individual his equal right to the use of the earth, it is also a proper function of society to maintain and control all public ways for the transportation of persons and property and the transmission of intelligence; and also to maintain and control all public ways in cities for furnishing water, gas, and all other things that necessarily require the use of such common ways." Henry George himself drafted the platform adopted in New York in 1890, including the final paragraph, and was chairman of the committee that reported it. As a member of the Conference at Chicago he opposed and voted against the alteration.

The platform as here reprinted was reaffirmed by the 1912 Single Tax Conference held under the auspices of the Fels Fund Commission (supra, p. 261).

poses, by a single tax upon land values, irrespective of improvements, and of the abolition of all forms of direct and indirect taxation.

Since in all our states we now levy some tax on the value of land, the single tax can be instituted by the simple and easy way of abolishing, one after another, all other taxes now levied, and commensurately increasing the tax on land values, until we draw upon that one source for all expenses of government, the revenue being divided between local governments, state governments and the general government, as the revenue from direct taxes is now divided between the local and state governments; or, a direct assessment being made by the general government upon the state and paid by them from revenues collected in this manner.

The single tax we propose is not a tax on land, and therefore would not fall on the use of land and become a tax on labor.

It is a tax, not on land, but on the value of land. Thus it would not fall on all land, but only on valuable land, and on that not in proportion to the use made of it, but in proportion to its value—the premium which the user of land must pay to the owner, either in purchase money or rent, for permission to use valuable land. It would thus be a tax not on the use or improvement of land, but on the ownership of land, taking what would otherwise go to the owner as owner, and not as user.

In assessments under the single tax all values created by individual use or improvement would be excluded, and the only value taken into consideration would be the value attaching to the bare land by reason of neighborhood, etc., to be determined by impartial periodical assessments. Thus the farmer would have no more taxes to pay than the speculator who held a similar piece of land idle, and the man who on a city lot erected a valuable building would be taxed no more than the man who held a similar lot vacant.

The single tax, in short, would call upon men to contribute to the public revenues, not in proportion to what they produce or accumulate, but in proportion to the value of the natural opportunities they hold. It would compel them to pay just as much for holding land idle as for putting it to its fullest use.

The single tax therefore would—

1. Take the weight of taxation off of the agricultural districts where land has little or no value irrespective of improvements, and put it on towns and cities where bare land rises to a value of millions of dollars per acre.

2. Dispense with a multiplicity of taxes and a horde of tax-gatherers, simplify government and greatly reduce its cost.

3. Do away with the fraud, corruption and gross inequality inseparable from our present methods of taxation, which allow the rich to escape while they grind the poor. Land cannot be hid or carried off, and its value can be ascertained with greater ease and certainty than any other.

4. Give us with all the world as perfect freedom of trade as now exists between the states of our Union, thus enabling our people to share, through free exchanges, in all the advantages which nature has given to other countries, or which the peculiar skill of other peoples has enabled them to attain. It would destroy the trusts, monopolies and corruptions which are the outgrowths of the tariff. It would do away with the fines and penalties now levied on anyone who improves a farm, erects a house, builds a machine, or in any way adds to the general stock of wealth. It would leave everyone free to apply labor or expend capital in production or exchange without fine or restriction, and would leave to each the full product of his exertion.

5. It would, on the other hand, by taking for public use that value which attaches to land by reason of the growth and improvement of the community, make the holding of land unprofitable to the mere owner, and profitable only to the user. It would thus make it impossible for speculators and monopolists to hold natural opportunities unused or only half used, and would throw open to labor the illimitable field of employment which the earth offers to man. It would thus solve the labor problem, do away with involuntary poverty, raise wages in all occupations to the full earnings of labor, make overproduction impossible until all human wants are satisfied, render labor-saving inventions a blessing to all, and cause such an enormous production and such an equitable distribution of wealth as would give to all comfort, leisure and participation in the advantages of an advancing civilization.

With respect to monopolies other than the monopoly of land, we hold that where free competition becomes impossible, as in telegraphs, railroads, water and gas supplies, etc., such business becomes a proper social function, which should be controlled and managed by and for the whole people concerned, through their proper government, local, state or national, as may be.

APPENDIX B

Summary of Votes on Single Tax Measures or Issues

Date	Place	Measure or issue	Vote for	Vote against	Per cent for
1896	Delaware	Campaign of Single Tax Party	1,173	37,000	3.1
1898	Washington	Local option in taxation	15,969	33,866	32.1
1902	Colorado	Local option in taxation (defeated by a close margin)			
1908	Oregon	State-wide exemption of most improvements and personal property	32,066	60,871	34.5
1910	"	Abolition of poll tax; local option in taxation	44,171	42,127	51.2
1912	"	Repeal of local option (proposed by legislature)	63,881	47,150	57.6
	"	"Graduated Single Tax and Exemption Amendment"	31,534	82,015	27.8
	"	"Single tax," Multnomah Co.	11,146	23,901	31.8
	"	"Single tax," Clackamas Co.	1,827	3,787	32.5
	"	"Single tax," Coos Co.	1,113	1,909	36.4
	Missouri	Gradual exemption of improvements and personal property	87,000	508,000	14.5
	California	Local option in taxation	169,321	243,959	40.9
	Everett, Wash.	Gradual exemption of improvements and personal property	4,858	2,637	64.8
	Seattle, Wash.	Exemption of improvements and personal property	12,191	28,180	30.2
1913	" "	Gradual exemption of improvements and personal property	10,578	21,260	33.2
	Pueblo, Colo.	50% exemption (1914), 99% (1915) of value of improvements	2,711	2,171	55.5
1914	Oregon	$1,500 exemption of improvements and personal property	65,495	136,193	32.5
	"	Graduated sur-tax on owners of "land and natural resources"	59,186	124,943	32.1
	California	Local option in taxation	267,618	375,634	41.6
1915	Pueblo, Colo.	Repeal of law of 1913	3,255	3,042	51.7
	Colorado Springs, Colo.	Exemption of improvements and personal property	944	7,241	11.5
	Denver, Colo.	Exemption of improvements and personal property	7,988	27,125	22.7
	Houston, Texas	Re-election of tax-commissioner Pastoriza over opponent on "single tax" issue	5,659	1,963	74.3

BIBLIOGRAPHY OF SELECT REFERENCES*

I. Bibliographies of the Single Tax Question

BULLOCK, EDNA D., Selected Articles on Single Tax (Debaters' handbook series), New York, H. W. Wilson Co., 1915, pp. 199.

DOLLFUS, ROGER, Über die Idee der einzigen Steuer, Basel, 1897, pp. 164. Short bibliography at head of each chapter.

JOSEPH FELS FUND OF AMERICA, Blymyer Building, Cincinnati, Ohio, Book List of selected books, pamphlets, and leaflets.

LIBRARY OF CONGRESS, Washington, D. C., Select List of References on the Single Tax, and Select List of References on the Taxation of Land Values (Typewritten manuscripts distributed to certain libraries).

PUBLIC, THE (537 So. Dearborn St., Chicago, Ill.), The Public's Selected List of Books on Questions of the Day: The Single Tax, Direct Legislation, City Administration, Proportional Representation and Other Social Science Subjects. Published from time to time in The Public. Cf. issues of Jan. 21, Mar. 3, and Apr. 7, 1916.

WASHINGTON, UNIVERSITY OF, Bureau of Debate and Discussion, The Single Tax, an Outline for Debate, University Extension Series no. 6, General Series no. 70, Seattle, Wash., 1913.

WASHINGTON, UNIVERSITY OF, Bureau of Debate and Discussion, Taxation of Land Values, a Bibliography, University Extension Series no. 13, General Series no. 85, Seattle, Wash., 1914.

* The writer believes that a short bibliography of select references is of greater value than either an enumeration of the sources to which reference has been made in the preceding pages, or a list of the controversial literature dealing with the single tax. The sources have been indicated in footnotes relating to particular subjects, and much of the controversial literature is of small value.

It should be added that one should refer to current single tax periodicals and to propaganda pamphlet literature in order to keep in touch with contemporary developments. The two main periodicals are the *Single Tax Review*, monthly (150 Nassau St., New York City), and *The Public*, weekly (537 S. Dearborn St., Chicago). For a further enumeration of periodicals, cf. supra pp. 248-50. For a list of pamphlets cf. Book List of the Joseph Fels Fund of America, Blymyer Building, Cincinnati, Ohio.

WILL, THOMAS E., Bibliography, Land and the Land Question, Arena, vol. 16 (1896), pp. 380-92.

II Biographies of Henry George

GEORGE, HENRY, JR., The Life of Henry George, New York, Doubleday, Page & Co., 1900, pp. 634.

PEDDER, D. C., Henry George and his Gospel, London, 1908, pp. 75.

POST, L. F., The Prophet of San Francisco, Chicago, L. S. Dickey & Co., 1904, pp. 61.

TAYLOR, E. R., Henry George, the Man, Single Tax Review, New York, July-Aug., 1912, pp. 1-13.

III. Select List of Presentations of the Single Tax Argument

FILLEBROWN, The A-B-C of Taxation, New York, Doubleday, Page & Co., 1909 (pp. 229), 1916 (pp. 236).

GEORGE, HENRY, Complete Works (Memorial ed., 10 vol.'s, including The Life of Henry George, by Henry George, Jr., New York, Doubleday, Page & Co., 1898-1901). George's books are as follows: Our Land and Land Policy, National and State, 1871; Progress and Poverty, 1879; The Irish Land Question (later published as The Land Question), 1881; Social Problems, 1883; Protection or Free Trade? 1886; The Condition of Labour, an Open Letter to Pope Leo XIII, 1891; A Perplexed Philosopher, being an Examination of Mr. Herbert Spencer's Various Utterances on the Land Question, with some Incidental Reference to his Synthetic Philosophy, 1892; and The Science of Political Economy (published posthumously), 1898.

GEORGE, HENRY, JR., The Menace of Privilege, New York, MacMillan Co., 1905, pp. 421.

HIRSCH, MAX, Democracy versus Socialism. a Critical Examination of Socialism as a Remedy for Social Injustice and an Exposition of the Single Tax Doctrine, London and New York, MacMillan Co., 1901, pp. 481.

HOWE, FREDERIC C., Privilege and Democracy in America, New York, Scribner's, 1910, pp. 315.

POST, LOUIS F., The Taxation of Land Values, Indianapolis, Bobbs-Merrill Co., 1915, pp. 179.

SHEARMAN, THOMAS G., Natural Taxation, an Inquiry into the Practicability, Justice and Effects of a Scientific and Natural Method of Taxation, New York, Doubleday, Page & Co., 1895, pp. 268.

IV. Select List of Arguments Against the Single Tax

CARVER, T. N., Essays in Social Justice, Cambridge, Harvard University Press, 1915, ch. on The Single Tax, pp. 281-303.

ELY, RICHARD T., Property and Contract in their Relation to the Distribution of Wealth, New York, MacMillan Co., 1915, 2 vol.'s. Cf. index under "George", "Land", "Natural rights", and "Single tax".

HANEY, L. H., The Single Tax, in Bull. of the University of Texas, 1915, no. 39, pp. 165-79, Studies in the Land Problem in Texas, Austin, Texas, 1915.

HARRIS, W. T., The Right of Property and the Ownership of Land, Boston, 1887, pp. 40. Reprinted from Journal of American Social Science Association, vol. 22 (1887).

HUXLEY, T. H., Collected Essays, On the Natural Inequality of Men; Natural Rights and Political Rights; and Capital —the Mother of Labour. These essays first appeared in the Nineteenth Century, vol. 27 (1890).

JOHNSON, A. S., The Case Against the Single Tax, Atlantic Monthly, Jan., 1914, pp. 27-37.

MALLOCK, W. H., Property and Progress, New York, G. P. Putnam's Sons, 1884, especially pp. 1-80.

RAE, JOHN, Contemporary Socialism, New York, Scribner's, 1901, ch. on The Agrarian Socialism of Henry George, pp. 441-500.

RITCHIE, D. G., Natural Rights, a Criticism of Some Political and Ethical Conceptions, London, George Allen Co., 1894, especially ch.'s 5 and 13.

SCOTT, W. A., Henry George and his Economic System, New World, vol. 7 (1898), pp. 87-102.

SELIGMAN, E. R. A., Essays in Taxation, New York, MacMillan Co., 1913, ch. on The Single Tax, pp. 66-97.

SHIELDS, CHARLES H., Single Tax Exposed, Portland, Ore., Oregon Equal Taxation League, 5th ed., 1912, pp. 63, and Seattle, Wash., The Trade Register, Inc., 7th ed., 1913, pp. 190.

STEBBINS, G. B., Progress from Poverty, Chicago, Charles H. Kerr & Co., 1887, pp. 64.

WALKER, F. A., Land and its Rent, Boston, Little, Brown & Co., 1883, pp. 232.

WILLOUGHBY, W. W., Social Justice, a Critical Essay, New York, MacMillan Co., 1900, ch. on The Labor Theory as applied to Property in Land, pp. 156-93.

V. General References

AMERICAN SOCIAL SCIENCE ASSOCIATION, The Single Tax Debate at Saratoga, Sept., 1890, vol. 27 (1890), pp. 1-124.

ANNALS OF THE AMERICAN ACADEMY OF POLITICAL AND SOCIAL SCIENCE, Philadelphia, vol. 58, March, 1915, pp. 149-227.

FINAL REPORT OF THE COMMITTEE ON TAXATION OF THE CITY OF NEW YORK, 1916, pp. 398.

HAIG, ROBERT M., The Exemption of Improvements from Taxation in Canada and the United States, a Report prepared for the Committee on Taxation of the City of New York, 1915, pp. 291.

HAIG, Some Probable Effects of the Exemption of Improvements from Taxation in the City of New York, a Report prepared for the Committee on Taxation of the City of New York, 1915, pp. 254.

MILLER, M. M., Great Debates in American History, 14 vol.'s, New York, Current Literature Publishing Co., 1913, vol. 10, pp. 52-109, Land Value Taxation (The Single Tax).

NATIONAL TAX ASSOCIATION, Proceedings of the Eighth Annual Conference (Single Tax Session), Madison, Wis., 1915, pp. 405-69.

INDEX

ity in, 132, 138; local option proposed in, 231
New York Tax Reform Association, 216, 230-31, 313
New Zealand, 156-57, 258
Nisbet, James, 40
Nye, A. B., 238

Oakdale, Cal., 208
Objections to the single tax, 299, 300-07
O'Connell, Daniel, 113
Ogilvie, William, 2, 5, 6, 276
Ohio, single tax activity in 133, 137, 138; single taxers work for direct legislation in, 166, 167, 239; local option proposed in, 233, 235, 236
Opponents of the single tax, see Adversaries
Opportunism of single taxers, 128-29, 140, 266, 311-12
Oregon, single tax campaigns, (1908) 163, 164, 168-70, (1910) 170-74, (1912) 174-80, (1914) 180-81; results of movement, 132, 182-83, 245, 288; direct legislation in, 166, 169, 170, 174, 180-81; local option in, 171 ff, 231-32, 234
Oregon State Tax Commission, 175, 179, 181, 182-83
Organization of the single tax movement, 64-65, 81, 104, 136-38, 246-48, 287-88
Osborne, E. B., 243
Our Land and Land Policy, see George, Works
Owen, R. L., 197

Paine, Thomas, 2, 6-7
Pastoriza, J. J., 145, 197-202, 256, 288
Payzant, Miss E., 185
Pennsylvania, single tax movement in, 138, 209-15
Pentecost, Hugh, 130
Periodicals, single tax, 109, 248-50
Perplexed Philosopher, A, see George, Works
Petition, single tax national, 133-38
Philadelphia, home of George, 27; independent single tax party in, 243-44

Philadelphia Single Tax Society, 149
Physiocrats, anticipation of George, 15-18; George's knowledge of works of, 25; see *Impôt unique*
Pinchot, Amos, 243
Pink, L. H., 224, 228
Pittsburgh, partial exemption of buildings in, 210-15, 225, 246, 281, 285; peculiar tax methods in 210-12; Board of Trade 213, 214; Chamber of Commerce, 214; Civic Commission, 212, 213, 214; Real Estate Dealers' Association, 213
Plagiarism, George accused of, 7, 24-25
Platt, T. C., 154
Plehn, C. C., 63, 161
Pleydell, A. C., 165, 218
Political activity, single taxers and, 105-07, 127 ff, 165, 244-46, 287; see Fillebrown, C. B.
Political Parties, relations of single taxers to, 123, 126 ff, 242-44; see Democratic Party, Progressive Party, Republican Party
Political theories of single taxers, 239-40, 261, 301-04
Poll tax, amendment to abolish in Oregon, 170-74, 176
Pollock, Frederick, 22
Populist Party, single taxers in, 242
Post, Louis F., 81, 83, 95, 96, 98, 99, 104, 105, 110, 118, 123, 130, 131, 133, 139, 149, 162, 230, 249, 257, 268, 269, 270, 279, 286, 306
Post, The San Francisco Evening, 54 ff
Portland, Ore., 168, 188
Poverty, single tax movement emphasizes problem of, 319
Powderly, T. V., 90, 91
Powers, E. P., 107
Precursors of George, see Anticipations
Preuss, A., 111
Privilege, single tax idea of, 294, 296
Progress and Poverty, see George, Works
Progressive Labor Party, 121, 123, 309

Date Due

Date Due			
APR 3 '62			
FEB 21 '64			
FEB 16 '82			
JAN 27 1982			
JUN 22 1982			
AUG 24 1982			
	PRINTED	IN U. S. A.